Susan Paul Pattie is an Honorary Senior Research Associate at University College London and former Director of the Armenian Institute in London. In recent years she served as Director of the Armenian Museum of America and was Program Manager of the National Armenian Genocide Centennial Commemorations in Washington, DC. She holds a PhD in Anthropology from the University of Michigan, Ann Arbor and is the author of an ethnography, *Faith in History: Armenians Rebuilding Community* (1997).

"*The Armenian Legionnaires* presents to an English-language audience an important but little-known aspect of Middle Eastern History in the World War I era. The Armenian legion was formed while the Ottoman Empire's genocide of its Armenian population was still ongoing, and this tale of its deployment, actions, and dissolution brings together the later passages of the Great War in the Middle East, the aftermath of genocide, Armenian hopes for the postwar future, resurgent Turkish nationalism and cynical great power politics."

Donald Bloxham, Richard Pares Professor of European History, University of Edinburgh

"This book, written lucidly and meant for the general public as well as scholars, is based essentially on published and unpublished memoirs by certain key volunteers. Because substantial excerpts from those eyewitness accounts have been included in translation from Armenian to English, the study renders a most valuable service to the non-Armenian reader as well. What is more, the numerous illustrations and maps certainly pump additional oxygen into the faces, situations, and places that come to life. All in all, it is a timely reminder of the oft-forgotten Armenian contribution to the Allied victories in the Levant during World War I. It is also a tribute to the young men and some women who put their lives on the line for a higher cause."

Vahram L. Shemmassian, Professor and Director of the Armenian Studies Program, California State University, Northridge

"This is a long-awaited book on the Armenian legion. The author has done a wonderful job by giving a voice to the main actors of this story, the legionnaires themselves, who through extracts from their memoirs make this book more vivid, concrete and comprehensible. The richness of the photographs of the legionnaires published in this book is also a very important contribution towards successfully reconstructing this crucial period of Armenian history."

Vahé Tachjian, Project Director and Chief Editor of Houshamadyan Project and Lecturer at the Péter Pázmány Catholic University in Budapest

Frontispiece. Early morning in Adana. American flag flying over Near East Relief building and below, workers going to the vineyards.
John Amar Shishmanian Papers, envelope B, Hoover Institution Archives.

THE ARMENIAN LEGIONNAIRES

Sacrifice and Betrayal in World War I

SUSAN PAUL PATTIE

with a chapter by
VARAK KETSEMANIAN

Published in 2018 by
I.B.Tauris & Co. Ltd
London • New York
www.ibtauris.com

Copyright © 2018 Susan Paul Pattie
Copyright © 2018 Varak Ketsemanian, Chapter 2

In collaboration with and sponsored by K. George and Carolann S. Najarian

The right of Susan Paul Pattie to be identified as the author of this work has been asserted by the author in accordance with the Copyright, Designs and Patents Act 1988.

All rights reserved. Except for brief quotations in a review, this book, or any part thereof, may not be reproduced, stored in or introduced into a retrieval system, or transmitted, in any form or by any means, electronic, mechanical, photocopying, recording or otherwise, without the prior written permission of the publisher.

Every attempt has been made to gain permission for the use of the images in this book. Any omissions will be rectified in future editions.

References to websites were correct at the time of writing.

ISBN: 978 1 78831 125 0
eISBN: 978 1 78672 454 0
ePDF: 978 1 78673 454 9

A full CIP record for this book is available from the British Library
A full CIP record is available from the Library of Congress

Library of Congress Catalog Card Number: available

Typeset by Initial Typesetting Services, Edinburgh
Printed and bound by CPI Group (UK) Ltd, Croydon, CR0 4YY

Contents

Foreword *K. George Najarian*		vii
Acknowledgments		ix
Note on the Contents of *The Armenian Legionnaires*		xiii
Timeline		xvii
1.	Armenians in a World at War	1
2.	The Armenian Legion at the Crossroads of Colonial Politics *Varak Ketsemanian*	8
3.	Recruitment and the Voyage	26
4.	Training in Cyprus	43
5.	Palestine and Preparation for Battle	59
6.	The Battle of Arara	73
7.	The Next Stages: Beirut	91
8.	To Cilicia, the "Promised Land"	103
9.	Repatriation and Increasing Uncertainties	128
10.	The Transfer of Power in Marash	145
11.	The Battles of Marash or "The Marash Affair"	160
12.	The Aftermath	181

Epilogue	205
Appendices	
A. Short Biographies	217
Dickran Boyajian *Marc Mamigonian*	218
Vahan Portukalian *Gagik Stepan-Sarkissian*	220
Hagop Arevian	221
Ovsia Saghdejian *Vahe H. Apelian*	223
B. Letters and Declarations	226
Official Declaration to the Armenian People	226
Letters of Commendation	227
C. "The French Record in Cilicia" from *The Christian Science Monitor*, 1921: An interview with legionnaire Lieutenant John Shishmanian	229
Notes	235
Bibliography	246
Glossary	248
List of Illustrations	251
Index	259

Foreword

As a young boy growing up in Cambridge, Massachusetts, the Armenian legionnaires were a part of my life for as long as I can remember. Born in Hyusenig, an Armenian village in Ottoman Turkey, my father Nishan Najarian emigrated to the United States before the Armenian Genocide of 1915 and settled in Cambridge. Despite his comfort and safety in the United States, like hundreds of other young Armenian men, he answered the call to join the Armenian legionnaires. He was 19 years old. At the end of the war he returned home, bringing with him a woman and her daughter, survivors of the Genocide. We don't know where or how he met them. We do know that when he was being discharged from the legionnaires he was told he could stay in the region or get on a boat back to the United States and take one other person with him. He said he wished to return but insisted on taking a mother and a daughter and wouldn't leave without both of them. He obtained the necessary permission, brought them to the United States, and eventually married the daughter, Arshalous, my mother.

The legionnaires who returned became close, lifelong friends whom we would see regularly. I remember going along to the legionnaires' picnics at Camp Hayastan in Franklin, Massachusetts, where the families gathered and the men would trade stories. A few times a year the legionnaires would get together and play cards and enjoy one another's company. Similar groups gathered informally in various cities: Providence, Rhode Island; New Britain, Connecticut; Troy, New York; Worcester, Boston, Cambridge, Springfield, Lawrence, Massachusetts.

When talking to non-Armenians about these young fighters, we would use the word "legionnaires" but in general conversation amongst Armenians they were known as the *Gamavors*, the Volunteers. These men fascinated me and inspired me: young men who willingly put their lives at risk to go back to their homeland and fight, who were committed to help free Armenia and rescue those in need.

This book is dedicated to the *Gamavors*, the Armenian legionnaires, the men whose idealism and courage fired their determination as represented in the spirit of my father, Nishan Najarian.

K. George Najarian

1. Upon discharge from the Legion, Nishan Najarian (right) returned to Massachusetts, bringing with him a mother and daughter, survivors of the Genocide. He later married Arshalous (center) and they raised four children together.

Acknowledgments

The author and sponsors have many people to thank for their contributions to this book. We are especially grateful to Baikar Press, Kevork Marashlian and Aram Arkun for granting permission to translate and use portions of Dickran Boyajian's *Haygagan Lekeone* [*The Armenian Legion*]. This lively book itself includes many perspectives from different legionnaires as Boyajian combines his own memoirs and research with the words written by his many comrades. Boyajian's book is the foundation of this one. Dr. Gagik Stepan-Sarkissian has done a meticulous job of translating these passages as well as others used for this book. For this, and equally, for his wise advice, constantly sought, we are very thankful.

The dream of publishing a book which tells the story of the Armenian legionnaires started with Michael Najarian, Sr. who, in the mid 1980s, began collecting letters, memoirs, and photographs from legionnaires who were friends of his father, Nishan. His brother George, shared his desire. George and his wife Carolann sponsored the taping of interviews with legionnaires by the Zoryan Institute and years later helped finance a major exhibition about the legionnaires at the Armenian Library and Museum of America along with a parallel traveling exhibit. Now, finally, using these efforts as inspiration, this book has become a reality.

Many hours were spent in the Legionnaires' Archive at the Armenian Museum of America (formerly the Armenian Library and Museum of America) and we thank the trustees of the Museum as well as Curator

2. Title page of Dickran H. Boyajian's *Haygagan Lekeone* [*The Armenian Legion*]. *Courtesy of Baikar Press.*

3. George Kolligian (fourth from right) and comrades. *Courtesy of the Armenian Museum of America.*

4. Légion Arménienne. Poste d'Erzine (also known as Yeşilkent), a town in the Hatay district on the Turkish coast. *Michael Najarian Collection.*

Gary Lind-Sinanian and Director Berj Chekijian for enabling the use of this important resource as well as permission to use many photographs illustrating this book. The Museum's archives are built on the resources gathered and texts written for the two exhibitions on the legionnaires and we thank Ardemis Matteosian, Arakel Almasian and Barbara Merguerian for generously sharing their thoughts and advice.

In Cyprus Susan was fortunate to have the advice of Ruth Keshishian, information and links provided by Anastasia Toumazou and an inspiring visit with Baret (Duke) Bedelian to sites important to the legionnaires, Monarga village and Kantara Castle. Our thanks to each of them and to the many other friends in Cyprus who shared their information and photos.

Images and illustrations have come from a number of sources, in addition to the Museum's collection. We are grateful to Project SAVE Armenian Photograph Archives and archivist Suzanne Adams, to the AGBU Nubar Library, Paris, and librarian Boris Adjemian, to the Hoover Institution at Stanford University, and to the many individuals who have lent their precious photographs and documents both to us and previously to Michael Najarian. Many thanks also to Marc Mamigonian at the

National Association of Armenian Studies and Research (NAASR) and to Misak Ohanian of the Centre for Armenian Information and Advice (London), to Vahe H. Apelian, Lynn Cadwallader, Michael Varadian, and especially, of course, Levon Chilingirian.

Note on the Contents of
The Armenian Legionnaires

This book includes eyewitness accounts, memoirs, letters, stories, documents and photographs passed down through families as well as excerpts from interviews with children and grandchildren of legionnaires about the memories passed on to them. Many of these were gathered by Michael Najarian in the 1980s and archived until the present.

The backbone of Chapters Three through Twelve is based on excerpts from Dickran H. Boyajian's *Haygagan Lekeone: Badmagan Hushakrutiun* (*The Armenian Legion: A Historical Memoir*, Watertown, MA: Baikar Press, 1965), translated into English for this publication by Gagik Stepan-Sarkissian. Some of the memoirs included by Boyajian were earlier published in Armenian papers such as *Hairenik*, *The Armenian Weekly*, *The Armenian Mirror Spectator* and *Haratch*. We are grateful to Baikar Press for consent to use extensive portions of the text of *The Armenian Legion*.

In 2001, Ardemis Matteosian, Arakel Almasian and Barbara Merguerian created an historic exhibition at the Armenian Library and Museum of America (Watertown, Massachusetts), "Betrayed Dreams: The Armenian Legion and the Great War", supported by George and Carolann Najarian. In 2007, a traveling exhibition on the subject, "Forgotten Heroes: The Armenian Legion in World War I" was produced by the Museum, also supported by the Najarians, and is available today for display.[1] Some of the material found in this book is in the archives of the Museum, collected and used in these exhibitions and generously made available for research and use for the present book.

Chapter Two, an original text by Varak Ketsemanian, provides an overall political and historical context for the personal experiences of the legionnaires, helping to make this book a lasting resource about the men and their times.

Regarding transliteration, Boyajian's original book is written in literary West Armenian and this text follows the spelling conventions of that variant of the language. Elsewhere, men's names are written as they did when using Latin letters. In the bibliography, Armenian names and titles are transliterated phonetically, where possible avoiding diacritical marks and other more scholarly conventions, hoping to make the list as accessible as possible.

5. Dickran Boyajian, author of *Haygagan Lekeone: Badmagan Hushakrutiun* [*The Armenian Legion: A Historical Memoir*]. *Courtesy of the Armenian Museum of America.*

 **FORGOTTEN HEROES** The Armenian Legion and The Great War 1916 -- 1920

6. Banner publicizing the 2001 exhibition at the Armenian Museum of America. *Courtesy of the Armenian Museum of America.*

7, 8. Postcard to Khan B. from "G", inscribed on the back: *To my Comrade Khan. In remembrance of Cilicia and Mesopotamia. This is how we started our work and we will continue in the same way. Some day we will remember these days. Your friend in ideals, "G".* Courtesy of Ardemis Matteosian (daughter of Khan B.).

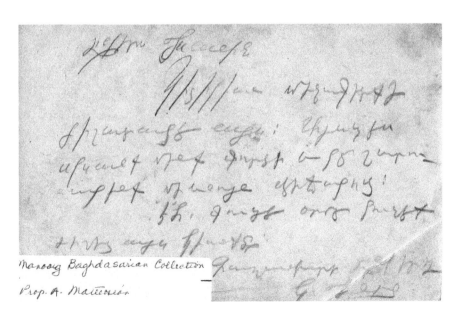

The Armenian legionnaires were also called *Gamavors* or Volunteers. There were other Armenian volunteers who joined the fight against the Turkish and German armies during World War I, many who fought on the Caucasian Front under General Antranig, as well as resistance bands (*fedayee*) of men and some women defending their villages and towns. Other young Armenian men joined the national armies and navies of their new countries, the United States and France. All of these deserve recognition.

This book, however, focuses on those who joined the Légion d'Orient (afterwards becoming the Armenian Legion) and primarily on those who left from the United States. The Légion d'Orient was later remembered as part of the French Foreign Legion, though it was an auxillary force with the French army (see page 17).

In the Epilogue, the reader will find photographs of men in uniform from all of these forces, on the different fronts posing proudly together at community gatherings. Their experiences and dreams could best be shared with each other and, according to family and friends, they did indeed remain comrades and patriots together to the end of their days.

Timeline

1914   World War I begins in Europe. The Allied (or Entente) Powers (Great Britain, France and Russia) against the Central Powers (Germany, Austro-Hungary, Ottoman Empire).

1915   February to November, 1916. Discussions with British and French take place regarding the creation of an Armenian fighting unit. Mikael Varantian initiates discussions, later led by Boghos Nubar, head of the Armenian National Delegation.

1915   April 24. Constantinople: Armenian intellectuals and community leaders arrested, deported, and most killed. Deportations and genocide of Armenian population of Ottoman Empire intensify.

1916   May. Sykes–Picot agreement signed after secret negotiations between France and Great Britain, agreeing to terms of settlement and division of the Middle East between them at the end of the war.

1916   November. Légion d'Orient formed, beginning with recruits from the refugees of Musa Dagh in Port Said, Egypt.

1917   January. 1st Battalion is sent to new training camp in Monarga, Cyprus, to assist in building projects, preparing for new recruits.

1917   January. Recruitment of legionnaires expands to Europe and North America, attracting over 1,200 men. Legionnaires also come from around the globe.

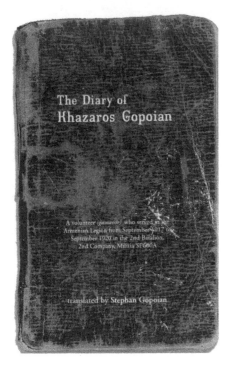

9. Original diary cover of Khazaros Gopoian, overprinted in English by his son and translator, Stephen Gopoian.
Courtesy of Ardemis Matteosian.

10. Diary frontispiece. In Armenian – "Notes of a Gamavor" by Kh. Gopoian
Courtesy of Ardemis Matteosian.

11. Khazaros Gopoian (top left) with legionnaire comrades.
Courtesy of the Armenian Museum of America.

1917   April 6. The United States declares war on Germany (but not on the Ottoman Empire).

1917   July. Legionnaires begin arriving from the United States. Some 1,400 men have arrived by end of summer.

1917   August. The Légion d'Orient begins training in Monarga, Cyprus.

1918   May. Legionnaires leave Cyprus after training. By July, there are 4,360 men, 58 officers.

1918   May until September. Legionnaire battalions undergo further training in Palestine preparing for battle as well as assistance to Allied Command in other places.

12. Hagop Minasian, Beirut.
Michael Najarian Collection.

1918   September 19. Battle of Arara: Under the command of General Allenby, Armenian legionnaires provide vital assistance in the key Megiddo Campaign, on the ridge of Arara, leading to defeat of Ottoman and German forces in Palestine.

1918   October. Legionnaires arrive in Beirut, having suffered the Spanish flu en route; assist in Allied occupation of Beirut and region.

1918   October. Légion d'Orient officially becomes Légion Arménienne.

1918   October 30. Mudros Agreement. Turkey signs armistice with Britain and Allies.

TIMELINE

1918   November 11. World War I officially ends with armistice between Germany and Allies.

1918   December. The Armenian Legion begins to arrive in Cilicia, assisting the French in its occupation. The majority of French occupation forces in Cilicia is composed of four battalions of the Armenian Legion.

1918   December through November 1919. The British troops are the primary occupying force in Cilicia until their evacuation at end of November.

1918   British and French encourage repatriation of surviving Armenian refugees. Over 120,000 return to their homes in Cilicia, believing themselves protected by the Allied Powers.

1919   March. "The Alexandretta Incident." The 4th Battalion is dissolved following armed hostilities between Armenian and Algerian legionnaires. Demobilization of the Legion steadily proceeds from this point.

1919   May. The Turkish National Movement officially begins under the leadership of Mustafa Kemal (later Atatürk), beginning a war of independence against the occupying armies.

13. Entry of the French Cavalry into Adana. *AGBU Nubar Library, Paris.*

1919	September. France begins to make changes in policy, showing openness to negotiation with nationalist forces in Turkey.
1919	November. British troops pull out of Cilicia, replaced by the French with far fewer men and supplies. Armed opposition by Kemalist forces increases fighting in regions around Marash.
1919	December. François Georges-Picot meets with Mustafa Kemal to discuss a possible accommodation.
1920	February. After protracted battles with Kemalist forces in Marash, French forces suddenly evacuate. Great numbers of Armenians try to follow them into a blizzard, thousands dying en route. Many left behind are massacred.
1920	April. French withdraw from Urfa but their troops are killed as they retreat. Massacres of Armenian and other Christian minorities continue throughout the region as other towns and villages fall to the Kemalist forces.
1920	August. Armenian independence briefly declared on the plain of Adana. French Command quashes declaration and also calls Col. Brémond back to Paris, accusing him of being pro-Armenian.
1920	September. The last members of the Armenian Legion demobilized. Some return to their homes, others remain to help, as civilians, defending remaining Armenian population.
1921	October. The Accord of Ankara is signed and France withdraws from all Turkish territory, including Cilicia.
1925	October 19–November 6. The bodies of the men buried near Arara in Palestine are re-buried in Jerusalem.

1

Armenians in a World at War

Introduction

A little-known aspect of World War I is the remarkable story of Armenian volunteers or *Gamavors* in the Légion d'Orient, an auxiliary force of the French army. Beyond their importance as a part of Armenian history, the experiences and perceptions of these men also provide important insights into relations between the Allied Powers (also called the Entente Powers) Russia, France and Great Britain during that period. We see the planning and decisions made at the uppermost levels through the lens of a small, powerless people caught in a war that was not their own but which had already destroyed their known world. Even today the rippling consequences of some of those decisions continue to undermine stability and efforts towards peace in the region.

This is the story of men who escaped death themselves and then returned to the battlefront to fight with the Allies, hoping to save their families, fellow Armenians and homelands. After a long training period in Cyprus, the Armenian Legion fought bravely under General Allenby in the Allied Forces' campaign in the Middle East, playing a crucial role in the winning of the Battle of Megiddo, known to Armenians as the Battle of Arara, in Palestine. Later, in Cilicia, members of the Legion faced a more protracted and complex struggle, there also performing acts of heroism.

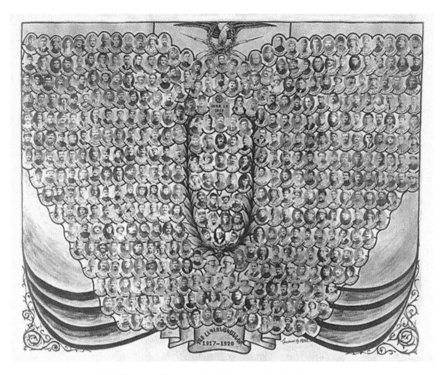

14. Plaque of portraits of Armenian legionnaires.
Courtesy of the Armenian Museum of America.

15. A portrait from the plaque, enlarged by his family. Legionnaire Hagop Shakarian. *Courtesy of Mayda Shakarian Tartarian.*

The legionnaires enlisted with the understanding that they would be fighting against the Ottomans in the area where their own ancestral homes had been. Should the Allies be successful, the Armenian legionnaires would be part of an occupying army in their homelands, laying the foundation for an independent Armenia. *The Armenian Legionnaires* describes these motivating dreams, the sacrifices made, the hard work involved in becoming soldiers, and their betrayal as the French and the British shifted their priorities and, at the end of the war, left these lands to the emerging Republic of Turkey.

Background

At the end of the nineteenth century, most Armenians were still living in their original homelands, in the Caucasus and in six provinces or vilayets of the Ottoman Empire: Erzurum, Van, Bitlis, Diyarbakır, Sivas and Mamuretülaziz. In addition, due to centuries of warfare throughout those lands, trading and other migration, many Armenians also lived in cities such as Constantinople and İzmir, in towns south of the vilayets mentioned above, such as Adana, Aintab (Gazianteb) and Mersin, and further south in the Antakya, Musa Ler, Kessab regions and beyond to Aleppo. The Armenian Kingdom of Cilicia (1199–1375) left the area with numerous Armenian-dominated small centers that thrived into the early twentieth century.

There is much evidence of insecurity, heavy taxation and periodic pogroms in the area, but Armenians and other minorities somehow adjusted to the demands of the government and regular raids by local bandits and Kurdish chieftains, rebuilding after the attacks. In spite of these difficulties, there is also clear evidence that Armenians were thriving throughout this region during the Ottoman period. While most worked the land of their ancestors, they were also quick to learn and use new techniques, both in farming and in the many new trades and skills that began to sweep across the region. Education for boys and girls began to reach the smaller towns and villages in the mid nineteenth century and by the twentieth century had become commonplace. Missionaries from the United States and northern Europe working in the area also introduced the possibilities of higher education. Many Armenians left to study abroad, becoming doctors and teachers, often returning to work with the people of their towns and villages.

From the last decades of the nineteenth century to 1915, there was a small but steady increase in migration, particularly of young men, away from the homelands towards the United States and Europe. The Hamidian massacres of 1895–6 and surrounding unrest had taken the lives of thousands of Armenians, destroying towns and villages. Famine in the region to the south also added to the insecurity and desire to move to safety and a better future, in any way possible. Some of the departing young men were married and intended to send for their families afterwards or return with new wealth to provide a good life in the old country. Even after many decades of loss, most Armenians wished to remain and hoped that the changes promised with new political reforms would bring a transformation of the situation in their homelands.

By the late 1890s, Armenians were not alone in their concern about the increasingly brutal rule of Sultan Abdulhamid II, and opposition grew among Turkish intellectuals who wished to modernize the state. A loose cooperation between Ottoman liberals and Armenian representatives seeking to reform the multi-ethnic society was complicated by European support, enabling opponents to claim there was danger of outside interference. The Young Turk movement, having begun with the desire for reform and inclusion of non-Muslim minorities, became increasingly concerned with the survival of what was left of the Ottoman Empire, its national character as Turkish and Muslim, and, connected to this, the development of an idea of the early origins of Turkishness and pan-Turkism. Agitation and unrest increased throughout the Empire as reforms provoked a fear of loss of control and power. The 1909 Adana massacre was the starting point for a new series of pogroms against Armenians in the region, resulting in the destruction of towns and villages and the killing of over 20,000 Armenians. A degree of order returned to the area but the resentment of the perceived special status of Armenians and other Christians was stoked by further developments, such as the resettlement of Muslims displaced from the Balkans. By the end of 1914, at official as well as popular levels, the ideal of Ottoman multinationalism had given way to an increasingly popular

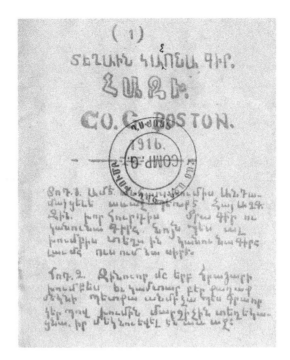

16. Page one of a booklet published in Boston in 1916, advising Armenians in the United States on how to organize paramilitary training in preparation for fighting for the homelands when the opportunity arose. Company G, Boston.
Courtesy of Ardemis Matteosian.

17. Rescue at Musa Dagh. Survivors of the 53-day siege are taken to the French ship *Guichen* and on to Port Said, Egypt.
Courtesy of Sona Najarian Touloumjian.

and narrowly defined "Turkism." Complete and rapid assimilation or brutal annihilation became the two alternatives. Unfortunately, many Armenians placed their hopes on the promises of intervention by the Western powers, particularly France and Great Britain. This proved to be a naïve and treacherous belief, but as it was, their other chances were slim or nonexistent.

On April 24, 1915 intellectuals and leaders of the Armenian community in Constantinople were arrested, deported to the interior, and most were killed. With this opening began months of mass deportations, rape, pillaging, executions and ultimately genocide throughout the Empire but particularly focused on the six vilayets and the area of Cilicia. Attacked by Kurdish bands, goaded to their deaths by Turkish gendarmes and soldiers, Armenians were driven from their homes and an entire culture and way of life indigenous to the area was erased from the region. Most of those who did survive owed their lives to the brave Turks, Kurds, Arabs and others, including Western missionaries, who took great risks to help Armenians as they were able. These included some important officials, both Turkish and Kurdish, mullahs, and many more ordinary folk who must be counted among the "righteous."

18. Some 40 women fought alongside the legionnaires in Cilicia. This (unnamed) woman was known as a "sharpshooter."
John Amar Shishmanian Papers, envelope B, Hoover Institution Archives.

Very few Armenian towns and villages took up arms to resist and defend themselves. All but two of these lost their greatly unequal battles. The people of Van were rescued after one month by the nearby Russian army and Armenian volunteers; the more famous resistance of the "Forty Days of Musa Dagh" (thanks to author Franz Werfel) also reached a successful ending as a French ship anchored near the bottom of the mountain and rescued the people. The fighters of Musa Dagh became an integral part of the story about to be told on these pages, eager to return to the battle, attempt to take back their homes and help create an independent Armenia. Others, much further away in Europe and North America, awaiting news of their loved ones, feeling a raw helplessness, were also ready to put their own fears aside and aid the fight to liberate the people and the land.

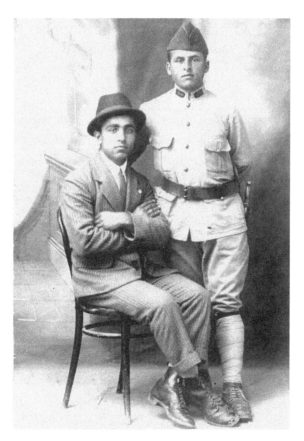

19. Kegham Aghjayan (standing).
Courtesy of the Armenian Museum of America.

2

The Armenian Legion at the Crossroads of Colonial Politics

VARAK KETSEMANIAN

This chapter presents the overall context within which the Légion d'Orient, later the Armenian Legion, was created. Relations between the Allied Powers are revealed through protracted negotiations concerning the Legion, both at the beginning and the end of its existence.

Much has been written on the atrocities the Armenians suffered during World War I. Yet a little-known aspect of the war is the compelling story of the Armenian Legion (*Légion d'Orient*, as it was first known), which served under the French banner and the British army, and contributed to the victory of the Allied or Entente Powers in the Levantine campaigns of the war. This chapter begins with the establishment of the Armenian Legion in 1916 and the clash of diplomatic interests that emerged soon after its creation as Armenian, British and French officials made conflicting plans regarding the purpose of this unit. While Boghos Nubar, the primary Armenian negotiator, hoped the Legion would serve as a first step toward the creation of an autonomous Armenia within the Ottoman Empire, the French and the British used the Armenian Legion as a colonizing tool for their imperial policies in the Near East. Finally, this chapter briefly touches upon the participation of the Armenian legionnaires in the Levantine battles of the war in

20. Boghos Nubar, Chairman of the Armenian National Delegation.

1917–18, among which the campaign at Megiddo, Palestine, was the most important.

The history of the Armenian Legion cannot be fully understood unless seen within the context of the deportations and genocide of Cilician Armenians in the summer of 1915. It was during those days when the inhabitants of Musa Dagh took up arms against the Ottoman forces as an alternative to the certain death that awaited them. This resistance, captured by Franz Werfel's *Forty Days of Musa Dagh*, ended with the rescue of approximately 4,000 Armenians when French vessels appeared on the Mediterranean coast on September 12, 1915. As explained below, the history of the Armenian Legion began with the arrival and encampment of Musa Dagh Armenians as refugees at Port Said in British-controlled Egypt.

The First Months of World War I and the Earliest Proposals

The earliest suggestion for using Armenians as auxiliary troops in Allied armies was made in November 1914, as part of a possible British landing at Alexandretta (İskenderun). Boghos Nubar, the chairman of the Armenian National Delegation (AND), drafted the proposal with the intention of protecting the Cilician Armenians, who he feared would be massacred by Ottoman forces in retaliation to Armenian volunteers joining the Russian Army on the Caucasian Front.[1] However, the French demand for a role in such a campaign, and the stalemate resulting from the unsuccessful attempt to force the Dardanelles with the navy alone in early 1915, compelled the Allied Powers to shelve the Alexandretta plan and reject the formation of an Armenian Legion to support it. The British feared that Armenian mobilization on behalf of the Allied Powers would lead to brutal reprisals by the Ottomans in Cilicia, and thus were hesitant to assume responsibility for such massacres.

Negotiating with British and French officials, Boghos Nubar called for an autonomous Armenia comprising the Six Provinces (Van, Erzurum, Bitlis, Diyarbakır, Sivas and Mamuretülaziz) in Eastern Anatolia, and Cilicia. This region would remain within the boundaries of the Ottoman Empire, yet be protected by the Allied Powers. He argued that an autonomous Armenia would remain neutral by the guarantee of world powers. His letter to Sir Francis Bertie, British ambassador to France, on May 27, 1915, attested to his dexterous diplomatic efforts to ensure the aid of one of the Allied forces during a time when massacres in Cilicia seemed imminent. Boghos Nubar claimed that "The Triple Entente inspires in us [Armenians] confidence for an approaching salvation and the accomplishment of our national goals, through raising their voices in favor of the Armenians, who have been subjected to Turkish harassments for centuries, and by officially declaring themselves protectors of our unfortunate nation."[2] However, Great Britain had no interest in the Armenian provinces at the time being, since its aspirations focused on northern Africa and Mesopotamia. Furthermore, the British were eager to force the capitulation of Constantinople before the Russian army marching from the east could reach the Ottoman capital. Thus, they concentrated the war effort on the Gallipoli campaign that had started on February 15, 1915.

The British continued rejecting proposals even in August 1915, arguing that the enlistment of Armenians in Allied armies would lead to brutal reprisals in Constantinople and elsewhere. Such arguments made the British and French positions specious, given that they were both fully aware of the already ongoing Armenian massacres in the Ottoman Empire and that they had condemned and held Ottoman officials responsible through a joint statement on May 24, 1915. Although the Armenians of Cilicia were not yet completely deported, the clash of imperial and colonial goals of Britain and France hampered all efforts to establish an Armenian fighting unit that could have protected the remaining Cilician Armenians, who were eventually deported. It is in this way that Boghos Nubar encapsulated the failure to convince the Allied Powers to make a landing in Alexandretta and thus, save the Armenians from total annihilation: "[Unfortunately], sometime later, when it was decided to land troops in Dardanelles, our plan [the establishment of an Armenian fighting force] was indefinitely postponed. Nevertheless, if we wait until the siege of Constantinople and for their landing troops on the Cilician coast, I am afraid that not one Armenian will be left in Cilicia."[3]

Throughout the early months of the war, Armenian officials of the AND remained active in the European capitals. In a correspondence with the French foreign minister Théophile Delcassé, Arshag Chobanian, another prominent member of the AND, suggested that the Armenians were willing to accept a French protectorate over Cilicia, given France's traditional interests in the region, provided that the French authorities would send military aid to the Armenians to resist Ottoman deportations that were already in their initial phase. As time went by, AND members became more anxious to establish any basis for a military assistance by the Allied Forces that would help Cilician Armenians survive the imminent massacres. The earliest deliberations regarding the formation of an Armenian legion, or at the very least arming Cilician Armenians for self-defensive purposes, showed the first clash of interests between the Allied Powers and Armenians officials.

Great Power Diplomacy and the Armenian Legion in 1916

The reluctance of the Allied Powers to relinquish their imperial and colonial claims for a concerted and coordinated effort to achieve a military breakthrough into Ottoman territories and gain a foothold in Asia Minor proved detrimental to the Cilician Armenians in August and September of 1915. The summer of 1915 witnessed an intensification of massacres and deportations in Cilicia. It was during that period when a handful of Armenians from Musa Dagh took up arms against the genocidal policy of Ottoman authorities as an alternative to the certain death that awaited them. The implications of the Musa Dagh resistance, and the Armenians' eventual evacuation to Port Said by the French navy, are significant to understanding both why the Allied Powers rejected the proposal for a Legion in 1915, and approved it only in 1916.

The Armenians' encampment at Port Said spurred a new wave of negotiations among Allied and Armenian officials around the possibility of enlisting these refugees as auxiliary fighters. It set the new stage for a French–Armenian collaboration; the refugees, looking to the French for help and in part owing their lives to the French humanitarian mission, were willing, as a sign of gratitude, to work loyally for France's success. Moreover, by the end of 1915, the Gallipoli campaign had become a dismal failure. Not only did this military fiasco compel the Allied Powers to look for a new front to outflank Ottoman forces and knock them out of the war, but also acquire the regions they considered postwar spoils, namely Mesopotamia, the Levant and Cilicia. Consequently, the French, who saw the Levant and Cilicia as their traditional zone of interest, feared their outnumbering by British troops in Egypt and loss of regional control.

The British were also disgruntled by the presence of Armenians at Port Said, whom they saw as a financial burden and prospective troublemakers. The scarcity of monetary contributions and relief from the Armenian community of Egypt exacerbated the situation. Confusion emerged about what to do with the Armenian refugees, and they became a matter of correspondence between the French Foreign Ministry and Armenian representatives in Egypt when efforts to send them to Italy, Cyprus and Morocco failed. British military authorities in Cairo inquired whether the French authorities proposed to make any use of the Armenians they brought there. Otherwise, the British planned to send them to Gallipoli and Mudros, where they would be of great use as workers on imperial construction sites, in exchange for their admittance to safety in Egypt. However, the French were not only pressured against this proposal by the AND, but had other intentions for the Musa Dagh Armenians. The French War Ministry thought it was necessary to form additional fighting units to counterbalance the British presence in the Levant, given the heavy casualties French troops had suffered at Gallipoli and the European fronts.

French and British diplomatic documents reveal that during that same period, General John Maxwell, Commander of the British troops in Egypt, and Brigadier General Gilbert Clayton, Intelligence Officer, proposed to the leaders of the Musa Dagh refugees that they prepare 500 capable men to serve in combat as part of an "Armenian Legion." In the fall of 1915, the Armenian National Security Council of Egypt, the body responsible for supporting the refugees, suggested to General Maxwell that in view of the growing enthusiasm of Armenians to participate in the war, an Armenian Legion should accept volunteers from Egypt, France and the United States. Nevertheless, the first proposals limited enlistment to Armenian refugees and some prisoners of war.

In addition to increasing the French forces, the congregation of Armenian refugees at Port Said presented the perfect historical opportunity to utilize their eagerness for revenge against the Ottomans, a factor in Allied military and imperial calculations. Both powers realized that the Armenians only needed the proper training, weapons and supplies to initiate their struggle against the Ottomans. As reflected in Boghos Nubar's private papers, the Armenians at Port Said were desperate to guarantee the aid of at least one Allied Power recognizing (willingly or unwillingly) their interests in the region. The French took this golden opportunity to exploit such calls for their own colonial prospects.

As these deliberations proceeded, French, British, and Russian officials were holding secret negotiations for the future of the Levant and Cilicia as well as the delineation of borders. It was mainly the outcome of these negotiations, known as the Sykes–Picot Agreement of 1916, that became the harbinger of the establishment of the Armenian Legion. After settling the postwar territorial disputes between the Allied Powers, this secret accord created a colonial framework through which the French would first form, and eventually deploy the Armenian Legion. The time was also "ripe" insofar as the deportations and massacres of the Armenians of Cilicia had already unfolded and thus the fear of reprisals was made redundant. The imperialist considerations demonstrated that the main obstacle against the establishment of an Armenian fighting force was not simply Allied fears of Ottoman retaliation, but rather undetermined colonial partitions that hampered all efforts in spite of the pleas of Armenian officials.

As the Allied Powers were busy making their postwar policies, the Armenian refugees were growing more impatient by the day. Not only did they want to avenge the deaths of their loved ones, but they were also eager to be a part of the final victory against the Turkish–German forces, catalyzed by the success of the Russian army on the Eastern Front. The French knew that an appeal to Armenian national and patriotic sentiments would not only mobilize the refugees in Port Said, but would also encourage thousands of Armenians worldwide to enlist in the Legion and swell the depleted French forces. This was a strategy that targeted the Armenian networks of France, Egypt and the United States.

Nevertheless, the Allied Powers were hesitant to incorporate Armenian volunteers into their armies and argued in favor of sending them to carry out incursions in Cilicia. By November, 1915, the French authorities prepared a plan to use the Armenian refugees as soldiers and send them to Syria on sabotage missions. They argued that the conscription of the Armenian refugees would first and foremost support the Allied military power in the Levant, encourage American–Armenians to join the ranks, and finally lessen the financial burden of the Allied Powers providing for the refugees in Egypt. Such proposals came in the midst of pressure from the Russians on the British and French to open a new theater of war in the Levant and thus relieve the Russian army on the Caucasian Front.

In May, 1916, the final version of the Sykes–Picot agreement was drafted and both Britain and France were ready to concentrate war efforts on their zones of interest. Nonetheless, the fate of the Cilician coastlands, though claimed by the French, remained precarious. An Allied expedition in Cilicia with a landing at Alexandretta had still not been completely denied by the British military authorities such as

General Maxwell. Nevertheless, the British, reluctant to displease their French counterparts, did not push the case for a joint landing. There existed a nexus of imperial interests which any of the Allied Powers was hesitant to undermine. Not only did the French official correspondence sent throughout late 1915 reveal the resuscitation of the proposals for a landing at Alexandretta but it also showed the French insistence that the campaign be a joint one, if any expedition were to take place at all.

The decision to establish an Armenian unit and incorporate it into the Légion d'Orient of the French Army came in this context. This time it was the British Brigadier General Clayton, in Cairo, who suggested to Paul Cambon, the French ambassador in London, that an Armenian Legion be formed and based in Cyprus. The proposal was subsequently approved by Boghos Nubar and the AND. What also led the Delegation to accept this proposal, was news of the victories of the Russian army on the Eastern Front, where seven Armenian voluntary battalions were also serving.

Boghos Nubar interpreted the formation of the Armenian Legion as a counterpart to the Russian–Armenian battalions, and a force that would attack the Ottoman Empire mainly through its southern flank in Cilicia. The Delegation approved the proposal on the condition that the Legion fight only in Cilicia and be exempt from deployment on other fronts. The French on the other hand saw the Legion as a counterbalance to the British troops in the Levant and a military maneuver to facilitate their armies' progression towards Ottoman territories from the south, an alternative strategy to Gallipoli. This was seen as a way to make the British comply with the terms of the Sykes–Picot agreement. Thus, the plan regarding the Legion was finalized in August, 1916, by the commander-in-chief of the French army, the French government and the AND.

Despite the partition of the Near East among the French, British, and Russians, Boghos Nubar still believed that the course of events would lead to the realization of an autonomous Armenia. In a letter sent to Catholicos Kevork V on May 16, 1916, he argued that Armenians ought to be flexible in their national demands, in that they should pursue national goals whose achievement was possible. Whether Boghos

Nubar's plans were "flexible" enough would only be tested at the Paris Peace Treaty of 1919. Allied diplomatic correspondence showed that the French wanted to utilize the Armenians, not as "liberators of their homeland," but rather an occupying army for postwar French colonies, given that the Armenians were familiar with the Cilician landscape. Furthermore, the British, eager to see the Armenian refugees departing Egypt, suggested that they be trained by French officers. The French, in turn, believed this would show their strength without enlarging their field of operations while also controlling the Armenian volunteers who might seek to create independent principalities in Cilicia.

In an attempt to avoid another military debacle, the Sykes–Picot agreement was a diplomatic turning point insofar as the British and French resolved to work together more closely. Although their imperial rivalry never fully dissipated, it was shrouded by the possibility of future colonial possessions, which necessitated a collaborative relationship, linking the successful conducting of the war with postwar imperial occupation. The Armenian Legion became the articulation of this cooperation.

The Organization of the Armenian Legion in 1917–18

After receiving British approval to create a training base for the Legion on the island of Cyprus (then under British colonial rule), General Pierre Roques, the French Minister of War, dispatched a military mission on September 23, 1916, led by Lt. Col. Louis Romieu. The intention was to assess the military situation in Cairo and Alexandria, and to inquire into the feasibility of establishing an Armenian military camp in Cyprus. The team was tasked with planning the preparation of the Armenian refugees of Port Said and some Ottoman–Armenian prisoners of war who were interned at a camp near Bombay, India, for a possible expedition to Cilicia. The French were careful to restrict the enrollment to a maximum of 5,000 men. This number included the qualified Armenians at Port Said, and potential legionnaires from other places as well. This is why the initial recruitment of the volunteers was confined only to the Armenian refugees of Port Said and the prisoners of war in India, suggesting that the French were reluctant to swell the fighting force to uncontrollable proportions that might lead to the eventual increase of Armenian control over Cilicia at France's expense. The mission was to conclude its report by October 1916. After initial inspections between 300 and 350 of the refugees were pronounced eligible for recruitment.

The early stages of organization of the Legion began in November 1916, and the first military camps in Cyprus were ready to welcome recruits by January 1, 1917. At the request of the AND, it was called the *Légion d'Orient* as a precautionary measure against possible reprisals from Muslims and in view of its potential to include those Christian Arabs who showed a willingness to fight the Ottomans. Nevertheless, it was apparent that the unit was primarily composed of Armenians who formed the Legion's first battalion. Despite the official promulgation of the Legion by French authorities, the judicial status of Armenian soldiers was still ambiguous. According to a French law adopted in August 1916, a national who held the citizenship of a country at war with France was prohibited from joining the French Foreign Legion. Therefore the Légion d'Orient was designated as an auxiliary force and was not yet completely incorporated in the French army. Furthermore, whereas Article 3 of the Legion's "organization manual" stated that "special instruction will fix their allocations which would be in principle equivalent to that of the regular French soldier," the Armenian soldiers did not receive familial allocations, or any other benefits. Nonetheless, there was an urge among the Armenians to take revenge and thus no special attention was given to these judicial issues, which were to contribute to the deterioration of French–Armenian relations in the postwar period.

The military leadership of the Legion was assumed by French generals and officers who chose Armenian adjutants among the legionnaires. Those who wanted to join the Legion had to first meet certain criteria: if a candidate's physical condition was deemed acceptable, he would then undergo medical examination. After successfully completing these tests, volunteers had to procure an official document from their respective countries or the French government attesting to their honest intent for serving in the Legion. Those coming from the Middle East were required to procure the document either from the French consulate at Port Said in Egypt or the Legion's commanding office in Cyprus. French concerns to keep enrolment below 5,000 made the selection process very rigorous. In a confidential dispatch addressed to Lt. Col. Romieu, the French Prime Minister Georges Clemenceau demanded that all recruitment activities stop and newcomers be rejected unless personally authorized by him. Such correspondence on the French official level demonstrated the enthusiasm of many Armenians around the world who hurried to join the Legion, which they believed was to be deployed for the sole purpose of liberating Cilicia from Ottoman rule.

By February, 1917, a squad of 400–500 men gathered at Port Said was joined by dozens of local Egyptian Armenians. Together they constituted the 1st and 3rd companies of the Legion. It was not until the end of July that the first group of American–Armenian volunteers arrived. By the end of the summer, when the recruitment stopped, 1,400 men had been recruited, comprising seven companies of 250 men each, six

21. Volunteers gather in New York before sailing to France and onward to Port Said. *Michael Najarian Collection.*

Armenian and one Syrian. The first four companies formed a battalion. Ahead of the possible deployment of the Legion, the French War Ministry decided in September, 1917, to form an infantry regiment of two battalions, each comprising three infantry companies, and a company of four machine gun units that were established by October. At the beginning of 1918, 1,700 men were already registered as official legionnaires. By July, 1918, there were three Armenian battalions with 58 officers and 4,360 soldiers including 288 Frenchmen, and a platoon serving two guns of 37 mm caliber.

22. Survivors of the Musa Dagh resistance at Port Said refugee camp. *AGBU Nubar Library, Paris.*

The first clash of interests after the formation of the Legion became apparent in July, 1917. General Bailloud, inspector-general of the French troops in Egypt, declared, after his inspection of the Armenian Legion, that a military expedition to Cilicia was no longer envisaged and that the Legion would be incorporated into a French expeditionary force destined for Palestine to fight alongside the British Army. Throughout 1917, Germany showed no signs of weakness on the Western Front and achieved impressive victories against Russia. Moreover, British Prime Minister Lloyd George hoped to achieve a breakthrough in the Near East, safeguarding British positions in Egypt. Dragging the French into this theater of war was seen by the British military leadership as the only viable option to protect British dominions. It is in this context that the frantic policy shift of the French came about. For the latter, the Levant was more important than Cilicia and they were determined to prevent any British encroachment upon French zones of interest. Numerous complaints on behalf of the AND followed, to the point where Georges Clemenceau intervened to assure Boghos Nubar that the French government had nothing to do with it, that the decision had been made by the French War Ministry. He assured Boghos Nubar that the government opposed the deployment of the Armenian Legion in Palestine, since this was a violation of the initial agreement.

23. Légion d'Orient. Armenian volunteers, 1918. *Photograph courtesy of the Armenian Revolutionary Federation Archive. Project SAVE Armenian Photograph Archives.*

The AND was faced with a dilemma: disband the Legion, an achievement for which it had been struggling since the beginning of the war, or conform to the new state of affairs. If the French authorities insisted on sending the Legion to Palestine, the only weapon that the Delegation possessed was the discouragement of further recruitments. Such declarations from the French authorities made their position vis-à-vis the Armenians dubious, as it was slowly becoming clear that the political ideals pursued by the AND did not really overlap with the postwar agenda of the French and British. The former, fearing an imminent British violation of agreements, were determined to do what it took to curb any leeway that their colonial rival might utilize at France's expense.

The "Baptism of Fire"

The Legion's "baptism of fire" came in the summer of 1918, when the British finally accepted the fact that the capitulation of the Ottomans and Germans could not be realized without a joint campaign with French forces. In July 1918, the Armenian Legion was incorporated into the French detachment at Mejdel, Palestine, and joined the British front. General Allenby, the commander-in-chief, decided to use the 5,000 men in the "French Detachment of Palestine and Syria". The Armenian Legion is mostly remembered for its significant contribution at the Battle of Arara in the larger military offensive that took place in the summer of 1918, known as the Megiddo Campaign. With the aim of forcing the Ottoman Army to capitulate without being able to organize reinforcement and supply lines, General Allenby dispatched a force of 35,000 to Palestine, supported by 400 artillery guns, against the 8,000 infantry and 130 artillery units of the German–Ottoman forces. Against the British and French advance stood the Ottoman 7th and 8th Army corps and a few battalions of the 2nd Army corps, as well as one German infantry brigade of 7,000 that was incorporated into the "Yıldırım" ("Lightning") Army commanded by Liman von Sanders. The Armenian Legion was to attack the Arara–Rafat front on September 19, 1918, at dawn.

Although the Legion was deployed far from its original destination, of Cilicia, many Armenian sources and memoirs translated for this volume demonstrate that the legionnaires were enthusiastic that the moment had finally arrived when they could avenge the Ottomans, be that in

24. Officers of the French Foreign Legion.
Lt. Col. Romieu is third from right, first row. *Courtesy of Ardemis Matteosian.*

Palestine or Cilicia. The general offensive began at the appointed hour. Facing the French troops, the 701st, 702nd, and 703rd German battalions, commanded by General von Oppen, were entrenched and held positions on the hill of Arara. They formed the most solid nucleus of the Yıldırım Army. A battalion from the Armenian Legion, commanded by Lt. Col. Romieu, marched and held positions on the right side of the French troops. The day before the attack, the 1st battalion had undertaken preparatory maneuvers. The next day, the 2nd battalion held position on Hill 26 after five hours of heavy fighting, notwithstanding the constant shelling and artillery fire from German forces. The legionnaires succeeded in capturing the first German defense line. Unwilling to come to terms with this strategic loss, the Ottomans resorted to counter-attacks. After five hours of battle, the German–Ottoman forces succumbed and began to retreat, giving way for the legionnaires to capture the 2nd and 3rd German defense lines. The 1st battalion succeeded in taking the summit of Arara.

25. Armenian women at Port Said made this flag for the 3rd Company, Légion d'Orient. However, the French would not allow it to be used as it carried the coat of arms of the ancient Cilician Armenian Kingdom.
John Amar Shishmanian Papers, envelope B, Hoover Institution Archives.

26. Armenian Legion on maneuvers near Adana. Photo by H. M. Berberian, Adana; legionnaire Aram Hovsepian is fourth from left. *Photo courtesy of Barkev Hovsepian. Project SAVE Armenian Photograph Archives.*

The Armenian Legion lost 24 men, suffered 80 injured and four missing in action. In a dispatch sent to the AND in October 1918, General Allenby highly praised the Armenian Legion and the sacrifices it showed on the battlefield, claiming that he was proud to have a legion of Armenians under his command. During the funeral of the fallen soldiers Lt. Col. Romieu eulogized the achievements and the commitment of the legionnaires. Although the Battle of Arara was the major offensive in which the Armenian Legion partook, it continued its campaigns with the French and British troops in Palestine and Syria, throughout the summer and fall of 1918, until the final capitulation of Ottoman forces on October 30 and the signing of the Mudros Armistice.

The French Occupation of Cilicia (1918–20) and the Armenian Legion

From December 1918 to November 1919 the four battalions of the Armenian Legion constituted the majority of French occupation forces in Cilicia. It was at this juncture that the Légion d'Orient was renamed the *Légion Arménienne*. Dickran Boyajian, whose translated memoirs constitute much of this volume, provides detailed information about the activities of the Armenian Legion in postwar Cilicia, as the legionnaires were stationed in various towns. The Legion became instrumental in organizing the relief efforts of Armenians who had survived the deportations and massacres, and were now returning to their villages and homes.

Soon after the French troops entered Cilicia, French foreign policy regarding the emergent Turkish Nationalist Movement changed. This led to the disarming and discharging of the Armenian legionnaires. After only six months of deployment in Cilicia, the French disbanded the Armenian Legion. "The nucleus of the future Armenian Army," as Boghos Nubar had envisioned it, was totally forgotten by the French and was never reinstated. The bitter experience of the shifting French policies left many Armenian legionnaires still in Cilicia totally disillusioned. For France, the Légion Arménienne had already served its purpose as a colonizing tool, and once this goal was achieved in the Levant, there was no need of an Armenian force.

Although the Legion did not form the nucleus of a future Armenian army, it demonstrated a spirit of devotion and patriotism. While the political intrigues of the Allied Powers prevented the creation of an autonomous Cilicia, the legacy of the Armenian Legion continues to make its mark on the pages of Armenian and French history. Its achievements concern a people who attempted to come to grips with the destruction and devastation of their nation. Its story also shows the union of hundreds of Armenians from different backgrounds for a greater cause. With the centennial of the Battle of Arara upon us, it is important to remember the Armenian legionnaires, who fought to keep the vision of an Armenia alive.[4]

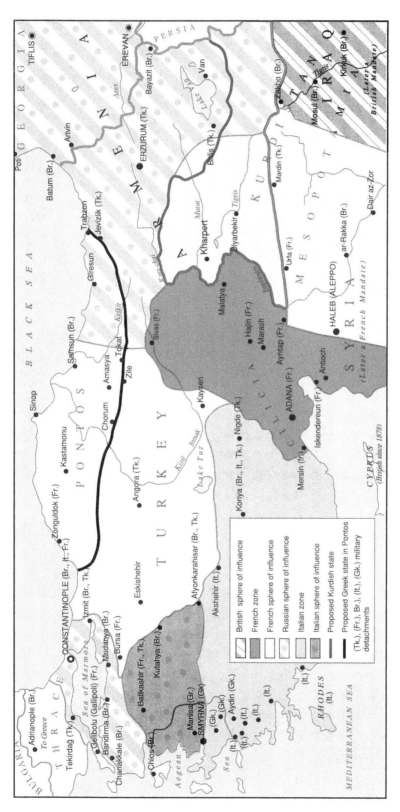

27. "The Proposed Partition of Turkey According to Various Secret Allied Agreements, 1916–1918."
Courtesy of Robert H. Hewsen, Armenia: A Historical Atlas. Original in color.

3

Recruitment and the Voyage

"Beginnings of Sorrows," the title of the first chapter of Dickran H. Boyajian's *The Armenian Legion*, refers not only to the ongoing genocide but also to a related source of disappointment and sadness, the perceived betrayal by the Allied/Entente Powers, for whom so many Armenians had great respect and upon whom they had laid all their hope. While this fractured relationship was outlined in the last chapter, here we return to the earlier period of hope and idealism when Armenian men uprooted themselves from their secure surroundings and returned to the killing fields of the Middle East, hoping to play some part in the liberation of their homelands.

Under the terms set out by the French Foreign Ministry, Armenian men joining the Legion would be placed in detachments according to ethnic group. Some Armenians already living in France had joined the French army as part of the regular forces. The Foreign Legion, however, as its name proclaims, was made up of non-French combatants. The Armenian National Committees in each country were designated as responsible for the transport costs of the volunteers from the United States to France, as well as from Egypt or India to Port Said. From Port Said, all volunteers would be sent to the camp in Cyprus for training. The French government promised to repay the Armenian National Committees for the expenses of those volunteers whose documents and physical health passed the tests for actual recruitment.

28. Legionnaires from Musa Dagh. *Courtesy of Karen Kludjian.*

The first to join were those already waiting in Port Said, the survivors of the siege of Musa Dagh. Roughly 600 of these men eagerly volunteered. Having proven themselves as agile and courageous fighters in their own struggle against tremendous odds, the men of Musa Dagh (also often called *Suediatsis*) were ready to do anything that might bring about the return of their beloved villages.[1]

While documentation for the men from Musa Dagh was being checked and their health and strength examined, preparations were beginning in the United States and France to allow more men to join. Much earlier, meetings had been initiated by the Prelacy of the Armenian Apostolic Church, joined by four Armenian political parties: Armenian Revolutionary Federation (Dashnaktsoutiune), Social Democrat Party (Hnchakian), Reformed Hnchakian, and Armenian Democratic Liberal Party (Ramgavar). However, unity eluded the group until March 1917 when the Armenian National Committee was formed by the four political parties with three delegates each and the Apostolic Church, the Armenian General Benevolent Union and the Armenian Evangelical Church with two delegates each.

The invitation to join and create a separate detachment affiliated with the French Foreign Legion was met with enthusiasm when members of the National Committee visited Armenian communities in North America. While most men shared similar motivations of revenge for their families' and fellow Armenians' deaths, many also hoped to play a part in securing the independence of a future Armenian territory, perhaps under a French mandate. Each had their own personal experiences propelling them towards this decision.

Memoirs of these men are often quite sparse at this first stage. It was almost taken for granted that they would join in fighting the war that had ravaged their homeland and taken away their families. Hovannes Garabedian, whose memoirs contain vivid descriptions of the Battle of Arara (see Chapter Six), begins in a typically concise and matter-of-fact manner: "I was born in the village of Perchen (District of Kharpert, Armenia) on August 28, 1891. I left my birthplace on March 30, 1912, and arrived in the USA on May 25, 1912. On June 30, 1917, I volunteered and joined the Armenian Legion to serve and protect the interest of the Armenian nation to the best of my ability. Few months later, our Legion left for France and on August 12, 1917, we were dispatched to Cyprus."[2]

Speaking in an interview in 1984, Mihran Guzelian remembered that men had come from Egypt in 1915–16, giving lectures and news from the homeland. He first heard of the Legion there when Ardavast Amirian, Mihran Damadian and Stepan Sabahgulian spoke of how an Armenian army was being organized to go and fight the Turks under the umbrella of the French army. He, his older brother and many friends joined.[3]

Other stories give a more detailed idea of the men's lives. Sarkis Najarian's daughter remembers her father telling her about life before his migration to the United States and his later decision to join the legionnaires: Born in Kharpert in 1896, Sarkis Najarian was the eldest of seven brothers. He later recalled that his mother wanted a daughter so badly that she made an oath to God. "Let me have a girl, even if I die!" She did have a daughter but died herself only six hours later. Sarkis's father could not cope with the death and the new baby and so she was taken to the mother's sister's home to be raised with that family.

29. Mihran Guzelian.
Courtesy of the Armenian Museum of America.

30. Sarkis Najarian. *Courtesy of Sona Najarian Touloumjian.*

The father remarried only a few months later and Sarkis was very unhappy. At 17 or 18 years old, he begged to be allowed to go to the United States to work. After resisting for some time, his father finally gave him his pocket watch and permission to go to his own sister's house near Boston. While living with his aunt and her family, Sarkis learned English and worked in a shoe factory but when the Committee came to ask men to join the French Foreign Legion, he joined them. By then he knew that his family had been deported and many killed and he wanted to find his sister, if she was alive.[4]

Stepan Dardouni, who later settled in the United States, spoke of how he first heard about the Legion. A native of Marash, he had somehow survived the deportations and, having lost track of his own family, joined a small group of other survivors from various towns, searching for ways to stay alive. One day he met a man who looked familiar. It was a family friend, Hrant, also from Marash. Hrant told him he was part of the Legion and Stepan decided immediately that he would also join. But Hrant said, "You're the only one left in your family now—have you

31. Vagharshag Vartabed Arshagouni, a priest serving in the Providence Armenian Apostolic Church, was remembered to have spoken at an Armenian Revolutionary Federation picnic in Syracuse, July 4, 1916. Funds were raised for refugees and Rev. Arshagouni asked for more: "He spoke with passion, extolling Armenia's revolutionary heroes, rejecting the tears of slavery and demanding revenge." (Mesrobian 2000: 51) *Photo courtesy of the Armenian Museum of America.*

30

32. American–Armenian men hoping to join the Légion d'Orient wait in Patterson, New Jersey, ready to sail to France and onwards to Port Said.
Courtesy of Ardemis Matteosian.

thought about that?" Stepan responded, "Yes. If I am the only one left, then what does it matter? On the other hand, if they are all alright, then again, what does it matter [if I am killed]?" Upon arrival in Port Said, Stepan was examined by the doctors and rejected as he was "too young, too weak, too small, not even a moustache growing yet." Stepan began speaking in French to the doctors and administrators, having studied it at school in Marash, telling them that he must become a *Gamavor*. "Oh! You speak French?" said the doctor. "That's good enough for us!"[5]

Guévork Gotikian outlines the strict process by which the volunteers were admitted, noting the steps that they were required to follow. Each volunteer was required to undergo a rigorous physical examination to determine their aptitude for battle. This would take place at the port where they disembarked: Le Havre, Bordeaux or Marseilles, or, for those in the Middle East, Port Said. They also needed a certificate signed by the French consul in the town where they were last living, stating their moral character. If this was not possible, then such a certificate signed by a member of the official Armenian National Committee could be accepted. Volunteers residing in France underwent the same process, presenting themselves in Paris or at the main ports, as did those in Port

33. Dzerone Hagopian, originally from Kessab, Syria, joined the Legion from the United States. *Courtesy of Arpi Hagopian Haboian.*

34. Kaspar Menag, legionnaire. "We are asked, Why, when life in the United States was so comfortable, did we leave and come to Cilicia when we knew that we were going into the jaws of death? Our response remains the same: What true Armenian would prefer a comfortable life when his family was under the yoke and being massacred by the Turks; when our entire nation was humiliated by the Turks and in the throes of the last moments of life? Of what use is the life of an individual when his entire nation is being murdered? You gladly sacrifice your life to justify your means of revenge." Menag, from Lawrence, Massachusetts, joined the Legion in 1917 and served in battles in Marash, Ceyhan (Jihan), and İslahiye. *Photo and text courtesy of the Armenian Museum of America.*

Said who went to the nearest French consulate.[6] A number of men were rejected at that stage, causing not only great disappointment but practical and financial problems for the men and for the National Committee which was responsible for paying for their expenses in France and return tickets if they were not selected.

The American–Armenian men were transported first to France. Boyajian describes his journey, leaving New York on July 9, 1917, for Bordeaux on the French steamship *L'Espagne*, noting that most of his group of 90 volunteers were originally from Kessab and Dikranagerd (Diyarbakır). The euphoria of setting off to engage in battle with the enemy was quickly tempered by increasingly frequent bouts of reality.

> From the very first moment, despite our mood of enthusiasm, we had more than one cause for complaint. Our boys were crowded into one of the lower decks of the ship surrounded by putrid and indescribable filth. It was impossible to comprehend such carelessness and neglect by any responsible captain or sailors. The food was bad and inadequate and no one gave any thought to its improvement.

35. The *Espagne* transported some of the legionnaires from New York to France. Built in 1909 as an ocean liner by Chantiers & Ateliers de Provence, it was used as a troopship during World War I.

> The hellish aspect of the threat of a more serious, more immediate danger appeared in our minds and engulfed us in fear. That was the threat of the German submarines.[7]

Once in Bordeaux the men were given a military contract to read and sign, though Boyajian writes that few of them understood French. They did, however, discover that one of the clauses included the stipulation that the men were agreeing to fight on any front and this troubled them greatly. However, they signed and undertook another journey, some 400 miles overland to Marseilles, in an open goods wagon. There they boarded a ship for Egypt, escorted by a small battleship, arriving after 16 days of a "slow, nerve-racking and dangerous voyage."[8] The danger was due to the constant presence of infectious diseases in their cramped and dirty quarters but also to the German submarines in the same waters. While Boyajian's group arrived safely in Egypt, another boat did not have the same good fortune.

At the end of August, 1917, some 85 American–Armenian volunteers set out on the *Amiral Orly* from Marseilles en route to Egypt, again escorted by a small destroyer. Legionnaires Diran Patapanian, Sarkis Najarian and Haygaz Aghayigian later recounted their experience to Boyajian and he included these in his own account.

> Our ship was going forward in zigzags in order to avoid German submarines. Every day we went through a drill so that each of us would be thoroughly familiar with his role. That way, if we were attacked, we would not be taken by surprise. [...]
>
> On the eve of September 1, everyone was in pursuit of a happy mood. It was as if all felt a foreboding that—who knows, perhaps tomorrow we too would be food for the fish. Eating, drinking, singing and dancing made us forget everything.
>
> Around 1 p.m. on September 1, as the soldiers were chatting on the deck, playing cards or sleeping, suddenly a terrifying jolt and a loud noise frightened everyone. Pieces of wood, iron and other items rose in the air like dust and came down on us as if turning into smoke, giving all of us a fantastical and unrecognizable appearance. The boats fixed around

the ship, except one, were cast in the water. The rout was indescribable.

The torpedo fired by the submarine had pierced our ship right in the middle, destroying the steam boiler and all its appliances. The ship was condemned to immobility but was bobbing up and down, fortunately.

With a great deal of difficulty, it became possible to restore some order. From the deck, we lowered a number of largish rafts into the sea, on which many of our friends and the Indochinese took their places. As the very last thing, we lowered the final boat following the captain's directions and the remainder of us were squeezed onto it. There was no room to move but we had to row to get away from the ship in order not to sink with her. A superhuman effort was required in order to be able to row. Finally, we were able to move a safe distance away from the ship. The rudderless rafts had floated away from each other and were bobbing aimlessly on the sea, here and there

36. Painting of the *Amiral Orly* sinking in the Mediterranean Sea. Many former legionnaires have a photographed copy of this and it seems that others may have recreated the painting itself. *Courtesy of Sona Najarian Touloumjian*.

37. Diran Patapanian.
Courtesy of the Armenian Museum of America.

becoming playthings for the waves. Everyone had undressed fearing sinking from the weight of wet clothes. It was summer and there was no fear of catching cold.

The warship escorting us continuously and swiftly circled our ship which refused to sink. It took hours to gather our boys together, one by one, squeezed onto rafts, and get them on board the destroyer.

We were all saved but our destroyer was floating around our torpedo-stricken ship. At that moment an English warship came to our rescue. The result of the deliberations of the captains of the two warships was that it was possible to plug the hole opened at the side of our ship and tow the ship to the island of Crete, which was not that far.

Words had not yet turned into actions when another torpedo passing under our destroyer fatally penetrated the stern of the

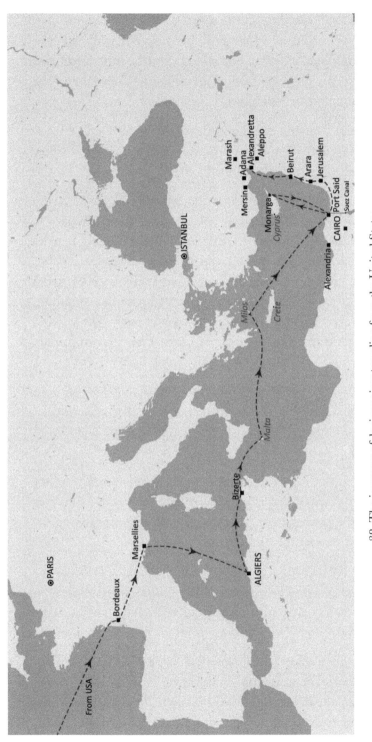

38. The journeys of legionnaires traveling from the United States. *By Anieka Sayadian.*

Amiral Orly still swaying on the sea. Our transport ship shook, twisted and raising her bow sank by the stern while we, the lucky ones, watched that horrible spectacle with terror and bewilderment. The God of the Armenians had saved our lives. We had not perished like dogs.

The English warship, feeling assured that we no longer needed her help, left us and we returned to the island of Milos, about 100 miles north of Crete in the southern waters of the archipelago.

Finally, a Greek ship arrived to transport us to Egypt. We ascended the deck crammed with around 150 Chinese people. It wasn't necessary to make a special effort to realize that we had been put on a rickety and defenseless ship made of wood ready to be broken into smithereens any minute by the lashing of sea waves. It neither had lifeboats nor guns. The French officials accompanying us did not embark on that ship; they stayed behind with the intention of joining us later.

We got together, conferred and decided to send a delegation to the captain of the battleship. We were not granted an audience despite our repeated and urgent demands and supplications.

We had no other way—disobedient but nevertheless an assured way—to force under duress the captain of the Greek ship not to set sail. A small English destroyer approached our ship and ordered the captain to set sail immediately. The captain replied that he was under threat and could not move.

You may call us whatever you wish: disobedient, rebellious, undisciplined. We had emerged victorious and had every right to be so. After a voyage of thousands of miles full of adventures, it was difficult to fall victim to an arbitrary and inhuman order.

We were temporarily transferred to another ship where we were all locked up in a cabin on the lower deck; we didn't know if it was a punishment or under constraint. Not long afterwards they brought us to the bridge where the admiral commander of the battleship and the captain of our sunken ship presented themselves to us. [The commander] reproached us a little for our rebellious stance and said: "This doesn't sit well with the disciplined and unflappable attitude you demonstrated during those difficult moments when your lives were in danger once your ship was torpedoed." The admiral praised us for that attitude as worthy of a soldier.

Barely a few days had passed when we had a most pleasant surprise. Another group of volunteers arrived in Milos from Marseilles. We were transferred to that ship, embraced each other tearfully and with emotion. We knew some of them but they were all dear to us. They were American–Armenians like ourselves. They clothed us. Together we drank, ate and enjoyed ourselves with boundless, indescribable enthusiasm.

We set out for Port Said. However, that wasn't the end of our travails. Our reputation as disobedient soldiers had preceded us to Egypt, where a court martial, conviction and exile could await us.

Fortunately, our situation was not that extreme. In Port Said we, the rebels, were assembled to one side and heard heavy words from the sergeant "trying" us who labelled us as cowards and men unworthy of a soldier's honor desirous of the liberation of the Armenian nation. Would that the ground opened and we were buried there. That is how we felt, all of us. Would it not have been preferable to have been on the ship when she was struck by the second torpedo and go to the bottom of the sea with her? No doubt we would have been considered heroes without firing a single shot against the enemy. Our names would have been inscribed in golden letters. And now? According to the French sergeant the story of our desertion would have been written in black letters.

The episode was soon forgotten. It was good that we had been a bit disobedient.[9]

18e RÉGION
PLACE DE BORDEAUX

N° 1174 du Registre d'inscription.

ACTE D'ENGAGEMENT

du nommé *Mardikian Nichan*

pour la LÉGION D'ORIENT

L'an mil neuf cent dix *sept*, le *douze Novembre* à *dix* heures, s'est présenté devant nous, ~~OHS~~, Sous-Intendant Militaire, résidant à BORDEAUX, le nommé *Mardikian Nichan* âgé de *33* ans, né à *Malatia (Arménie)* fils de _____ " _____ et de _____ " _____ résidant en dernier lieu à BORDEAUX (Gironde). Taille d'un mètre *soixante-six* centimètres, cheveux *et* sourcils *noirs*, front *étroit*, yeux *noirs*, nez *régulier*, bouche *régulier*, menton *régulier*, visage *allongé*. Marques particulières *néant*.

Lequel en présence de M. *Edilian Caporal Légion d'Orient*, Interprète, a déclaré, après avoir pris connaissance des conditions du service à la Légion d'Orient fixées par l'Instruction Ministérielle n° 7.966 9/11 du 26 Novembre 1916, vouloir s'engager pour la durée de la Guerre dans la LÉGION D'ORIENT, ~~en vue de combattre contre la Turquie sous le Drapeau~~. A cet effet, il nous a présenté un certificat d'aptitude délivré le *10 Nov. 1917* 191_, par M. GUY, Lieutenant-Colonel, Commandant le Recrutement de BORDEAUX, et constatant qu'il n'est atteint d'aucune infirmité, qu'il a la taille et les autres qualités requises pour le service de la LÉGION D'ORIENT.

Il nous a présenté en outre un sauf conduit délivré par le Consul Général de France à *New York* le *19 Octobre* 191*7*.

Nous, ~~OHS~~, Sous-Intendant Militaire, après avoir reconnu la régularité des pièces produites par M. *Mardikian Nichan* lui avons fait expliquer par l'Interprète qu'il devait s'assujettir à toutes les charges de la Discipline Militaire et en particulier à la juridiction des Conseils de Guerre français.

Ensuite de quoi, nous avons reçu l'engagement de M. *Mardikian Nichan* lequel a promis de servir avec honneur et fidélité sous le Drapeau Français, à partir de ce jour jusqu'à la fin de la Guerre.

Lecture et traduction faites par l'Interprète à M. *Mardikian Nichan*, il a signé avec nous.

L'Intéressé,
Signé :
Nichan Mardikian

POUR COPIE CONFORME :
Le Sous-Intendant Militaire,

Le Sous-Intendant Militaire,
Signé :
Imbert

39. "*Certificat d'Engagement*" showing that Nishan Mardikian has been accepted into the Légion d'Orient. *Michael Najarian Collection.*

Sarkis Najarian, in a separate personal account, writes: "When I write these words tears flow from my eyes."[10]

In Port Said, the waves of *Gamavors* arriving from or by way of France assembled and looked for ways to pass their time. Boyajian writes that it was a boring time for them and certainly other observers, such as the French and British officers in charge, were also concerned. These men and those in the Musa Dagh refugee camps of Port Said were eager to be on their way and fighting the enemy. The officers in charge allowed them to visit Cairo where they were greeted and embraced by members of the Armenian community there. The men stayed in a hotel and took in the local sites, including the pyramids and the banks of the Nile.

> One evening there was a tea reception in honor of the volunteers in the presence of the Armenian elite of the city. Time passed very slowly in Port Said. There was nothing to do and we were impatient to do something. Occasionally we were allowed to go into town to get away from the monotony. [...] Generally,

40. The first departure of legionnaires from Port Said, en route to Cyprus.
AGBU Nubar Library, Paris.

the places we would visit were smoke-filled coffee shops where one could see persons of every class and character.[11]

Boyajian gives a flavor of the time and place with the teasing remarks of the backgammon players as they battled against each other contrasting with the serious deliberations of the "diplomats" huddled over their drinks, discussing international politics.

> The group of "diplomats." Their number is not important. In front of each there is a never-ending glass of beer or arak (*oghi*).
>
> "The state of France appears to be dismal. She cannot hold out for long if the American soldiers don't show up" predicts one of the "diplomats."
>
> "You there! Are you out of your mind? France will not be defeated easily. She will fight to the last soldier and will surely overcome," ripostes another, "especially because she has standing next to her such a noble country as England."
>
> "What did you say?" protests a third in an indignant voice. "That perfidious, selfish and haughty Albion? Is she going to be the one to triumph over Germany? Can't you see? The war has been going on for three years and England's participation has only been half-hearted."[12]

When the soldiers sailed to Cyprus, their connections with Cairo continued in important ways. Egyptian Armenian ladies became "godmothers" (Boyajian uses the French word *marraine*) to many of the men and sent letters, socks, underwear, shaving blades and other small items to them. They also assisted when serious health issues emerged, hosting soldiers who needed special attention in Cairo.

4

Training in Cyprus

Cyprus, a British colony at the time, was chosen as the training ground for the new legionnaires. As allies in the war, both the British and the French had interests in the actions of the Légion d'Orient and arranged to work together on their training and deployment.

Guévork Gotikian notes that the siting of the training camp in Cyprus required protracted discussions between the French and British. Permission was finally granted by the British High Commissioner, Sir John Clausen, but the men were put under the direct command of a French officer, Lt. Col. Romieu. The village of Monarga (now called Boğaztepe) was chosen as the site of the proposed camp. Some 24 kilometers north of Famagusta—Αμμόχωστος (Ammochostos) in Greek and Mağusa in Turkish—Monarga was chosen, according to Gotikian, because it was far from Greek or Turkish Cypriots and they wished to avoid local problems.[1] However, Boyajian notes that the small farming village of Monarga itself had been evacuated and its residents moved further inland. Though the area was not densely populated, indeed there were both Greek and Turkish villagers in the area as well as in the town of Famagusta as becomes evident in the legionnaires' memoirs and the local history written by both Greek and Turkish Cypriots.

The eastern coast of Cyprus, looking straight across the water towards Syria and Cilicia, had flatlands as well as rocky, stubbled hills

41. Armenian Legion tents pitched at Monarga, Cyprus. 1917.
Michael Najarian Collection.

42. Lt. Col. Louis Romieu. *Courtesy Ardemis Matteosian.*

where the men could practice their maneuvers. Just a kilometer inland from today's coastal town of Boğaz, Monarga was indeed very close but not close enough to Cilicia and the Armenian homelands.

The men from Musa Dagh, or the Suediatsis, as they were called, arrived in Cyprus several months ahead of the other legionnaires. They had begun their military training while still in Port Said and continued in Cyprus while also building the first camps. Eventually, three main camps were built, one just below Monarga, where the Suediatsis lived, the second in Monarga itself for the officers, with mess hall and other shared facilities, and a third in the valley just beyond Monarga where the rest of the recruits set up their tents. This dispersion was in part due to the lack of sufficient water at any one of the sites as the numbers swelled. Later, following local disturbances involving a few of the legionnaires, another group was moved to a new camp, on the northern side of the Kyrenia Mountains.

While the move to Cyprus did take them several steps further on the journey to the battlefield, many of the men were impatient. They were disappointed at the treatment they received as enlisted soldiers and in the time that it was taking to reach their goal. Boyajian sums up these feelings: "There were rude, ignorant, uncivil and cruel minor officials, corporals and sergeants, lording it over us. It was as if the riffraff and the most useless soldiers of the French army were gathered together and

43. Adrian Barracks, Monarga, Cyprus. The back of the photo is signed by Romieu, noting the building is the "Foyer des soldats." *AGBU Nubar Library, Paris.*

appointed as captains and trainers of the Armenian volunteer groups. We were heavily disillusioned. There was no escape route nor would we have contemplated taking it, had there been one."[2]

By the time Boyajian and his group arrived, other companies had been at the camp for some time. He describes being greeted by the Suediatsis as well as other soldiers who had come from the United States. He writes that the welcomes lasted into the night with conversation, laughter and even jokes. But the next day, reality returned with a meager breakfast of "a piece of dry bread, a slice of cheese and a cup of tea without lemon or milk. Eat and be content!"[3]

In his interview, Stepan Dardouni also speaks about strict routines and drills set out for the men as well as the camaraderie between them. When asked about the age range of the legionnaires, he answers that there were young boys like himself of 16, or even younger, as well as men with grey hair, perhaps 50 years old. But, he says, all mixed together: "We were close like brothers and also sharing a deep love for the nation." However, when Dardouni was initially assigned to the telephone room, he refused the work. "I didn't come here to answer telephones! I came to fight." Initially accused of insubordination, he was saved by a comrade and somehow convinced the officer that he should be a combatant.[4]

The men settled into a routine in the camp, rising at 7:00 in the morning, resting after 5:00 p.m. The newly arrived soldiers continued the construction of buildings that the Suediatsis had begun. But, Boyajian notes, the men wondered why they were building semi-permanent structures. How long would they be in Cyprus and why were these needed? The soldiers were suspicious of the discrepancies they noticed between the promises made during the recruitment and their present situation. They were eager to fight and felt they were wasting their time. However, the men kept their thoughts to themselves initially.

Boyajian reports that one of the soldiers did object to a certain job, which involved heavy work carrying large rocks. He was taken to a military tribunal and sentenced to hard labor in Tunisia. Generally, Boyajian writes, the men began to feel that the French were taking advantage of them and drawing out their time in Cyprus for no apparent reason. The men of Musa Dagh in particular had been waiting for many months and felt their training was complete. Boyajian uses such words as "useless" and "barren" to describe the soldiers' life in limbo[5] and observes that dissatisfaction grew as the newcomers added their complaints to those of the Suediatsis.

Later reflecting on that period, Boyajian discussed the men's discontent.

> We the newcomers began to justify their [the Suediatsis] position, because we too were dissatisfied with our incomprehensible internment and were impatient and wanted as soon as possible to confront the brutal enemy bent on exterminating our race. We didn't understand, or perhaps didn't want to understand, that our waiting could have been due to very valid reasons. Our youthful enthusiasm, our vengeful anger and our inexperience as well as our proud attitude would not allow us to reason dispassionately that we were going to be an insignificant part of a big army being made ready to fight on the Palestinian Front.
>
> Discrimination by the Frenchmen against the Armenians was a glaring reality. There was even prejudice towards Armenian officers and minor officials. There were occasions on which an Armenian sergeant major refused for months to join the French officers' table as a protest against their attitude.
>
> Among Armenian soldiers there were a considerable number of educated young men who could have been trained for the rank of officer. Not only was there no desire shown to encourage these men, but also there was obvious opposition towards the mere idea. Even those who had served for many years in the American army were admitted as privates in the Legion and only months later promoted to the ranks of sergeant, adjutant or at most, second lieutenant.[6]

As the men finished the building projects, they found other ways to keep themselves busy. In addition to the military parades, training in target-shooting, musketry, one-to-one combat, and other forms of fighting, the men also took part in jogging, wrestling, gymnastics, and the singing of patriotic songs in Armenian and French. These included:

"*Loosin chgar*" ("There was no moon"); "*Tartsyal paylets*" ("It glimmered again"); "*Grvetsek dgherk*" ("Fight on, lads!"); "*Heravor yergir*" ("Far country"); "*Pam porodan*" ("Boom! They rumbled"); "*Arik haygazoonk*" ("Armenian bravehearts"); "*Im chinari yare*" ("My love is like a plane tree"); "*Dalvorigi zavag em kach*" ("I am a brave son of Dalvorig"); "*I zen, hayer*" ("To arms, Armenians!"); "*Hay abrink yekhpayrk*" ("Let's live as Armenians, brothers!"); "*Tzayne henchets Erzroomi hayotz lerneren*" ("not a sound rang out from the Armenian mountains of Erzurum"), and many others. The French songs listed in Boyajian's memoirs are "*La Madelon*" and the "*Marseillaise*".[7] Among the soldiers were musicians, including singers and instrumentalists, actors and those who could recite poetry and stories. The violin, mandolin, oud, flute, cornet, qanun and other instruments were played.

Throughout his book, Boyajian includes extracts from the memoirs of his fellow legionnaires. Here Lt. Vahan Portukalian also discusses the relations between the men and the commanding officers as well as the ways in which the men passed their time while in Cyprus. In general, the Commander, Lt. Col. Romieu was widely respected and appreciated as an exceptional leader.

44. Legionnaire musicians in Monarga. Mgrditch Garinian with mandolin.
Courtesy of Mrs. V. S. Gulezian. Michael Najarian Collection.

> Lt. Col. Romieu, the Legion Commander, brought an Adrian Barracks[8] over from Egypt [...] He designated it as a meeting place for the legionnaires, furnishing it with fixtures for non-alcoholic beverages and ordered Armenian and French newspapers and magazines for reading. A few days passed. Not a single legionnaire set foot in the hall. The reason was simple. A sign was placed on the door of the Adrian Barracks with the inscription "Meeting Place for Native Legionnaires" [The French word *indigène* (native) is used in Armenian transliteration in the text.] The wording was put together by a non-commissioned officer from North Africa or from colonial regiments who had no idea who the Armenians (or Syrians) were. The Armenians did not accept the designation "native" or indigenous, first of all because they were not natives of Cyprus and secondly because they were aware that in that context "native" meant belonging to an "inferior race."
>
> The Colonel immediately had the inscription erased and had the word "native" replaced by "auxiliary" which was the term used in the Legion's statute.[9]

Portukalian goes on to describe an outing to view the ruins of a tenth-century castle in the nearby Kyrenia Mountains. Kantara Castle straddles the mountain range, with stunning vistas both north and south but also east and west along the range itself. The men called the ruins "Levon's fort" after the last king of Armenian Cilicia. Lusignan royalty in Cyprus, who intermarried with the Cilician Armenian royal family, spent time in the castle, hunting and relaxing. Eager to see this physical connection to their own history, the men set out at dawn. Their enthusiasm grew as the sun appeared and they began singing Armenian patriotic songs, by now familiar even to the French officers.

> We passed through Greek and Turkish villages where we reminisced about village life back in Armenia. Our imagination took us back there where we lived our teenage years of happiness and sadness. Gloomy feelings encircling our hearts, we felt our spirits collapsing as we thought about all those charming

> places, now deserted. […] We set up our tents in a grove and started preparing for meals. Each section of ten soldiers made their own hearth. Everyone was busy, some bringing water, some making fire and others preparing meals.
>
> [After visiting the ruins of the castle] we were hoping that the day wasn't far off that we would set foot on Cilician soil as victorious soldiers, and then … [10]

Portukalian leaves the sentence to be completed by the reader and continues his memoirs with notes on daily life in the camp, including new pastimes invented to alleviate the boredom.

> The wrestling match between Vartan from Kharpert and a soldier from Brusa has stayed fresh in my memory; the first entirely inexperienced and only relying on his strong muscles and the latter an experienced wrestler, heavy set and strong.
>
> The experienced wrestler […] was mercilessly tormenting poor Vartan who through superhuman efforts was trying to keep both his shoulders away from the ground. We were following

45. Kantara Castle, north of Monarga in the mountains.
The legionnaires visited "Levon's Castle." *Courtesy of Susan Paul Pattie.*

every single move, sometimes in horror, especially when the wrestler putting Vartan's head under his arm, was squeezing it forcefully or when laying Vartan down on his face, was crossing his legs and squeezing and squeezing them with the cruelty of a savage beast. "Let him go, man, it's enough torturing the poor boy! Look here, have you no pity?" some were shouting. The wrestler had no pity whereas Vartan was enduring the pain with inexplicable patience. He could not yield or concede defeat. No one had succeeded in making his back touch the ground; was this Brusatsi savage going to frighten him? No. Vartan was determined to defend the honor of Kharpertsis. His defeat was going to be inevitable if others hadn't intervened. The honor of Kharpertsis was outwardly saved.[11]

Vartan's story does not end with that, Boyajian continues:

Once we had a day off and went to Famagusta along with Vartan. Altogether there were six of us. We went into a restaurant and you can imagine what our first order was going to be—*oghi*, plenty of salad with lemon and olives. Our heads were already turning before the main meal arrived. We ate, drank, sang, and danced. At least for a day we had left soldiery behind at Monarga […]

Evening came. The sun was setting and we had to be back in camp. Everyone was awake, whereas I had just started to doze off. They dragged and hauled me out onto the street. Wherever we stopped, I would sit down and sleep. The boys were looking for a cab to hire. I don't know how a brawl started between our boys and about ten Greeks. They were fighting for an empty cab: "I must have it! You cannot have it!"

Vartan was in his element. He snatched a piece of wood from the hands of a Greek and fell upon them at the speed of lightning. Whoever got hit, fell to the ground. He had already split the heads of six or seven people.

Policemen intervened. The fighting stopped. The Famagusta

46. Inscribed on back of photo: "Future Armenian soldier." (Note the boy is also in fig. 43 with the musicians.)
Michael Najarian Collection.

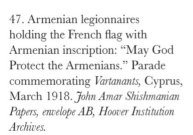

47. Armenian legionnaires holding the French flag with Armenian inscription: "May God Protect the Armenians." Parade commemorating *Vartanants*, Cyprus, March 1918. *John Amar Shishmanian Papers, envelope AB, Hoover Institution Archives.*

postmaster, the late Roupen Herrian, rushed in. I was now completely awake but had missed the brawl. He approached me and with an angry tone, though not devoid of pity, said "Dikran, you too got drunk? Aren't you ashamed of yourself, lad?" Roupen Herrian could not believe that I too could get drunk. The cabman had fled and we were forced to spend the night in Famagusta, sitting up until the next morning without a bed. Mr. Herrian telephoned the military authorities of our brigade, informing them of the situation, lavishing praise on us who had been able to oppose around one hundred Greeks and had put them to flight. Of course one hundred was an exaggeration, whereas twenty would have been nearer the truth. One ought to confess that even if those who got in a fight with us had numbered one hundred, we would have won, thanks to our Vartan.

We set out early in the morning for Monarga. We had hardly left the town, when we saw a cab approaching from behind. We stopped it. It was the cabman of the previous evening who had refused to take us to camp and had fled. His fare was a Turk. When the cab stopped, he got out discreetly and disappeared. All six of us got in the cab and went to Monarga in all comfort. The cabman was so frightened of us that he did not ask for money.[12]

During the long months in Cyprus, the legionnaires created their own community, papering over their peacetime differences, whether these arose from hometown allegiances or political affiliations. Boyajian goes so far as to claim that party connections were never mentioned while in the Legion. However, several disturbances were reported between certain soldiers and local Cypriots.

The period of waiting brought some 4,000 men together with minimal supervision, anxious, overheated minds and bodies aching to fight. The street fight in Famagusta ended in injuries. Other incidents were even more dangerous. Andreko Varnava, writing about Ottoman Famagusta during World War I, describes how much pressure was put on the local policing and colonial forces of the island. Varnava writes about the Cypriot Muleteers who were training in the same area before joining the war, noting the problems they created with their misbehavior. However, he claims that the legionnaires stretched the local police far further with brawls between legionnaires and the local people.

48. Men marching on parade, honoring the Armenian national holiday, Vartanants. *John Amar Shishmanian Papers, envelope A, Hoover Institution Archives.*

49. Legionnaires. *Michael Najarian Collection.*

These incidents, found in the State Archives of Cyprus, reveal that the clashes between Cypriot natives (Greek and Turkish) and the Armenian legionnaires were continuous, rather than occasional incidents. Noting the Cypriot villagers' prejudice against outsiders as one factor, Varnava also describes the Armenians' drunken behavior, including abusive language, theft, disrespectfully "propositioning women," many fights in which men on both sides were gravely wounded, and a major crisis occurring over two weeks between December 1917 and January 1918.

Lt. Col. Romieu defended the men, saying that "he could not guarantee the morality of 3,000 'Oriental volunteers';" particularly "those coming from America have, as all other inhabitants of new worlds, a rather lively temper." The situation continued to worsen with new police stations opening up near the villages in order to protect the people. The long stay of the legionnaires was soon to end, leaving the villagers to return to their old lives. Unfortunately, the actions of a small minority had exacerbated the suspicions of the surrounding Cypriot villagers who had originally hoped to earn money from the new strangers through their shops and restaurants.[13]

50. Lt. John Shishmanian (seated) with fellow legionnaire at Salamis, Roman ruins north of Famagusta, Cyprus. *John Amar Shishmanian Papers, envelope B, Hoover Institution Archives.*

51. Karnig Berberian (far left) and fellow legionnaires.
Courtesy of the Armenian Museum of America.

During this period, Boyajian received news of his mother's death. He stayed in his tent, remembering the last time he had seen her.

> That morning I was not at the military parade [*rassemblement* – the French is used in transliteration]. Our company was due to go on a military tour. Lieutenant Louis Schlinker, the noble French officer who was handsome like Apollo, had noticed my absence and had enquired after me. He came through the tent opening and found me in bed. Instinctively, I got up. He made a sign for me to sit down. He too sat next to me. He was moved on hearing the news of my mother's death. He talked to me, exhorted and advised me to put on my clothes and join the others. "In the field, together with your friends, your sorrow will be assuaged," he said with the compassion of a brother. "Put on your clothes and come."[14]

The relations between the legionnaires and their French officers were sometimes at this individual, more human level, with some men forging lasting friendships. More often it seems that the relations reflected a difficult combination of innocent but misguided hopes and dreams projected onto the French state, represented by these officers, many of whom apparently did not sympathize with the particular aims of the Armenian legionnaires, nor were they generally interested in their troubles. Indeed the French and British showed themselves to have their own priorities, contrary to promises made and agreements earlier signed.

Time dragged on and as months passed by, Boyajian writes that the men became very impatient being in one place for so long, doing the same things every day, seeing the same things and the same people. The men had great difficulty understanding what could be the purpose in leaving them in this limbo state for so long when they ached to be using their strength and skills on the battlefield. It was eight months of training for Boyajian's group and much more for the Suediatsis who had arrived ahead of the others.

> Reluctantly, we had started to think that the French had apparently deceived us. Yes us, who making every sacrifice had left our peaceful and safe surroundings in places far off, crossing thousands of miles to perform our national duty, obeying the

52. Lt. John Shishmanian "with my boys."
John Amar Shishmanian Papers, envelope B, Hoover Institution Archives.

final call of our martyred people. And now we were condemned to be imprisoned on this island, away from our fatherland, away even from our enemy.

Easter Sunday was approaching. We had already celebrated Christmas in an inglorious and sorrowful manner and this circumstance awakened in our memories occurrences that made our protector-friends hateful in our eyes. We remembered the presents sent to us from Egypt, America, France and other places, barely a quarter of which had reached us.[15]

One distraction provided to Boyajian during those long months was the assignment of giving English lessons to one of the officers. Captain Azan had recommended him as a teacher for First Lt. Pianelli and their lessons took place twice a week. Boyajian wrote that he enjoyed "the thorough respect that a student shows his teacher." As Easter grew nearer, Boyajian dared to ask him. "*Mon Lieutenant*, is it true that soon the Legion will set out for the front?" He looked at me in amazement. My question was unexpected. He knew that the soldiers had become impatient and I was no different. He didn't want to lie to me. Therefore, without hesitation, he replied, "It is true, we will leave in a few days."[16]

5

Palestine and Preparation for Battle

On Easter morning, the troops received the news that they would be setting off immediately. Boyajian writes that the next day, the 1st, 2nd and part of the 3rd Battalions began leaving Monarga in turn, arriving first in Famagusta where they boarded the *Saint Brieuc*, going to Ismailia via Port Said. Some members of the 3rd Battalion remained in Cyprus with a commanding officer and others were sent to perform guard duty on Kastellorizo Island just off the south coast of Ottoman Turkey, and another group to do the same on Rouad (Arwad), off the Syrian coast. These men joined the others later in Beirut and Cilicia.

53. Ardashes Arakelian and comrades.
Courtesy of the Armenian Museum of America.

Life on Kastellorizo

Onnik Sinanian[1]

Kastellorizo was a mountainous, rocky little island facing the Adalia Mountains at a distance of almost 2,500 meters. Our company was assigned to watch over the four separate extremities of the island.

Apart from a few Turks, the entire population of Kastellorizo consisted of Greeks, and according to their recounting, the town had lost a lot of its charm since the beginning of the war. The people had left little by little, shops were closed and their owners left for other places. There were barely one or two sailing ships remaining in the harbor, whereas before the war, countless ships were visiting from various ports of Greece, Rhodes, İzmir and other places.

The poverty prevalent amongst the remaining Greek population in the town was not to be envied. Meat was sold in the town on rare occasions and, as in countries involved in the European war, a certain amount of bread was given to each individual.

Only once every four to five weeks a small steamboat would cast anchor at the southern part of the island at night, leaving a little bit of provisions, and would leave the same night without being observed by the Turks. The Turks had once sunk a steamboat with one discharge of cannon right in front of the town.

And it happened that for six to seven weeks we would not be favored by the visit of the steamboat. That was when our situation, both mentally and physically, became intolerable, because simultaneously we were deprived of letters and provisions. It happened once that for two weeks we ate macaroni and rice cooked only in water and thus, as a result of a penury of provisions and food, the goats belonging to two or three Greek goatherds of Kastellorizo started disappearing in a mysterious way. Almost every day complaints were addressed to the military commander who promised to put harsh measures into action and yet, the goats continued their mysterious disappearance.

In Ismailia new problems emerged, adding to the frustrations already building for so long. While the men knew they were finally preparing for battle, it was clear that the battle would not be in Cilicia but in nearby Palestine, helping the British and French against the Germans and Turks on that front. Boyajian empathizes with the plight of the Musa Daghtsis, away for so long in Monarga, now faced with their original refugee camp and families across just a short stretch of water. However, he notes that the incident that followed could have had even more serious repercussions had not the "Armenian military and national authorities acted prudently." He quotes the account of Vahan Portukalian, printed in *Haratch*, August 15, 1964.

> After the arrival of the first company in Port Said, the Musa Daghtsi legionnaires found themselves almost face to face with their former tent city, where their families still lived and whom they had not seen for over two years. Between them passed the Suez Canal, which meant nothing to the Musa Daghtsis. Some would swim across to the other side at night and return in the morning. Soon dozens were following their example. At first the military command tolerated this. It was understandable that men about to leave for the front would want to spend a few more hours with their families. It would have been best if regular permits had been issued [...] It was said that the English High Command had not been willing.
>
> One day those who had gone succumbed to the lure of the family and did not return. With their simple reasoning, they did not realize that they were committing mass desertion, a most serious transgression. Col. Romieu, who was well disposed towards Armenians, did not want to resort to repressive measures immediately. He first ordered the Musa Daghtsi officers [...] to persuade the transgressors to return. That attempt was not successful. The colonel appealed to the religious authorities but their efforts were likewise fruitless. Finally, the National Union, which was the colonel's last hope, also failed.

54. (From left) Lt. Vahan Portukalian, Lt. John Shishmanian and Lt. Papazian.
John Amar Shishmanian Papers, envelope B, Hoover Institution Archives.

> There was no other means but to bring back the disobedient soldiers by force. A detachment of fifty soldiers from the second company was ordered to accomplish that duty. The second company consisted of Turkish Army prisoners of war who had done military service for years. For them discipline did not depend on one's whim. From a psychological point of view, perhaps it ought to be considered that these natives of Greater Armenia [the Armenian Highlands] had not seen their families for years and were no longer going to see them.
>
> Unfortunately the Musa Daghtsis also had their own psychology and most importantly, their rock-solid stubbornness. Only after bayonetting a few of them was it possible to bring the others back to Port Said where they were imprisoned awaiting court martial.
>
> The court, presided over by the French Col. Renié, was lenient and handed down a mild condemnation. They were allowed to leave for the battlefield with the Legion.[2]

Boyajian notes that this was not the only problem for the men while on their second stay in Egypt. By then the hot summer months were upon them, but they were more troubled by a feeling that their French officers were developing a "repressed antipathy" towards them. After their drill one day, they returned to their canteen, tired and hungry.

> As soon as the trumpet sounded, we ran to the kitchen and every group of ten soldiers went to the canteen after receiving their share of the meal. We looked at the food a bit astonished. Why was it so dark? We were hungry, we tried to eat. It was bitter and tasted putrid. We were obliged to return the meal to the kitchen, silently without complaint, without making a fuss, because we knew from past experience that complaints and protests made our situation worse. We returned to the canteen, brokenhearted, satisfied with the bread given to us.
>
> Barely 10 minutes later the captain of our 6th company came in. We all rose, by force of habit. Captain Azan appeared angry. His

eyes were red. He ordered us to sit down and began to speak to us through an interpreter. He strongly condemned our rebellious behavior. He reminded us of the inevitable difficulties of military life, its constraints and vexations. We understood all that and become red-faced. If only we had not taken the food back to the kitchen and had not shown signs of dissatisfaction. After all, we were soldiers and we could not forgive ourselves for appearing in a mutinous position. Captain Azan continued in an unforgiving spirit, as if we had attempted a mutiny within the army. He was beside himself and even became impatient with the interpreter for translating his words slowly. The French captain delivered his last utterance with bridled articulation and carefully weighed words, understood by everyone: "This behavior of yours leads me to the conclusion that the Turks were justified to take up disciplinary measures against the Armenian people."

55. A. Ajemian (standing), Cairo, June, 1918. *Michael Najarian Collection.*

56. Lt. Hagop Arevian. *Courtesy of the Armenian Museum of America.*

> The blow was unexpected and terrible. We were all shaken. We looked at each other stupefied, as if numbed. There, in front of our eyes stood a high-ranking French officer who had the duty of leading us in battle against an enemy whose monstrous acts he was justifying.[3]

One of the few Armenian officers, Lt. John Shishmanian, was consulted and on his advice, a delegation was sent to Captain Azan to ask for reassurance that they had misunderstood his words. Though he received the delegation, Captain Azan insulted them further, accusing them of insubordination. Boyajian and the others lost hope of any advancement, which turned out to have been the correct intuition.

On July 2, 1918, the troops prepared to leave for Mejdel. Unexpectedly, as relations between the military authorities of the Legion and the National Union of Egypt had been severed following the problems with the Musa Daghtsis, the National Union, along with men and women from the Armenian community, visited the legionnaires to bid them farewell. How this came about is described by Vahan Portukalian who begins by noting that Lt. Col. Romieu, believing that the ruptured relations between the legionnaires and the community of Cairo was not beneficial to the men or their purpose, had given him orders to somehow re-establish the cooperation that had worked so well in the past.

> In keeping with the colonel's bidding, I paid a visit to the French ambassador, M. de France, who received me benevolently and gave encouragement. I went to the headquarters of the National Union.
>
> At the end of a vast hall, next to the window, I observed someone sitting at a desk, reading a newspaper, spread widely. Hearing footsteps he raised his eyes and, seeing a French officer, raised the newspaper to his eyes, pretending he couldn't see me. However, when I approached the table he was forced to lower the newspaper and, in a rather dry tone, asked in French, "What is it that you want, sir?" Instead of replying, I introduced myself: "Lieutenant Portukalian." He jumped to his feet and nearly hugged me. It was Sooren Bartevian. We talked. I

didn't have a great deal of difficulty in making Col. Romieu's perspective acceptable. All members of the National Union, headed by Dr. Nevrooz, were patriotic and dedicated activists.

To mark the agreement in principle, I suggested that the National Union visit Ismailia, the Legion's headquarters, to bid farewell to the legionnaires. Sooren Bartevian hesitated for a moment. "How would they receive us?" he asked. "With honor," I assured him. People living with no communication with each other often acquire prejudices. I insisted that other compatriots, and in particular ladies, accompany members of the National Union in order to give the visit a wide national character. And so it was arranged.

On my return, I reported the result of my mission to the colonel who thoroughly approved.

57. H. Derderian, B. Zakarian, N. Karnakian.
It was common for photographs to be taken of men posing, as if in battle.
Photo Khazaros Gopoian Collection, Courtesy of the Armenian Museum of America.

On the designated day, the entire board of the National Union came to the Ismailia headquarters, accompanied by other compatriots and a number of ladies. The legionnaires had gathered in front of a podium onto which members of the National Union and the other visitors proceeded to ascend. On my order the legionnaires saluted all together. I announced that the National Union had wished to express their gratitude and bid farewell to Armenian volunteers and then gave the floor to the Union's speaker. The moment was awe-inspiring. Sooren Bartevian had the disposition and talent of a true orator. He delivered a patriotic and stirring oration addressed to the newly born Armenian army, upon which so many hopes were placed.

Afterwards, the visitors freely strolled around the headquarters, chatting to the legionnaires. On that day, the nation was one with one will.

Following a reception, the visitors returned to Cairo. The Legion continued preparations for departure. The last day was approaching, when a telegram arrived from Paris in which the President of the Republic congratulated the Legion on the occasion of their leaving for the front.[4]

In his autobiography, Hovannes Garabedian describes the following days, the transition from army-in-waiting towards the actual battlefield.

After ten months of intensive military training in Cyprus, we left for Ismailia, via Port Said (Egypt), to face the murderer of the Armenian nation (The Turks). We found the enemy in a well-prepared and fortified position. The Turks had concentrated about 100,000 troops and 70,000 camels to cross the Suez Canal and capture Egypt.

Fortunately, the military intelligence of the allies (French and British) had detected this concentration of troops right on time and by cannon fire from their battleships destroyed the enemy's military strength. When we arrived at Mejidel (a small town inhabited by Moslem Arabs) which was captured by the British

58. Hovannes Garabedian (right) and comrade.
Courtesy of the Armenian Museum of America.

three months before our arrival, we were told that the following day, July 14, the National Independence Day of France [sic] will be celebrated.

The Armenian Legion also participated in the festivities; infantry was on the first line, next followed the cavalry and then the artillerymen. After marching about thirty minutes, we arrived at headquarters, where we were welcomed by the Allied High Command (French and British officers). After four hours of parading, picture-taking and cannon fire, in a jubilant and triumphant mood, we returned to our barracks.

On August 1, 1917, a general military exercise was performed under the command of a British general for a night attack. The Armenian Legion was divided into two groups—the enemy, which was hidden behind a hill, and our group with all sorts of armaments, was placed under maximum alert for the attack. At 12:00 midnight, with the help of intensive searchlights, we found the enemy's location, surrounded them and with a swift, surprise attack, captured them as prisoners of war.

On August 23, we left Mejidel and with 70 pounds of load on our backs, started marching towards Turkish positions to face the enemy. It took us seven days (ten hours march daily) to reach our destination—the second line of Turkish fortifications.[5]

While in Mejdel, the legionnaires were joined by 250 Syrian volunteers and reorganized into troops ready for battle. This consisted of three

59. Legionnaires Haig Panossian (left) and Ardasher (family name unknown).
Courtesy of the Armenian Museum of America.

60. Camouflaged tent of Lt. Shishmanian on the ridge of Arara where he spent 15 nights.
John Amar Shishmanian Papers, envelope B, Hoover Institution Archives.

battalions, a company of machine-gunners, the small group of artillery and the Syrian company. The problems of the past weeks and months must have seemed quite distant as the men turned their thoughts to the reality of what lay ahead of them. In a more intimate passage, Boyajian tells of an evening walk and reflections with a comrade.

> The stroll with my legionnaire friend Khosrov Nargizian is still very fresh in my memory. [...] We were walking amongst the olive trees with no intention of reaching anywhere. We talked about old and recent things, remembered the senseless and sterile [Armenian political] party quarrels. Neither of us made any attempt to justify any reprehensible act by parties to which each of us belonged. Khosrov

was a Dashnak while I was a member of the Reformed Hnchakian party. Both of us were deep down, by nature, upbringing and inclination, nationalists. Socialism for Khosrov was a point of view that made no sense for a people who were not free and independent. And now that the Mother Country was emptied of its Armenian population, discussions about abstract ideologies would have been mere prattle.

We didn't know what the near future had in store for each of us. If we lived, we were again going to devote our lives to our nation, selflessly and without sectarian fanaticism. The moon was a witness to our covenant. Nothing was going to break the affection initiated and developed between us, two comrades in arms.[6]

Boyajian continues, writing that the legionnaires reached the district of Rafat in Wadi Balut on August 30, some four to five miles behind the front lines of one of the strongest positions of the Turkish army.

61. "Armenian–American legionnaires refused to give up this American flag and carried it through Palestine, Syria, and into Cilicia. Lt. Arevian is the tall man on (sic) left; Manasse, standing under the flag, was killed in the Battle of Arara. This flag was brought from the U.S., was ordered destroyed, but every time turned up," writes Shishmanian. Though Shishmanian writes that Manasse was killed at Arara, he is not listed among the war dead. It is possible that this is a nickname, that he died of wounds a little later, or that Shishmanian misremembered his name.
John Amar Shishmanian Papers, envelope B, Hoover Institution Archives.

62. To the firing line.
John Amar Shishmanian Papers, envelope B, Hoover Institution Archives.

The soldiers were to receive their last orders there and Boyajian notes that for the first time, they had a feeling that their weaponry was inadequate. Their cannons, of 37 millimeters, would be unable to do much damage to the enemy positions. A few days later a new shipment arrived and the men had to acquaint themselves with the new weapons quickly.

Boyajian himself was assigned work as the personal secretary to Dr. Louis Roland. Together, after nightfall, the two of them sought a safe position for the medical station, walking until they reached the village of Dayr Balut. There they found an abandoned house with enough walls standing to be useful for their medical aid center.

6

The Battle of Arara

On the night of September 14, 1918, Boyajian writes that the Legion moved to the frontline and a decision was made to place the 4th, 5th and 6th companies (mostly Armenian–American volunteers) in the foremost position. The attack was to take place on September 19 at 4:30 a.m.

Legionnaire Sharam Stepanian provides the following account of the night before the assault (from *The Volunteer* published in 1928, Cairo).

> It was evening; here and there under the olive and fig trees and in trenches clusters of volunteers were having intimate conversations and conveying wishes and requests to each other in case they did not return from the frontline.
>
> An abundance of dishes was laid out on the ground; it was the last evening and we were spared no pleasure. "Let's drink this cup to tomorrow's victory," shouts one, visibly moved.
>
> And the cups of wine were emptied of their contents.
>
> "Let's sing 'Our Fatherland' [*Mer Hayrenik*]" shouts another, and they all sing together.

On the fifth anniversary of Arara, Boyajian gave more details about the topography of the battle. Writing in the occasional journal of the

Armenian Legionnaire Association he describes the positions of the soldiers.

> Throughout the length of the front in Palestine, from the Dead Sea to the eastern coast of the Mediterranean, there wasn't a position as difficult to penetrate and perhaps as impregnable as the position assigned to the Armenian Legion on the western flank of Arara. It was said that towards the end of spring 1918 the 3,000 English soldiers had on several occasions led attacks against the Turkish trenches and were repelled sustaining great losses.
>
> The 600 soldiers of the Armenian Legion fought along a two-mile stretch. Ahead of them there were three high hills behind which were built, successively, the first, second and third lines of Turkish defense. The left flank of the Legion was taken by

63. *The Gamavor*, published in Cairo in 1928, tenth anniversary of Arara. *Michael Najarian Collection*

a battalion of Algerians, whereas the village of Rafat was situated on its right, built on the west flank of Arara, the defense of which was entrusted to the Syrians who did not even fire a bullet throughout the entire course of the battle.[1]

Hovannes Garabedian, mentioned earlier, continues with this account in his autobiography:

> On September 18, we descended into our fortified trenches and waited for nightfall. At 3:30 a.m., the offensive began. Each commander, with his troops, followed the front line intelligence and moved towards the enemy trenches—a mountain top where they had placed their machine guns. Under the heavy burden of ammunition and provision, we moved down the valley; and then with the utmost caution, up the mountain from three different directions to encircle the enemy. As we got closer, the enemy detected our approach and opened concentrated machine-gun fire at our positions. A few minutes later, our artillery, wisely placed about a mile in the rear, responded with cannon fire. In response to this, enemy cannons started rumbling; all sounded like a horrible clash of fire power, as if heaven and earth had collided in the darkness of the night. But for us (the Armenian legionnaires), it looked like a wedding party. Filled with profound feelings of revenge against the Turks, each one of us had become a wild lion looking for a prey. Perfectly armed, bayonets firmly attached at the end of our rifles, we felt as if no fear existed on earth. Our primary objective was to settle accounts with the enemy for the Armenian genocide and bring to justice as many Turks as possible. As the enemy machine-gun fire was showering us like early spring hail, we moved forward without hesitation or fear. Under extremely difficult conditions, hanging so many times between life and death, at last we got to the top of the mountain and with a final blitzkrieg captured the enemy fortifications with countless casualties and 28,000 prisoners of war. During the main battle that lasted about thirty hours, our casualties were twenty-four killed and seventy-five wounded. After this successful military

64. Khazaros Gopoian, author of "Notes of a Gamavor."
Courtesy of Ardemis Matteosian.

65. Two pages from the diary of Khazaros Gopoian, showing the battlefront of Arara. *Courtesy of Ardemis Matteosian.*

operation, we were ordered to lay down our arms and take a temporary rest.

In the darkness of the night, we started moving down the mountain towards the valley, where the enemy had regrouped, presumably, for a counter-offensive. The same night, from 11:00 p.m. to 12:00 a.m., I was given the front-line guard duty to monitor enemy movements. About twenty minutes after assuming responsibility, I heard a distant noise that was coming closer gradually. I listened carefully but failed to understand anything from their Arabic conversation. Immediately, I dispatched news to the headquarters to check, find out what was going on and report to the high command. Our intelligence determined that they were Arab peasants living in the area, who informed us that the Turks were taking advantage of the night and had abandoned everything and fled away. The news of Turkish flight caused us profound anger, for we wanted the enemy to continue the face-to-face battle so that we could satisfy more and more our thirst of [sic] revenge.

The next morning, we went up the mountain again and inspected the enemy trenches; they were filled with corpses. The ones who were not totally dead proved to be the most unfortunate. The memory of yesterday's genocide (the loss of our parents, children, sisters, brothers) was so fresh in our minds, the thirst for revenge was so profound in the hearts of the Armenian legionnaires, the wounded Turks found no mercy. They were finished in their trenches.

Thus, the Turkish fierce resistance was totally crushed, and in disarray the enemy withdrew towards the interior of the country. We interred our killed brothers with full military honor on the mountain, right at the location of the battlefield called "Arara". While lowering them into their graves, we all in unison prayed the Hayr Mer [The Lord's Prayer] and "Let God bless your souls and illuminate your graves forever. Amen."[2]

66. Mihran Guzelian.
Courtesy of the Armenian Museum of America.

A similar account is given by Mihran Guzelian in his memoirs, describing the anger and revenge that was the driving force behind the men's bravery.

> Firing opened up on both sides and the battle between the Armenians and Turkish forces had begun. The brave Armenians, without any hesitation, immediately became the attacking force. From their shelters the Turks tried vainly to stop the advancing Armenians. They opened up with their German machine guns and field artillery thus creating an immense firing line. The Armenian soldiers hollered in Turkish "We are Armenians, and we have come to even the score." With daring

and bold movements, the Armenian soldiers forced the Turks to abandon their first line of defense. The Armenian 4th, 5th and 6th company of the 2nd battalion jumped into battle and started fighting toward the top of Arara.[3]

In another article in the fifth anniversary edition of *Arara*, legionnaire Stepan Kinosian describes days preceding the battle and also another observation on the fighting.

> Three Turkish airplanes attempted to cross over to our side but were prevented by anti-aircraft fire hitting two of them which crashed behind our positions. English aircraft approach Turkish positions and taunt them by aerial acrobatics, infuriating the Turks.[4]

From the medical station, with Dr. Roland, Boyajian was able to watch as the legionnaires began the attack. In his own account, he notes that after seven hours of artillery barrage and intense fighting, the enemy retreated, abandoning their frontline of fortifications. With the enemy in retreat, a group of soldiers led by their officers gathered the bodies from the battlefield and transported them to a space near the village of Rafat where they were buried in a humble grave. Mihran Guzelian describes this experience:

> Suddenly the sound of a bugle reached our ears; it was the call for assembly, so we immediately ran toward the point of origin, and the entire army gathered together in a very short period of time. The order was given by the commander to gather up the corpses of our martyred comrades and put them together at a designated spot.
>
> We placed our heroes on our tents tied to two rifles and began to transport them to the cemetery designated for their burial. Everybody was silent; they slowly approached the site from all sides, in groups, without hymns, without chorister or priest.
>
> A large ditch had been dug, in which our immortal heroes would lie, embracing one another. There was neither incense smoking there, nor candles to burn; there were neither mothers

weeping over their young braves, nor fathers and friends. Thus, holding our weapons perpendicular like unlit candles, we offered our deep military respects to our proud heroes who became martyrs, as worshippers of ideals, lovers of freedom, and fighters for the future betterment of mankind.[5]

By 11:00 a.m. when the bombardments stopped, the fighting had gone on for seven hours non-stop. When the fighting resumed after midday, the German gunners were unsparing in their onslaught, though Boyajian observes that "through a lucky ruling of Providence, most shells falling on the ground would not explode." Bombardments and rifle-fire continued until sunset when the fighting stopped for the night. Before sunrise, the legionnaires were ordered to attack but the enemy positions were silent. Scouts were dispatched and confirmed that the enemy had fled during the night. The legionnaires were victorious.

Twenty-one Armenian lives were lost on the battlefield and three more men died three days later. One of these was Lt. Joseph Arditti, whom Boyajian describes as "a noble Jew, born in 1895 in Beirut who mixed his blood with that of Armenian heroes on the frontline of Arara, symbolizing and evoking the affinity of two historic races struggling and suffering for similar ideals."[6]

Boyajian lists the injuries and injured and says that the number of the injured, Armenian and non-Armenian, was nearly 80, some very lightly, although others had deep but treatable wounds. Garabed Yegavian was the first to come to the medical station. "He asked Dr. Roland to dress his wound and allow him to return to the frontline. Permission was not granted and Yegavian was transported to hospital."[7] During the attack, the chaplain of the Legion, the priest Vagharshag Vartabed Arshaguni also carried out nursing duties in the medical station.

With the enemy in retreat, a group of soldiers led by their officers gathered the bodies from the battlefield and transported them to a space near the village of Rafat where they were buried in a humble grave. Guévork Gotikian includes an official French proclamation and the words of Romieu and Allenby in his description of the graveside service.

> In an official communiqué published on September 20, 1918, the Légion d'Orient was praised for its comportment: "The

67. Mardiros Jingirian (seated), killed in the Battle of Arara, with Stepan Piligian. *Courtesy of the Armenian Museum of America.*

68. Hovannes Kouyoumdjian, killed in the Battle of Arara. *Courtesy of the Armenian Museum of America.*

69. Kourken Zildjian, killed in the Battle of Arara. *Courtesy of the Armenian Museum of America.*

70. Sgt. Arditti and Dr. Grunberg. *John Amar Shishmanian Papers, envelope A, Hoover Institution Archives.*

diplomatic agency of France in Egypt is proud to be able to pay a tribute of admiration to the Armenians and Syrians who have just given, in the ranks of the French army, the full measure of their patriotism and military virtues." On September 20, Lt. Col. Romieu gave a vivid tribute at the funeral of the soldiers and officers who had fallen in the field of honor. "In the name of all the leaders, officers and soldiers of the sector of the right, I salute our Armenians who died in combat yesterday. They have fallen in this place where we have come to make a poignant pilgrimage, where we are also reminded of the tremendous victorious result, having liberated the land to the horizon, as far as the eye can see. [...] The tenacity of your race—which has made possible your survival over centuries of trials—has never been put to better use. You all deserve the Croix de Guerre, you are all leaders, the saints of the Légion d'Orient. Sleep in your glory, you have opened the road to justice and to the rights that have been chased from this region for centuries. [...] I make this oath over your tombs, in front of this cemetery, that we will create a monument of glory and that we will call this the cemetery of Arara, to bring together this name with the memory of our dead, of their sacrifice, of their victory, and of the horizon that they have opened for the national aspirations of their compatriots." On October 12, General Allenby, in turn, presented his congratulations to Boghos Nubar Pasha: "I am proud to have had an Armenian contingent under my command. They have fought brilliantly and have taken a large part in the victory."[8]

Boyajian gives a similar description of the service and speeches, adding that even Captain Azan, the commander of the 6th Company, representing the 2nd Battalion, the same officer who had so insulted the soldiers in Port Said, now had changed his mind. "That day, standing at the head of the grave of the heroes immortalized in death at the flank of the hill of Arara, Azan was a different person, someone acknowledging the value and spirit of sacrifice, an officer accepting and appreciating the Armenian's indomitable character, admirable vigor and unsurpassable bravery."[9]

I desire to convey to all ranks and all arms of the Force under my command, my admiration and thanks for their great deeds of the past week, and my appreciation of their gallantry and determination, which have resulted in the total destruction of the VIIth and VIIIth Turkish Armies opposed to us.

Such a complete victory has seldom been known in all the history of war.

26th September, 1918.

Allenby
General
C.i.C.

71. Message to the legionnaires and officers from General Allenby, telling of his thanks and appreciation for their great deeds, gallantry and dedication.
Courtesy of Ardemis Matteosian.

72. Legionnaires gather to bury their comrades. *John Amar Shishmanian Papers, envelope B, Hoover Institution Archives.*

73. Burial site at Rafat–Arara. Shishmanian notes, "The boys placed a barbed wire fence around the plot and wrote, *Mort pour la Patrie*." *John Amar Shishmanian Papers, envelope B, Hoover Institution Archives.*

The War Dead and their Origins

Listing the war dead and their origins, Boyajian shows that the men came from many different towns and villages of historic Armenia:[10]

Sgt. Arsham Amerigian from Kghi

Simon Antaramian from Kharpert

Arshag Arslanian from Sepasdia

Cpl. Mardiros Babayan from Chnkoosh

Cpl. Hagop Bedigian from Aintab

Boghos Bouloudian from Dzov

Nigoghos Derderian from Sdanos village of Sepasdia (died of injuries a few days later)

Sgt. Manoug Der Hagopian from Albistan

Sgt. Mardiros Der Kaprielian from Anchrti village of Arapgir

Sarkis Dilikjian Delligian from Suedia

Ghughas Ghugasian from Chmshgadzak

Sgt. Misak Havounjian from Ekbez

Mardiros Jingirian from Hyusenig

Sarkis Kassabian from Arapgir
Hagop Kehiaian from Gesaria
Sahag Kiskinian from Sepasdia
Cpl. Hovannes Kouyoumdjian from Bandrma
Dzeron Messirlian from Kessab
Dikran Bzarian from Kessab
Misak Taslakian from Suedia
Boghos Trekjian from Chnkoosh (died of injuries a few days later)
Melkiseteg Zanoyan from Chnkoosh
Sgt. Koorken Zildjian from Constantinople

Mihran Guzelian describes two of the fallen men.

Of our 23 Martyrs, I would like to mention a few words about two of our heroes. The first, Kevork Chiljian, Bolsetsi of our known Chiljian family, left his comfortable and free United States and two brothers and joined the Armenian forces in Cyprus becoming a member of the 5th Armenian company. This young Armenian hero was an athlete and in his training he was immediately made a non-commissioned officer, taking charge of an attack force of 50 men. His squad reached the top of Arara and after fierce fighting he was hit with a bullet in his chest. In a wounded condition, knowing his men have been observed by the enemy, he secured their positions and after establishing a line of defense, died knowing that his men were safe. [The name Kevork Chiljian does not appear in the lists provided by Boyajian and others, but Koorken Zildjian, of Constantinople, does. This is almost certainly the same man and perhaps the "known" family is the famous Zildjian percussion and cymbal-makers.]

Hagop Bedigian, Ayntabtsi, also came from America. A modest soldier, he also joined the 5th Company. He immediately rose to the position of a squad leader of 10 men. When training in Cyprus he was given the job of company clerk responsible for the purchase of rations. After finishing his first tour of duty on this job, he refused to remain and wanted to join combat forces. He said he came from America to fight the Turk. He did join the combat forces and during the fighting, while leading his men toward an enemy machine gun position, this hero lost his life.[11]

With the battle over and the enemy gone, the victorious Armenian Legion reassembled a few miles away from the frontline near the village of Mejdel-Yaba to await further orders. While there, the soldiers received a letter from the National Union of Egypt sent to the chaplain of the Legion who had conveyed to them the glad tidings of the victory of Arara. The National Union expressed their pride and happiness at the news and promised to take care of the soldiers: "We will try to send a delegation soon to the hospital at Lyud (Lod), to visit and bring presents to our wounded soldiers. We have already sent chocolates with Takakjian; the *cantine* should have arrived in Lyud and be in the process of being installed. The boys should want for nothing—cigarettes, etc.—from now on."[12]

Reburial of the Fallen

Seven years later, the grave at Arara had not been visited and it was decided to transfer the ashes of the fallen heroes to Jerusalem where a memorial would be erected on the grave. Legionnaires living in Egypt and Jerusalem worked together to plan and carry out this difficult work. First it was necessary to find men who were familiar with Palestine and would be able to actually find the original grave. Hampartsume Nazerian was one of those who had fought in the battle and then had the sad task of helping to dig the grave afterwards. He was especially determined and took every care to ensure the success of the reburial operation.[13]

It was difficult to find the exact spot for several reasons but particularly because there were two places called Arara. Boyajian explains that actually, the Armenian legionnaires had occupied Rafat, the fall of which resulted in the surrender of the nearby hilltop of Arara, surrounded by

74. "Six Armenian officers decorated for bravery in battle. Top, from left: Portukalian, Sahatjian, Papazian. Bottom from left: Bablanian, Shishmanian, Arevian." *John Amar Shishmanian Papers, envelope B, Hoover Institution Archives.*

the British 10th division and also Mesha and Bedié. "Arara and the hamlet of Rafat are the two summits of the same ridge."

On October 19, 1925, after a long and arduous journey, the small group found the correct site and began the difficult work of digging up the remains, cleaning them, and arranging and placing the bones in special boxes to transport them to Jerusalem. There a religious ceremony was held on October 25 and they were placed on a catafalque in the church of Holy Etchmiadzin, a chapel adjoining the church of St. James.

Boyajian discusses the reasons why the difficult decision was taken to move the remains of the men, rather than building a monument on the site of their first burial.

> The idea conceived by our patriotic people to erect a monument to the Armenian legionnaires on the spot was beautiful and honorable but it was not considered practical or feasible for those who were familiar with the local conditions in Palestine.

> The conditions prevailing at European frontlines during the General war [World War I] and those measures that were implemented there after the war to respect the graves of soldiers

75. Cover of *Arara*, 1923, showing a possible design for the future reburial site of those who fell at Arara. *Courtesy of National Association for Armenian Studies and Research (NAASR).*

fallen on battlefields differed in reality from the conditions in Palestine. There [in Europe] the operations of fighting armies took place in densely populated regions, where every spot would easily be found, because they are shown on exact and detailed maps while first-rate roads connect European villages to each other and to large centers, thus greatly facilitating transportation and communications. In addition, it is customary amongst Western countries to respect each other's graves, cemeteries and monuments, which remain as reminders of struggles and suffering in periods of war.

In Palestine, apart from large towns connected by vehicle-worthy routes, in peace times the majority of villages and places of no significance are in want of tracks that can be called roads. [...]

Therefore, to erect a monument in such a place, aside from difficulties of transportation and communication, would have entailed considerable expense and would have necessitated the placing of permanent guards on site to prevent possible destruction and desecration.[14]

7

The Next Stages: Beirut

The battle, of course, left the fighters physically and emotionally weakened. Those most affected by the experiences were allowed leave to go to Cairo for rest and recuperation. Boyajian was part of that group and thus able to attend the wedding of Dr. Roland who also left after the battle in order to marry a Frenchwoman he had earlier met in France. Boyajian not only attended the wedding but also the wedding breakfast where only the three of them shared the meal. The new Mme. Roland asked Boyajian to tell her about his life, curious about the young man who had earned the trust and affection of her new husband.

> With meticulous detail I described the village of my birth, my student life, the harshness of our family's poverty, the abuse, oppression and plunders of Turkish *beys*, the loss of my father in my teens. I told of leaving my mother, sister and other family members aged fifteen and setting out for America, the torments I suffered during my journey, being sent by unscrupulous travel arrangers from Antwerp, together with five other young men, to South America on board a cargo ship. Halfway through the voyage, we disembarked at Las Palmas of the Canary Islands, suffered various there after which I returned to Marseilles, went on to Liverpool and finally I related my clandestine entry to the city of Boston in America as a fugitive and going to Providence at night by train.

76. Dr. Roland, the Chief Medical Officer of the Armenian Legion, is described in *Arara* 1919.

Dr. and Mme. Roland listened to this story without interrupting, every now and then looking at each other and exchanging glances in amazement. I recounted the difficulties of my student years and leaving off my university course in order to enlist in the volunteer movement. Dr. Roland was familiar with the rest. When my story ended, Mme. Roland got up and kissed me on both cheeks with maternal affection. Dr. Roland watched this moving scene with a smile. He knew me better now and was going to show more affection and look after me from now on.[1]

Boyajian was fortunate to have made this personal connection. There were difficult days ahead. For those remaining near Arara, the next stage of the journey came after some days of rest when the 1st and 2nd Battalions set off for Beirut. Garabed Torosian describes the trip.

Before setting out for Beirut, we were told that ships would be made available and we would initially be transported by ship from Haifa to Beirut. Soon, however, we were informed that finding a ship was impossible and we had to make the trip on foot.

Provisions started running short. For days, we were only eating English biscuits out of tin boxes. Very often when we would open the box, the greater part of the contents would be spoiled; we could barely find a few undamaged ones but those had become so hard that they would not get soft even when soaked in water. Nibbling on these hard biscuits made our teeth go so soft, as if we had eaten something sour. However, all these tortures could not put in despair the Armenian who had a build, but above all a will of steel. They never ceased their daily songs, dances and jokes. For example, a tall soldier walking alongside his shorter companion would say, "Armenian lad, take bigger steps so that with each step you will be nearer Armenia by seventy-five centimeters!" The other would reply: "Follow the road and don't rely that much on your height; I will get to Armenia before you."

77. Starting north along the Mediterranean Sea.
John Amar Shishmanian Papers, envelope B, Hoover Institution Archives.

The tough young men from Chnkoosh were more remarkable; no matter how tired they were, they had to dance their special group dance every evening, creating a festive atmosphere all round.

Along the route, the soldiers were joined by Armenians, mostly women and children, from Arab villages along the way. Torosian continues:

> We had been traveling for ten days. One evening we stopped at the foot of a hillock to spend the night. We were busy with the arrangements when we saw a man standing on top of a hill, watching us. Brigade Master Arevian [see Appendix A], the officer we liked most, was issuing orders in Armenian, shouting at us. Suddenly we saw the man on the hill letting out a cry, running towards us. We stopped working to see what was about to happen. When he came near us, he stopped, looked at us and said in Armenian, "I can tell from your faces that you are Armenians."

78. Hagop Arevian (in white) and members of his battalion.
Courtesy of Ardemis Matteosian.

"You are right," we said, "we are all Armenians." Hearing these words, he hugged a soldier and kissed him, and then another and another. The man was laughing loudly with joy and at the same time, copious tears were running down his shrivelled cheeks.

Responding to our questions, he told us that he was living nearby in an Arab village. He had nothing there apart from an acre of millet and he muttered, "Let their millet go to hell! I will never be separated from you."

Like him, fifteen to twenty more Armenians, mostly women and children, were found and followed the army. A few days later, we came across a full, flowing stream. Since leaving Egypt we had not come across such an abundance of water. The surprising thing was that it was much colder than expected. We threw ourselves on it and began to drink. Our elders cautioned us, but no one paid any attention.

The next day, we would sometimes hear a cough. The following day the number of people coughing increased and on the third day the physician informed us that the Spanish Flu had reached us. A few days later I too succumbed.

79. Refugees in Palestine, trying to go home.
John Amar Shishmanian Papers, envelope B, Hoover Institute.

80. Freight carriers for the Legion.
John Amar Shishmanian Papers, envelope B, Hoover Institution Archives.

81. Villagers speaking with legionnaires along the road.
John Amar Shishmanian Papers, envelope B, Hoover Institution Archives.

Every day thirty to forty soldiers were falling behind. Eight hundred fell ill. According to the information we received, there were six casualties. We finally reached Beirut. That gruelling march lasted twenty-one days.

We camped in a Catholic monastery to the south of the city. We had our meals in the open air within the compound. The local people would usually beg for bread from us. We could no longer eat our bread and would distribute our portion of bread to them, in particular the children. The officials noticed that in doing so we were going hungry and stopped us eating outside.[2]

82. Lt. Portukalian and Lt. Papazian.
John Amar Shishmanian Papers, envelope B, Hoover Institution Archives.

Boyajian includes here in full an article written by Vahan Portukalian and published in *Haratch* in 1964. Portukalian also succumbed to the Spanish Flu epidemic and excerpts from that account follow.

At dawn the army took down the tents and left. The sick, Armenians, Frenchmen, Algerians—I cannot remember how many dozens—were left on the sand. Cabs were supposed to have come to transport the sick to the infirmary. Hours passed. The sun started to burn. Finally, an officer of the general staff passed us at a gallop. He told us that the cabs had been assigned to another task and it was useless waiting for them.

As I was the only officer amongst the sick, I decided to go to Haifa to seek some sort of arrangement. Walking with difficulty on sand and under the burning sun, I reached the first houses of the town and there I met two French soldiers with Red Cross armbands. Seeing the state I was in, they ran towards me and offered to take me to a dispensary. I wanted to see the physician first of all. They put me in a car and took me to a doctor with the military rank of a major. […] Having barely heard me, he declined to deal with us. "Mr. Chief-Physician," I said, "I can look after myself. However, I wanted to let you know that there—on the sand—nearly one hundred military personnel are waiting to receive medical attention on orders from the Military Command. I am no longer responsible." Upon hearing this, the attitude of the doctor changed and he sent me to an Arab house serving as hospital. I was in a pitiful room where there was already a French officer lying in bed who did not hide his pessimistic view of medical treatments given. […]

After two days, the patients, some few hundreds, were transferred to tents outside the town and next to the cemetery. The condition of many became worse. The reason was not the proximity of the cemetery, but rather the choice of the land. It used to be the municipal rubbish dump.[3]

83. Lt. John Shishmanian at Beirut Hospital.
John Amar Shishmanian Papers, envelope B, Hoover Institution Archives.

While in Beirut, after recovering from the flu, the soldiers were given other duties, helping the French manage the city. Sometimes the tasks were more difficult than could be imagined, as Yenovk Ashtaraketsi writes:

> For us the most bitter pill to swallow was guard duty in front of one of the most luxurious hotels [of Beirut], where some Turkish military and civil officials were supposedly being held in custody. They enjoyed all types of freedom in the third-floor rooms of the hotel. They were not spared copious dishes of many kinds, coffee, smoking items and frequent visits from outside. Their only punishment was not to leave their apartments. And why would they need to leave? They wanted for nothing. And downstairs we had to guard them on our feet and then tired and exhausted, return to camp where even the food was not enough.[4]

As the time in Beirut neared the end, an incident occurred that in retrospect was a harbinger of things to come, a small, seemingly unimportant indication of the impending chaos that would fatally harm the pre-war promises and expected structure. Again, Portukalian tells the tale.

84. Nurses at Beirut Hospital.
John Amar Shishmanian Papers, envelope B, Hoover Institution Archives.

85. Armenian legionnaires with Sikh soldiers from the British Army. *Courtesy of Ardemis Matteosian.*

A number of legionnaires, having made a purchase from an itinerant merchant in Beirut central square—Place des Cannons—made their payment in Egyptian banknotes, which is how they were getting paid by the army. The seller demanded Turkish banknotes and threw the Egyptian banknotes on the ground with disdain. A quarrel ensued. A local policeman—a remnant of the Turkish rule—instead of approaching and getting to know the problem, took out his pistol and fired into the air. Immediately, as if on cue, armed men emerged from different places and attacked the legionnaires. The latter were unarmed and resorted to self-defense, using any available objects.[5]

While the legionnaires were still waiting in Beirut for further orders, the Armenian National Delegation (AND) reached an agreement with the French authorities granting the Legion permission to occupy Cilicia. Georges-Picot, co-author of the famous Sykes–Picot agreement of 1916, arrived in Beirut at roughly the same time as the Legion. He requested a memorandum on the reorganization of the Eastern Legion from Lt. Vahan Portukalian. Excerpts of Portukalian's memorandum are included in Boyajian's book:

> The Armenian military units that form part of the Eastern Legion are destined to become the nucleus of the future Armenian army. The Armenian military groups from the Caucasus and Persia would be incorporated within that army and would be reorganized according to its model.
>
> As for the Armenians, I can say that they consider the grouping of Armenian soldiers within an autonomous Armenian Legion to be their most immediate need. The designation "Eastern Legion" impairs the Armenians' military successes, an issue which hurts their national pride and causes desperation in the best of them.
>
> It is desirable that the reorganization take place as soon as possible. It is evident that very few Armenian soldiers would re-enlist in an army that would not be national-ethnic and autonomous. It must be noted that the Armenian press, as if heeding an order from above, no longer talks about the Eastern Legion but uses the term "Armenian Legion" instead.[6]

Soon after this, the Eastern Legion changed to the Armenian Legion.

8

To Cilicia, the "Promised Land"

From the first mention of the formation of the Legion, the goal was to reach Cilicia and defend what was left of the Armenian people, their towns and villages. The hopes of the legionnaires were focused on their original lands, the fate of their families, and on building a future out of the ruins. Independent Cilicia was the dream and until the end, the men were frequently encouraged by the colonial powers to believe this could be achieved. Boyajian mentions that high-ranking French officials and officers spoke about this with them, including his friend, Dr. Louis Roland, the chief physician of the armed forces, who later commanded considerable authority. Apparently, he expressed the opinion that in a short time the creation of a Cilician republic for Armenians would cease to be only a wish and would become a reality. Col. Édouard Brémond, Chief of French supervision in Cilicia, initially presented himself as the "Governor of Armenia and Cilicia."[1]

Following the Armistice of Mudros in October 1918, ending hostilities in the Middle East, the region was divided between the British and the French. However, in a further complication of this process, it became clear that the French were not prepared to expend further lives and financial resources on its occupation where serious resistance was found. Such resistance was presented in Cilicia, exactly the area where the Armenians had believed they would receive the support of the French and British.

In December 1918, the men finally boarded ships to be taken to Mersin and Alexandretta. Under French command, the men were dispersed to assist in creating order in the region. Memoirs of that period reveal variations on similar scenes, depending on where the soldier was stationed. Hovannes Garabedian included a passage in his autobiography about this arrival stage. As for a number of others, for him this was initially a thrilling opportunity, then a heart-rending, utterly disappointing period and, at the end, also an occasion for the beginning of his future personal happiness. Here he describes his arrival in Cilicia.

> On December 6, a Navy ship took us from Beirut and on December 8, we arrived in Alexandrette (now Iskenderoon [İskenderun], Turkey). On December 19, 1918, we started marching towards Adana; after crossing through several Turkish villages, such as Payas, Dort-yol (the town of oranges) and Ersin, we arrived in Toprak Kaley. From Toprak Kaley, we took the train and as we approached Adana, a large Armenian crowd had come to the railroad station to greet us. Their warmth and enthusiasm were beyond description. They were so delighted and excited to see triumphant Armenian soldiers at home that, with tears in their eyes, they were welcoming and embracing us as if we were God-sent Heavenly Angels. We spent the night at a Turkish hospital that belonged to the Armenians in the near past. The next morning, we took the train and on December 25, 1918 we returned to Adana again where we stayed until April 7.
>
> In the meantime, the Turkish officials were contemplating how to bribe our officers and move us out of Adana. Finally, they succeeded in their plot and on April 8, we moved to Ayram (a railroad station surrounded by huge mountains) where we established our military quarters and remained there until October 28.[2]

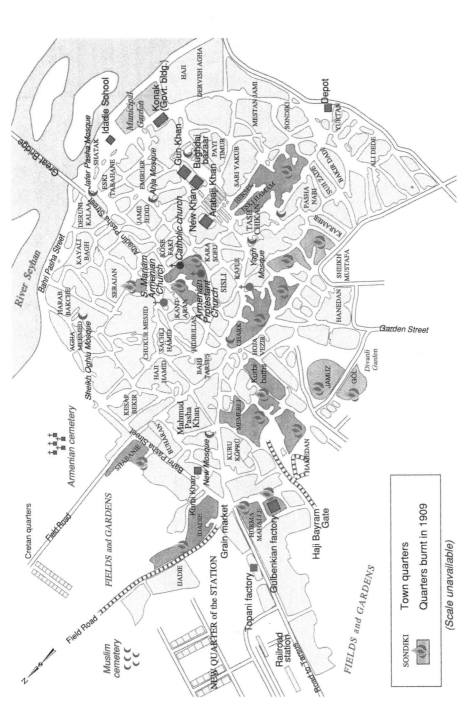

86. The City of Adana. Fire symbols show destruction in 1909. *Courtesy of Robert H. Hewsen, Armenia: A Historical Atlas. Original in color.*

87. Aram Hovsepian, writing in *Arara*, recalled: "The first time that I set foot on Armenian soil, I piously knelt, kissed the ground and put a pinch of soil in my mouth as a relic. My sergeant, Lavarel, interpreted this action of mine differently and in the prejudicial spirit specific to the French stood erect in front of me displaying a grotesque demeanor and shouted, became enraged, derided me and decreeing a punishment went away. The next day the commanding officer of my company summoned me to his room. [...] For your misdemeanour of yesterday, Sergeant Lavarel has decreed four days of restriction for you, but I understood from your Papers that so far you have been a good soldier and have changed it to 15 days' imprisonment." *Arara*, 1923: 30. *Photo courtesy of the Armenian Museum of America.*

Boyajian includes a number of excerpts from men whose accounts overlap with and extend that of Garabedian. Upon landing in Mersin, Boyajian himself gives the following account:

> At the seashore amongst the curious crowd there were children and old women. A grandmother dressed in rags approached me with an almost naked child at her hem. She caught my hand and instinctively, without warning, kissed it. In her hollowed eyes the tears had gone dry. In a quivering, barely audible voice she said: "Welcome, my children, may I be a sacrifice to your souls. But, you came late. You came to see a wasteland. You came to search for the proof of the crucifixion of our people. But you are welcome. We, the survivors, will have a place for you in our worn-out arms and withered hearts, in order to be revived and heartened by you."[3]

Later, as the men arrived in Adana, Boyajian writes of angelic Armenian girls, dressed in white, adorned with tricolor ribbons. The group found Janjigian's restaurant. "We went in and found ourselves unexpectedly amidst a crowd. As if the town's elite had assembled to entertain us."

88. Legionnaires salute the flag at the new station, Adana. *Michael Najarian Collection.*

The Janjigian restaurant became even more important to Boyajian as he grew friendly with the family. He writes that during his first days in Adana, he and a group of legionnaires became acquainted with the entire Janjigian family and their home became a regular meeting place for them. He lays claim to being the "luckiest of all" as he was chosen to teach English to the two elder daughters.

> Barely one month had passed since we were acquainted when one evening, visiting the family in a group, with the help of Vahan, I asked for the hand of Ardemis. I received a positive answer two days later and on February 13, 1919, on the anniversary of Mr. and Mrs. Janjigian's wedding, a magnificent reception celebrating our engagement took place in the presence of Dr. Roland, high-ranking Armenian and French officials, a large number of legionnaires and the Armenian elite of the town.[4]

The returning residents of Adana did indeed hold the legionnaires in high regard, both for what they had already accomplished and of course, for their dedication to the shared goal of securing the homeland. Karnig Tourian, the son of another Adana family restaurant-owner, remembered how the news of the Battle of Arara had influenced even his own name.

> I was born in Adana on 19 September in 1918, the day of the victory of "the battle of Arara Heights." Accordingly, I was baptized and given the name of "Arara," although I did not have the chance to use that name for long. When I was still very young, my father found an abandoned little girl in the street whose parents and younger brother were massacred by the Turks. Her name was Takouhi. My father brought her home and persuaded her that I was her brother Karnig. From that day on, my name was changed to Karnig.
>
> According to what my mother used to tell us, in Adana my father had a big restaurant, next to a big hotel. Most of his clients were the Armenian volunteers of the French Foreign Legion, stationed in or around Adana, and the chorus girls

89. Legionnaires gather at the Adana restaurant of the Tourian family.
Courtesy of Anahid Tourian Eskidjian.

performing shows in the hotel next door. Besides the tasty meals, my father also prepared delicious oriental sweets and pastries. For these he had a big shop window.[5]

At that point, many still believed they would be able to raise their new families in an independent Cilicia. But as Boyajian continues,

> Unfortunately, this favorable state of affairs did not last long, because of diplomatic expediency. Little by little the French high-ranking officers showed friendly disposition towards the Turks to the astonishment and detriment of the Armenian people.
>
> The Turks resorted to every means to improve this about-face in their favor. They organized balls, dinner parties and all sorts of receptions in their honor in order to win over senior and minor French officials."[6]

This, Boyajian writes, was occurring everywhere the French occupied, including Beirut, Alexandretta (İskenderun), Marash, Beylan and Aintab. In addition, Boyajian and others also saw Turks as taking every opportunity to create problems between the Armenian legionnaires and Algerian Muslim soldiers, also working with the French. Gradually, Boyajian writes, the French authorities became more suspicious of the Armenians, whom they believed to be vindictive and unreliable. The Turks demanded the removal of Armenian soldiers from Beylan but another incident in Alexandretta further undermined French authority and resulted in the occupation of several Cilician towns by British soldiers. According to Boyajian, it also meant the dissolution of one of the Armenian battalions and the severe punishment of half of its men, perceived as utterly unfair by their comrades.

The Alexandretta Incident

Following the signing of the Armistice, the French occupied Alexandretta. Initially a company of Algerian riflemen (called by an Armenian transliteration of *tirailleurs* in Boyajian's text) were brought in and then joined by the 1st Battalion of the Armenian Legion. An Algerian major was thought to be sending "deceitful reports" about the Armenians, showing a hostile attitude towards them. The 1st Battalion was replaced by the 4th, arriving from Beirut and, according to Boyajian and his sources, the situation worsened by the day. The men felt that the Algerians were looking for excuses to pick a fight and the French allowed this to deteriorate.

Soon such an "excuse" did occur. On February 10, 1919, some Armenians came to the aid of a drunken English soldier who had been attacked and robbed by Algerian riflemen in a brothel. Fighting broke out and the Armenians helped the English soldier recover his stolen money. However, on their way back to camp, the Armenians were fired upon and wounded by Algerians. Following the advice of their officers, the Armenians did not seek revenge but this was not the end of the story.[7]

> [A few nights later] a trivial argument arose in a coffee shop between Armenian and Algerian soldiers about Armenian songs being performed there. The Algerians insisted on singing Arabic songs. When the musicians refused this demand, the Algerians seized the violinist's violin and smashing it into pieces,

threw it to the ground. Seeing this, the Armenians fell upon their opponents. The Algerians fled but instead of returning to camp, hid behind walls awaiting the Armenian soldiers in order to take revenge. Their departure en masse awakened suspicion amongst the Armenians and indeed, when the Armenians left the coffee shop, the Algerians opened fire on them and two Armenians were injured. Enraged, the Armenian soldiers ran to their camp, picked up their weapons and returned to chase the Algerians. The skirmish continued for a long time. A bullet fired from a nearby Turkish house seriously injured an Armenian soldier. The Armenians smashed the doors of the house of that savage Turk who was well known for his past wickedness. The criminal fled and the mob—Armenians, Greeks and the *fellahin*—plundered the house and set it on fire. At this moment, an Armenian soldier was killed by bullets fired from Turkish houses. Following this, the angry Armenians attacked Muslim shops and ransacked them.

The consequence of this incident was that an Armenian was killed and three were wounded, one seriously. The Algerians incurred no losses. It should also be noted that at the same time a group of Algerians and Turks ransacked Armenian and Greek shops, entered Armenian houses and subjected women to beastly violations and seized their jewelry.

The next morning, February 17, all officers of Armenian soldiers—corporals and sergeants—were arrested and imprisoned by the French military authorities, despite the fact that they [the Armenians], with a few exceptions, had not even left their quarters throughout the incident. The French commander had not even left his house to put an end to the conflict and arrest the guilty, which was his duty. The Armenian soldiers in town who served in the 10th and 13th companies of the 4th Battalion, a majority of whom were volunteers from Damascus previously serving in the Turkish army, received the order to assemble in the camp. The French officers then ordered the Armenian soldiers to hand over their weapons. The Armenian soldiers refused. At that juncture, the *commandant* closed off all access points around the camp and placed machine guns everywhere. Once all these preparations were over, the soldiers were ordered to come out on the street for a drill. The Armenians, suspecting that an ambush has been laid for them, refused to come out unarmed. In the afternoon, the battalion commander invited the Armenian and French officers over and appointed two people amongst them, entrusting Adjutant Kevork Tavitian with the task of mediating with the insubordinate soldiers in order to disarm them. The Armenians refused to disarm, objecting that the Algerians were not subjected to similar harsh measures. Being aware of the fact that the Turks massacred the Armenians after disarming them, the Armenian soldiers did not trust the French authorities either.

The Armenian camp was near the seashore and as the French warship *Coutelas*[8] approached the shore, the military commanders ordered the rebels to give themselves up in an hour, otherwise the camp would be shelled. Perceiving the danger, the English Lt. Col. Eastwood who had been following developments from the nearby English hospital, wished to intervene in order to put an end to further bloodshed. He took along Dr. Krikorian, who served as a physician in the English hospital, and begged the Armenian soldiers to lay down their arms, promising to do his best to resolve the issue in an equitable manner. The detained soldiers surrendered their arms to the English commander whose intervention with the French governor allowed them to be freed.

While the Armenian soldiers were thus being disarmed, another game was being played out in the town. The shops were shut and streets deserted because a group of Algerians, accompanied by their officers, had blocked the roads and had placed machine guns here and there.

One kilometer away from the camp, Armenian coachmen and mule keepers returning from work encountered a French sergeant major who ordered them to return to camp immediately and take up arms. When thus armed the Armenians arrived in front of the police station in the town center where a lieutenant, gun in hand, ordered them to lay down their arms. The Armenians obeyed promptly. Then he ordered them to raise their arms and kneel, while the Algerians accompanying him prepared to fire their arms. The mule keepers knelt in front of the officer and beseeched him to spare them, but the furious officer fired his gun and killed one of the Armenians. Then he ordered the Algerians to open fire on the others. Thirteen people were killed and three taken to hospital.

The next morning the French authorities searched the Armenian church and interrogated the local priest about the flower wreaths prepared for slain Armenian soldiers. The officer then made the following announcement: "We have already buried those who died yesterday outside the town." It isn't difficult to understand the fury and resentment of the Armenians, reacting to this ruthless and cruel treatment, not even able to give their unfortunate victims a decent church burial.

The Armenian soldiers who were involved in this terrible incident in Alexandretta were either imprisoned or sent to internment camps where they were subjected to harsh and cruel treatment.

At the military tribunal convened on February 26, March 7 and 15, presided over by Captain de David-Beauregard, seven legionnaires were found guilty and received the following sentences: one person to fifteen years of hard labour, two persons to ten years, one person to eight years, one person to five years and one person to one year. Only two Algerian riflemen received a prison sentence of one and a half years and ten ordinary citizens received various punishments.[9]

The 4th Battalion was dissolved after these awful incidents. Four hundred of the men were reassigned to the other three battalions of the Legion but the 400 men in the 10th and 13th companies "were exiled as convicts," according to Boyajian.

90. Shishmanian labels this a sketch of an old Armenian castle in Cilicia.
John Amar Shishmanian Papers, envelope B, Hoover Institution Archives.

It became clear that the three remaining battalions of the Armenian Legion were not enough to maintain order in occupied Cilicia. However, there was no sign of new troops being sent from France and the legionnaires became aware of a changing attitude towards the future in the region. Boyajian gives an example of these concerns noting that in December, 1918, Col. Édouard Brémond's title was "Governor of Armenia and Cilicia" but in January, 1919, it changed to "Governor General of Occupied Enemy Northern Zone Territories."

The Search for Armenian Women and Children

While taking on the full impact and sorrow of the "Alexandretta Incident," the legionnaires were preoccupied by another aspect of their own mission, which was to seek out any Armenian women and children who were still alive and return them to their families or to an orphanage where they would be cared for as Armenians, rather than as Kurds, Turks or Bedouins. Legionnaire Krikor Muradian remembered that he and his companions saw trains from Mosul, Dikranagerd and

Aleppo heading towards Bozanti, Bursa and Konya which were full of "Turks who had wrung Armenian bones to the marrow, laden with priceless loot, Armenian riches and also Armenian girls." He wrote that the Armenian legionnaires, where possible, would burst into the train coaches and were sometimes able to free the women.[10]

A number of stories exist which show the complexity of this situation, some several years after abductions or adoptions had taken place. Boyajian includes excerpts with several examples of this from the memoirs of Yenovk Ashtaraketsi.

> We enjoyed the hospitality of the director of the telegraph office in Yenice. He gave us the impression of being a sincere Turk. Once or twice every week he would invite us to take coffee which was offered to us by an eight- to ten-year-old beautiful girl, of whose Armenian identity we had no idea. One day an Armenian lady informed us that the little girl was Armenian. We were surprised. We considered it our immediate duty to rescue her. Indirectly we asked our host about the identity of the girl. We learned a few days later—and in a pleasing way—his response. The Turk was ready to deliver the Armenian girl to us together with three gold coins, six sets of clothes and a large parcel of other necessities. After a few days, we sent the little orphan girl to Adana, after which we completely lost her trace.
>
> We received intelligence that in trains traveling from Aleppo to Constantinople there were often Armenian women forced to become Turks. These trains would stop for 15–20 minutes at Yenice station. Sometimes we succeeded in removing from coaches Armenian women whose identities had been established beforehand. Amongst them were some who refused to be separated from their Turkish husbands and our harsh way of acting resulted in complaints being addressed to the French authorities, thus creating an undesirable situation for us.
>
> We received intelligence that amongst a group of women placed in one of the coaches of a train bound from Aleppo to Constantinople was an Armenian woman who had to be rescued at all cost.

> When the train stopped, we took with us the clever Haroutiun, an Armenian sergeant in the Turkish army. We entered the coach in one corner of which four or five Turkish officers with their swords sat talking. The women's group was separated from the men by a curtain. We opened the curtain. We saw facing us a group of veiled women, one of whom, we were told, was Armenian. We asked: "Is one of you Armenian?" There was no response. One of the women furtively pointed the Armenian woman to us. Haroutiun removed her veil and told her that she was free to leave the coach with us. The woman, whose chest was adorned with gold, refused to be separated from the group.
>
> To apply force would have been imprudent. We left the coach and immediately sent word to legionnaire guards at the next station who through a more audacious deed removed the woman from the train and on the spot married her to the legionnaire who had rescued her.[11]

Sarkis Najarian had told his family of a similar situation, as his daughter Sona remembered.

> While in Cilicia, Sarkis had became a postman or a courier on the Adana–Mersin rail route. One day he saw a rich Turkish family traveling with a pretty girl whom he thought must be Armenian. He decided he would find a way to separate her from the family and take her away. When they got to the station and the family was disembarking, Sarkis managed to make a big fuss and distract everyone while separating the girl from them and keeping her on the train. As the train pulled away from the station, he told her to be honest with him—was she Armenian? She was afraid but she said yes. He told her that they were now on their way to Mersin where he would put her in an orphanage where she would be safe.[12]

There are also stories of women who told their would-be rescuers that it was "too late." At that point, they preferred to stay where they were, particularly if they had children who would be left behind. Sarkis

Najarian's own story took a different turn when he tried to save his own sister. In Mersin, he married Siranoush who had been orphaned by the Genocide and after the armistice, they went to Beirut where he had contacts and believed he could find another job. His daughter Sona continues with his story:

> In Beirut, a telegraph came from relatives in Aleppo. "Sarkis—we have found Nishan!" Thirteen years old, his brother Nishan had been walking through Aleppo with camels. A relative saw him walking and said, "Doesn't he look like Nishan?" The boy heard him say the name and ran over—"*Ana Nshan!*" in Arabic. I'm Nishan! They understood that he was Najarian and explained to him that he had a brother—a rich one—in Beirut. He was leading the camels through the street and said, "I have to take them back or they will kill me." So, the men said, "OK. Do that and tomorrow come back here and we will put you on the train to Beirut." He did come back and they had bought him a ticket and put him on the train. He had long dirty hair, unwashed, filthy clothes but he went. The men sent a telegraph ahead to Sarkis to go to that train and meet him.

91. (left to right) Brothers and sister, Nishan, Yeghsabet and Sarkis Najarian, Beirut.
Courtesy of Sona Najarian Touloumjian.

92. Armenian legionnaires in Adana. Photo by H. Fermanian.
Courtesy of Sona Najarian Touloumjian.

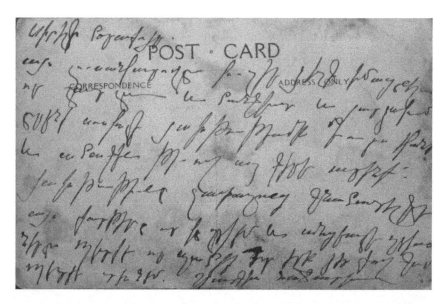

93. Back of Sarkis Najarian's group photo: "Dear Aunt, With this photograph, I wanted to let you know that I am very well and comfortable. We made an attack and emerged with a spectacular victory, taking a great number of prisoners. The victory was greatly appreciated. You must keep these postcards that I'm sending you—and those I sent earlier—so that, when I come to you, I can see them. Sarkis Najarian." *Courtesy of Sona Najarian Touloumjian.*

When the train arrived, Sarkis began shouting, "Nishan! Nishan!" so that he would find him. He came and they went to the house. Siranoush was shocked – he was so dirty. Sarkis took him to the hamam immediately and had to teach him how to get cleaned. Nishan thought the soap was a rock at first. The next day he got new clothes and the day after that, he began to learn Armenian. He learned quickly as it began to come back to him after a little bit. He spent two years with Sarkis and his family and then was sent to military school.

One day Nishan told Sarkis that he had a sister in the deserts of Arabia. [This was actually Sarkis's sister and Nishan's stepsister, as the mother's sister was Nishan's birth mother.] Sarkis wanted to go immediately and find her. They got in a taxi and when they drew close, Nishan went first to where she was and found her. She was already engaged and gave Nishan money to go away and said they would kill him if they found him. She herself wanted to stay and did not want to go with him. She wanted to marry the man. Much later, Sarkis went back and found her again, married to a rich Bedouin, tattooed—and happy. Later they visited each other, back and forth and were very close. Her name was Yeghsabet before she was adopted and married into the Bedouin family.

When she would visit Sarkis and his family, he would take her to church and they lit candles. But she would also do her Muslim prayers in their home. He said to her, "Yeghsa, you used to be Christian. Don't do *namaz* in our house please." She said that she would pack up her bags and go home then. "I have Armenian blood but I was raised a Muslim. When I hear the call to prayer, I have to do my prayers until the end of my life." Sarkis changed his mind and they continued to visit with each other.[13]

Some of the stories told by the men and their descendants open up many more questions about modes of survival during the Genocide years. How did some people manage to stay in their villages while others were ripped from their hiding places? How did some neighbors

94. Armenian girls, tattooed by Arab Bedouin, found (Shishmanian states "bought") by legionnaires and brought to doctors in Cilicia.
John Amar Shishmanian Papers, envelope B, Hoover Institution Archives.
Rebecca Jinks notes that the practice of tattooing women in Bedouin communities was thought to accentuate beauty, and occurred at life-stages such as puberty, marriage, or childbirth. The tattooing of Armenians 'absorbed' during the Genocide thus denoted acceptance and inclusion: but for those Armenian women and girls 'rescued' after the war, their tattoos were often felt to be a source of shame. Surgical removal of the tattoos was not uncommon, as appears to be the case with these two girls pictured. See Rebecca Jinks, "'Marks Hard to Erase': the troubled reclamation of 'absorbed' Armenian women, 1919–1927."
American Historical Review 123, no. 1 (2018): 86–123.

manage to hide Armenians or bribe officials to look the other way? By the time of writing memoirs, and particularly by the time of writing books in the twenty-first century, many stories have become reduced to their bare bones—but are still both moving and fascinating. Levon Saryan remembers the story of his own father's rescue from the village of Piran. The power of family reunions and the resilience and courage of the young children involved comes through clearly.

> My father was still living in Piran, his native village in the Taurus Mountains, with his grandmother. His father's younger brother, Simon Sarkisian, had arrived in the USA a few years before 1915 and was living and working in Providence. He had joined the Armenian Legion movement, and reached Aleppo around 1919 with the rest of his comrades. At that point, he deserted from his unit for a few weeks and made his way to Piran located in the mountains to the northeast. Reaching the village, he found my father, then about nine years old, who had escaped the deportations of the summer of 1915 by going into hiding. Simon decided to bring my father to Aleppo and then to the USA.
>
> The two of them set out to the south towards Diyarbakır and Mardin. At the city of Mardin was a train line, and they were to take the train from there westward to Aleppo. When the once-per-week train arrived, there were throngs of expectant passengers trying to get on board. As they tried to board, a tug-of-war ensued, and the pair was separated, my father making it onto the packed train wearing his uncle's *Gamavor* cap, while uncle was left on the platform. His uncle told him that when he reached Aleppo, the other soldiers of his unit would recognize him by the cap that he was wearing and would make sure he was taken care of until the uncle could join him the following week. Meanwhile, Simon also arranged to find himself a wife in Aleppo.
>
> Eventually, my father's uncle was able to return to the USA and in the following year, he sent enough money for his nephew

95. Sarkis Saryan, Simon Sarkisian, wife Shamiram and baby George Sarkisian. New York, 1931. *Courtesy of Judith Saryan.*

and his new bride to come to the USA. When Simon arrived at the dock, however, he found only my father waiting for him. The woman had been spirited away by some members of her family who had arranged to take her to Chicago to marry her off to someone else![14]

The search and rescue operations were taking place in an atmosphere of increasing turbulence in the area as the Allied/Entente Powers scuffled with each other around conference tables in Europe, dividing up the Middle East between themselves. Still hoping to be the vanguard army of a new Armenian territory, the legionnaires performed their duties (and beyond) faithfully, even when their suspicions were aroused that the outcomes were not favorable for their own goals. The men were caught in the diplomatic tensions between the French, the British, the new Turkish Republic and also Arabs seeking independence themselves. Yenovk Ashtaraketsi continues with further observations on this in his memoirs:

> The only way they could have stopped our patriotic efforts would have been to disarm us and send us away from the places we had conquered. And they did just that. From Bozanti to Yenice they removed the Armenian legionnaires from every station and replaced them with Algerian Muslim soldiers. There is no doubt that this turnaround was not only as a result of the undisciplined conduct of the Armenian legionnaires, but also—and especially—because of the change in French foreign policy thanks to which the Turk became more audacious and the position of the Armenian Legion in Cilicia faltered.
>
> Thus, they gathered the soldiers of the 3rd Company from everywhere and brought them to Tarsus telling us that we were free to be demobilized and go wherever we wanted—whereas when our company first arrived in Tarsus, they had officially informed us that the number of the legionnaires would be increased to 12,000 and that we were even going to capture Sepasdia [Sivas]. The announcement of demobilization was the death knell of the Armenian Legion and the collapse

of the hope for the formation of an Armenian army. The hope of liberation of Cilicia dissipated into thin air with this announcement.[15]

Some men thus began leaving the Legion while others, whose companies and battalions had not been demobilized, continued with their duties, as ordered.

Sgt. Doud

Lt. John Shishmanian relates the dramatic story of Sgt. Doud who began as an Armenian officer in the Turkish Army where a general took a special interest in him. While stationed near Aleppo, Doud's sister visited him. Afterwards a Turkish colonel demanded that Doud come to his tent and told him, "I would have children by such a beautiful woman." Doud ignored this command twice but on the third time, he brought a gun and killed the colonel.

The General was forced to send him for a court martial but also sent a letter by two couriers to Jemal Pasha, commander-in-chief, living in Jerusalem, "explaining that the young man had taken the colonel's life in pursuit of his duty." The courier gave the letter to a red-haired woman at Jemal Pasha's apartment. The woman, Jemal Pasha's mistress, took it inside, returning it signed and sealed in wax with the signet ring.

Meanwhile, Doud, condemned by the military court, was waiting to be shot. As he smoked his final cigarettes, the breathless courier arrived with the reprieve. Back in Aleppo, the general gave Doud a furlough which Doud used to go and thank Jemal Pasha personally.

In Jerusalem again, he made his way to the apartment. There the attractive woman who answered the door smiled. "I gave you your reprieve. I am a Jewess. You are an Armenian. I sympathize with your people. The day the courier arrived, Jemal Pasha was drunk. I took his signet ring and made out the paper for your reprieve. He is in his office now and in a good mood. We'll go and tell him this story."

Jemal Pasha laughed at the story but afterwards, Doud was concerned that the commander would have second thoughts so he deserted and joined the legionnaires. After fighting "valiantly" with the Legion, losing an eye in a landing on the coast of Asia Minor, Sgt. Doud was demobilized and began serving as an officer in the Beirut police force, under the French. He was awarded the Médaille Militaire.

96. Sgt. Doud. *John Amar Shishmanian Papers, envelope B, Hoover Institution Archives.*

The Military Police

In spite of, and throughout the surrounding problems, Boyajian notes that it is important to mention that the Military Police, who were created from the soldiers of the Armenian Legion in Adana, played an honorable role in maintaining peace. One of these, Manoog Khan Baghdasarian, wrote an article included in Boyajian's book.

> *The Military Police was formed from chosen soldiers who were not only mere policemen, but also linguist interpreters and agents of the secret service. In collaboration with the military police and secret service of the English army they watched over the general security of Cilician towns. Before the start of the battles in Hadjin,*

97. Military Police of the Armenian Legion, Adana, Turkey, 1919. Photo by H. Berberian. Manoog "Khan" Baghdasarian (seated far right), a volunteer in the military police of the French Armenian Legion. Beginning in 1914 with training in the United States, he served two years with General Antranig in Turkey, Russia, and Persia, and two years with the French in Syria, Egypt, Arabia, and Palestine. In 1920 he married and came to the United States. *Courtesy of Ardemis Baghdasarian Matteosian. Project Save Armenian Photography Archives.*

the military policemen supplied a sufficient amount of arms and ammunition, with the cooperation of the Armenian Legion guards. [These guards] were entrusted with the task of watching over the arms and ammunition seized from the Germans. They sacrificed their night's sleep and rest and, with the agreement of the French Captain [...] made half the depot's ammunitions disappear and handed them over to the Provisions Body of the National Union in order to secretly arm Mountainous Cilicia.[16]

9

Repatriation and Increasing Uncertainties

As the legionnaires were making their own way from Palestine and Beirut northwards to Cilicia, survivors of the Genocide were also preparing to return. It is difficult now to imagine the tumultuous scenes that were taking place as these desperate people were given hope of returning home. For some, the option of emigration to join extended family in other countries was a possibility. For others, returning to their homes, the life that they had left, and the possibility of great improvements under the new regime, was the natural action to take. Some had no other options, others were driven by a belief that indeed the time for an autonomous Armenia had come and they must do their part. Many simply loved their hometowns and villages and wished to try again.

Boyajian relates how after the British began their occupation of Ottoman lands, following their victory in Palestine, a public meeting was held in Aleppo. On December 4, 1918, many thousands of refugees and local Armenians gathered and together decided to present a letter to the leader of the Armenian National Delegation (AND), Boghos Nubar Pasha. The letter, addressed to Boghos Nubar on behalf of 50,000 survivors, men, women and children, expressed abhorrence of Turkish atrocities and demanded the following: immediate evacuation of Turkish forces from Armenia and Cilicia; declaration of Armenian independence; protection of Armenians still under Turkish rule; the return of possessions belonging to Armenians who had been killed;

reconstruction and indemnification; the liberation of kidnapped women and children; and punishment of those guilty of massacres.[1]

From that point, refugees began to flow away from Aleppo towards their villages and towns. A variety of plans were proposed for organizing this return migration but disagreements and shifting priorities resulted in chaos all around. The British and French each had their own reasons for wanting the Armenian refugees to leave Aleppo, all agreeing that the sooner Armenians were home and working again, the fewer refugees there would be to take care of. However, transportation, protection and support until they were safely in place were haphazard at best and much of the local administration in those zones remained in the hands of the original Turkish officials who often proved reluctant to return Armenian homes, farms and businesses to the returning refugees.[2] Vahram Shemmassian quotes a realistic observation by Sir Mark Sykes of the British Foreign Office: "Indications show that unless steps are taken by Entente to supervise repatriation, Turks will grow more obstructive as they know that while Armenians remain exiled birth rate is diminished and death rate is increased." He accordingly offered a scheme to "organize, cover and protect, the repatriation of deported Armenians."[3] However, those returning were subject to bandits, demobilized Turkish soldiers, and hunger and thirst en route without such organization as proposed by Sykes. Timelines were discussed with little agreement, and responsibility was also divided inconclusively.

98. In Aleppo, the first group of survivors prepare to return to their homes.
AGBU Nubar Library, Paris.

While most refugees in Aleppo waited for permission and a way to return, some discovered a quicker way to do so. Young men began to enlist in the French Foreign Legion again. "By mid-October 1918, 903 eligible men had conscripted in Damascus. On October 28, 750 left for Cilicia via Beirut after receiving the blessing of Catholicos Sahag II Khabayan (Sahak Khapayan) the head of the Armenian Apostolic Church of Cilicia, the previous day amid thousands of cheerful [sic] compatriots."[4] However, the remaining 153 men were not allowed to proceed to Cilicia and further conscription was suspended as again disagreements arose between those in charge. Briefly, there was a new influx for the Armenian Legion.

In some places, such as Kessab and its villages, closer to Aleppo, refugees returned of their own accord, assisted by each other. The people themselves set up a structure, protection, and their own "government" led in part by legionnaires originally from those villages (see the Epilogue, below). Elsewhere, the sheer numbers, distance and lack of preparedness of the military authorities made this impossible.

By October 1919, the migration away from Aleppo was no longer voluntary but made mandatory by the British and French for their own reasons. Just as the British were concerned that the refugees in Port Said were a long-term burden for the British government, so too were those in Aleppo. For their part, the French tried to prevent migration to Cilicia by any Armenians who were not originally from those towns and villages, expressing concern over the "legitimate protestations of the Muslim population."[5] This would prove to be another harbinger of future developments in French–Armenian relations in Cilicia.

Settlement in Adana

Boyajian notes that, of course, the task of settling the refugees was very difficult. As refugees were funnelled from Aleppo to Adana, this process was undertaken voluntarily by Dr. Roland with Lt. James Chankalian as his aide.[6] The refugees were encouraged to go back to their villages rather than stay in Adana, in order to ease overcrowding. Orphanages were set up, housing some 10,000 children. More orphans were to have

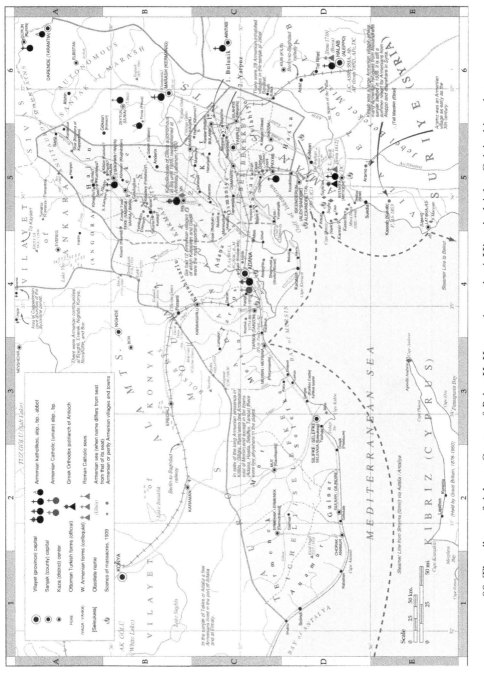

99. The vilayet of Adana. *Courtesy of Robert H. Hewson, Armenia: A Historical Atlas.* Original in color.

100. Early morning in Adana. American flag flying over Near East Relief building and below, workers going to the vineyards.
John Amar Shishmanian Papers, envelope B, Hoover Institution Archives.

come from Aleppo but it was not possible. Dr. Roland did more than find housing, and created work for the refugees. Boyajian writes,

> In order to encourage the Armenian's spirit of entrepreneurship, [Dr. Roland] succeeded in securing credit from the French authorities to establish a carpet and handicraft factory within the Apkarian school, under the careful supervision of Lt. Jim Chankalian. Employment was secured for nearly 300 persons in this factory.[7]

101. Nurse Marie Dertadian worked at the French Hospital in Adana. Marie later married Manoog Khan Baghdasarian (see fig. 96).
Courtesy of Ardemis Matteosian.

102. Captain James M. Chankalian, decorated with the *Médaille Militaire*.
Courtesy of the Armenian Museum of America.

An excerpt from a letter from James Chankalian (in English) dated 1920 is included in this description.

> Many women under my care have been taken from Turkish harems. Previously they were in an abominable state but, after a little care, they became entirely new women. I don't have access to funds to carry out such work. I am spending all my monthly salary on them, but this is not enough.

> This is the greatest and most necessary work that we can do. These unfortunate women are all young. They flee from Turkish houses almost naked. It is impossible for me to see all this and not be affected. I enjoin them to be good, but how can they be content with half a loaf of bread daily? When they are naked and hungry, how can we expect them to be virtuous? My

friend, this is the state of our exiled sisters. It has been eight months that I am busy with this work, but I have yet to receive any support from Armenian organizations. The funds given to me from the French government are absolutely inadequate.[8]

Dr. Roland, who had worked so hard to help the legionnaires and the refugees, met a sudden end. On the night of August 19, 1919, his wife heard gunshots and rushing to his side, found him sprawled on the floor of their home. A telegraph was sent to Dr. Altoonyan of Aleppo but his arrival was too late to save Dr. Roland. Boyajian writes, "Dr. Roland, the affectionate father of the Armenian refugee and orphan breathes his last on August 21."[9] A special ceremony was held for him with the Armenian Primate, representatives of the Jewish community, delegates from AND and many thousands of mourners.[10]

Demobilization Continues

As rumors circulated about disagreements between the French and the British, the Armenians became more and more uneasy and less motivated. Their perceptions of hostility on the part of the French continued to concern them. As Boyajian observed, the legionnaires were now in Cilicia and "justly considering themselves to be at home, were hoping to have the privilege of acting fearlessly and freely. Unfortunately, the reality was not like that."[11]

With the end of the war, major questions emerged. Their military service was ending—would they be completely demobilized? They could see that there were no significant foreign troops occupying Cilicia as the British continued to withdraw. The legionnaires, in spite of losses and partial demobilization already, had grown to more than 5,000—but this number was not sufficient to control such a large area. Further, local (Turkish) civil servants remained in place, where they had been before the war. Boyajian notes that

> It had become impossible to lay hands on any information on their past bad deeds because at the time of their retreat the Turks had destroyed the documents and correspondence

103. Legionnaires. *Courtesy of Michael Najarian Collection.*

related to all the crimes perpetrated against the Armenians—massacres, deportation, kidnapping, plunder, etc.—and it had not been possible to find any unfavorable information about them.[12]

Afterwards, following the occupation of Cilicia, on the basis of a decision taken by the French and with their encouragement, more than 100,000 refugees were transferred to various towns and villages of Cilicia in the course of a few months. If the French had any thought of evacuating Cilicia, then why this repatriation, was the reasoning of every Armenian and especially every legionnaire.[13]

As these concerns and questions continued and grew, other factors that might have been overlooked also took on new and bigger dimensions. Boyajian lists again the discriminations that the men felt were unfairly put upon them, and the favoritism shown the local Turks, their receiving less pay, less nutritious food and, what he says was most frustrating, the lack of promotion for the promising young Armenian men. Questions about leadership went beyond the French military. Boyajian discusses this and includes a letter that outlines issues troubling the Armenian Delegation.

> Unfortunately, in this state of crisis, there was no effectual leadership on the part of the Armenians. The National Union was powerless and had not yet been able to establish and maintain a link with the National Delegation which probably could have prevented the complete disbanding of the Legion. Naturally it was expected that as soon as the legionnaires arrived on Cilician soil, representatives or a representative of the National Delegation would follow. A close link between the Armenian army and Armenian political authorities could have played a major role in maintaining a high morale amongst the soldiers.[14]

An unsigned document, dated March, 1919, found in the archives of the National Delegation presents a discussion of the reasons for disbanding the Armenian Legion and what could be done about it.[15] Noting that everything was contingent upon the Peace Conference and the mandate issue, the letter states clearly that until then, one could not find a way to transform the Legion into an Armenian national army. However, it was better to continue in the hope that the present soldiers would form a nucleus of the national army. Related to this, the letter suggested the dissolution of the Armenian Workers' Camp in Port Said. The authors also wrote that the Delegation must demand that French Legion officers show more respect and kindness, provide better food, train men to be officers and promote those few who already were.

Important political points were broached as the letter also

104. Hovsep Ajemian.
Courtesy of Michael Najarian Collection.

105. Military Police pass belonging to Hovsep Ajemian.
Courtesy of Michael Najarian Collection.

demanded that demobilization be suspended, that they be able to see General Hamelin's file on reorganization, that the condition of joining the Legion be changed from "serving in the East" to "serving in Armenia" and that the committee be able to see the files on the Alexandretta Incident and the disbanding of the 4th Company.

Finally, it was noted that the Armenian Legion felt abandoned by the Armenian nation and suggested that General Antranig be brought to investigate the situation and encourage the men.[16]

Boyajian goes on to describe how different the situation could have been, given that amongst the refugees there were many young men who wished to join the legionnaires. He mentions that around 800 men came on foot from Aleppo to Adana, wishing to enlist. "There was every likelihood that the number of volunteers in the Armenian Legion could have reached 20,000, if only this were allowed. But the French command with its reprehensible conduct refused new enlistings."[17]

The demoralization of the legionnaires continued and many expressed a desire to demobilize at that point. Others were not given a choice and were forced to leave. Portukalian lists the following figures:

This is the exact situation:

- ◊ First Company: Almost all the soldiers, apart from 50–60 souls, have asked to be discharged.
- ◊ Second Company: Nearly 300 souls have asked to be discharged. There remain 5–600 soldiers.
- ◊ Third Company: Nearly 300 want to be discharged. There remain 650 souls.
- ◊ Fourth Company: Entirely disbanded. After the incident in Alexandretta half the company was discharged; the remaining half was divided between the other companies.[18]

Lieutenant Portukalian adds that the applications to enlist from 700 men coming from Aleppo, 600 men sent from Constantinople and many others in addition have been rejected.

A committee was set up to look into the reasons behind the discouraging situation in which the legionnaires found themselves. Boyajian lists a number of the factors enumerated and these begin with the continuing powerlessness the men felt as the French continued to postpone the transformation of the Armenian Legion into the Armenian National Army. The committee suggested that the National Delegation first remind the French government that, in spite of a few instances inaccurately interpreted as insubordination, the Armenian Legion had behaved well, according to the testimony of their commanders, and their presence was necessary to keeping the peace in Cilicia. It was further demanded that better food be provided along with wages equal to those of a French soldier, that their families be supported according to basic living costs, and that a retirement pension be granted to those rendered disabled during military service.

Today these would seem very ordinary demands, though sadly not always met with acquiescence. The committee went further, demanding that the organizational structure of the Legion be changed so that Armenian soldiers would be promoted according to ability, that both the officer corps and the administrative authority consist of more

Armenians, that courses be provided to train new officers, mounted and military engineering forces be formed, a representative of the AND liaise with the military command of the Legion and that an official appeal be addressed from AND to the Legion.

The commission set out certain measures that AND should adopt should the French government insist on disbanding the Armenian Legion: specifically, to immediately take a decision to launch a fund of 1 million francs to implement the necessary measures demanded by the situation; to employ every means possible to ensure that the existing military union would not be disbanded; and to use the legionnaires for the purpose of occupying the Armenian Provinces and maintaining their security, and either join them to the volunteers from Mesopotamia or put them at the disposal of the government of the Republic of Armenia.[19]

106. Neshan Mardikian, Certificate of Good Conduct,
April, 1919, Adana.
Courtesy of Michael Najarian Collection.

All of these letters and reports show the level of crisis felt by those trying to support and even enlarge what remained of the Armenian Legion. They also betray a degree of confusion within, some focusing on the region of Cilicia, others (as shown in the last point above) linking the independence of Caucasian Armenia with Cilicia. More letters follow (as collected by Boyajian), including one from Boghos Nubar on behalf of AND to Mihran Damadian, nominating him as AND representative to the National Union, the Armenian communities of Syria and Cilicia and the British and French civil and military authorities. Nubar notes that "The issues of the Armenian Legion would require your entire attention."[20]

> When Mr. Damadian arrived in Adana in the month of June, most legionnaires had already been discharged from the army. The discharge of those still under arms was only a question of time. Learning that most of those who had been demobilized wished to leave Cilicia, the President of the National Delegation appealed to General Commander General Allenby, firstly to introduce the representative of the United Delegation and afterwards to request that discharged Armenian legionnaires be allowed to remain in Cilicia, and if needed to be used as auxiliaries to British troops in order to occupy the Armenian provinces.[21]

A letter from Nubar to General Allenby, dated July 1, 1919, includes this excerpt:

> As far as our volunteers of the Armenian Legion are concerned, the discharge of most of them deeply grieved us; those young men who had been engaged to fight against the Turks and help liberate their homeland have offered to re-enlist if they were given the assurance that tomorrow they would be integrated within the Armenian national army. As their request was not accepted, they have been discharged and we learn that most of them have been sent to Port Said. We should be grateful if you were able to do your best so that those Armenian soldiers, who had been so well trained and had received the honor of

your precious praise, were not dispersed. We hope that you would be kind enough to allow them to remain in Cilicia until the Armenian Question is resolved, or employ them as auxiliaries for the British forces in order to occupy the Armenian provinces.[22]

Allenby's reply is not included here but by this time, Cilicia had been designated as "French" and the British were making their own plans to exit the area. The letter betrays what can politely be called "wishful thinking" as France and Britain had already put barriers in place to Nubar's proposed solution and it is surprising that Nubar does not appear to take this seriously in his own thoughts about the future of Armenian Cilicia.

Some Armenians would continue to serve, but in ever-diminishing numbers. None of the demands had been met, none of the demobilized men were able to return. However, in the increasing chaos of the Legion, some new men did continue to enter, as already noted. As the hoped-for plan unraveled ever more quickly, Boyajian realized that

107. Old Roman bridge across the Djihan (Ceyhan) river. Lt Shishmanian's headquarters were at the left end of the bridge in this photo.
John Amar Shishmanian Papers, envelope B, Hoover Institution Archives.

the men alone could not change the direction of the decisions. He and others hoped that their own political leaders, in particular those heading the cross-party or neutral-political committees, would have the courage and the wisdom needed to persuade the Allied Powers to consider their plight and make good their earlier promises. It was not clear which of the leaders had the necessary charisma, and the ability to communicate both with foreign powers and with the Armenian soldiers. An open letter written by Damadian to the remaining legionnaires, dated July 24, 1919, is revealing in its rather clumsy attempt to encourage and direct the men by criticizing them.

Initially the letter describes how the men are "greatly appreciated" by AND, the French commanders and the entire Armenian nation. He begs them to stay on until the peace treaty is signed with Turkey, after which time new recruits will arrive to take their places. However, he then complains that some men are saying that their work is over and all should be demobilized. Here he changes tone and tells them it is not their job to "dabble in politics."

> As I see it, one of the issues that weighs heavily on your mind is the notion that has taken root amongst you that the Nation has forgotten you and that the Delegation and National Unions are not interested in your situation. Now, I sincerely assure you that this opinion of yours is completely wrong.
>
> [He continues to exhort them to] have confidence in national bodies, to show respect to their French officers and obey them. A soldier does not argue, does not reason, does not squabble, but obeys.[23]

Following the inclusion of this letter in full Boyajian writes, "Despite its diplomatic turns of phrase and ambiguities, Damadian's letter was surely able to stop the complete dissolution of the Armenian Legion. However, it was not possible to swallow the pill of extreme military submission that he was offering. […] We don't think that Damadian believed in what he was saying. His position was very delicate. He was a diplomatic representative and it was his duty to talk and operate like a diplomat."[24]

108. Legionnaires and children near Adana. *Courtesy of Michael Najarian Collection.*

While all of this correspondence was taking place on one level, the remaining men of the Armenian Legion continued as best they could. Many men continued as legionnaires, in spite of the grievances, the troubles and the disappointments, believing that they could at least help their compatriots with their resettlement of the homeland, protecting them as they rebuilt their homes. Some also would have hoped for a reversal of their fortunes and, somehow, a miraculous return to the promises made to them when they enlisted and indeed repeated to them only a year earlier. They could see that they were needed where they were. In fact, they were to see more and longer battles than they had in Palestine. However, earlier they had been part of a large war machine; now, it often felt like they were on their own.

10

The Transfer of Power in Marash

In 1914 some eighty-six thousand Armenians lived in Marash and its neighboring villages. By January 1923, none of them remained.
—From the Preface to the *Lions of Marash*
by Stanley E. Kerr

While the winners and losers of the Great War jockeyed for positions and territories, the small number of Armenian legionnaires remaining tried to follow orders and also protect the surviving Armenians of the towns and villages and each other. Some considerable confusion seems to have surrounded the forces as they carried on with what turned out to be their final months of work. The British and the French, working through their plans to divide the Middle East, were focused on their own postwar concerns. Neither they nor the Armenians realized that the era of empires was passing, and not only for the Ottomans. The Armenians hoped for an autonomous region under a protectorate. Britain concentrated on controlling Mesopotamia, Palestine and Transjordan, and France on Syria, including the Hatay, and Lebanon. During this transition, concern about the fate of the Armenians and other local minorities seems to have slipped entirely away. The ramifications of these maneuvers are still playing out in the twenty-first century.

Many significant changes took place in the spring of 1919. Lt. Col. Romieu, General Commander of the Legion, took early retirement, it was said at his own request. Col. Flye Sainte Marie took his place and Col. de Piépape was given the title of "Commander of the French Forces in Cilicia." Boyajian comments that this is a "vague" title because apart from the Armenian Legion, there were no other French forces in Cilicia. While this is not literally true, it is clear the French were very severely, indeed fatally, understaffed and the Armenian Legion itself became fragmented and greatly diminished.

In spite of this, Boyajian reflects that the year 1919 had been exceptionally successful for the returning Armenians in other ways. Many building activities were carried out, crops were harvested, people were even achieving economic successes. However, uncertainties were plaguing the people and certainly the legionnaires as well. The departure of the British, the increasing lack of trust with the French, the dispersion of the legionnaires: all were at great contrast with these gains.

Boyajian himself was demobilized from the Legion in May 1919 and decided to visit Marash (modern Kahramanmaraş), his family home,

109. Marash, 1919. Photograph by Stanley E. Kerr. Under the protection of the British and French troops, Armenian deportees return to Marash from exile in the Syrian desert. *Photo courtesy of Rev. Vartan Hartunian. Project SAVE Armenian Photograph Archives.*

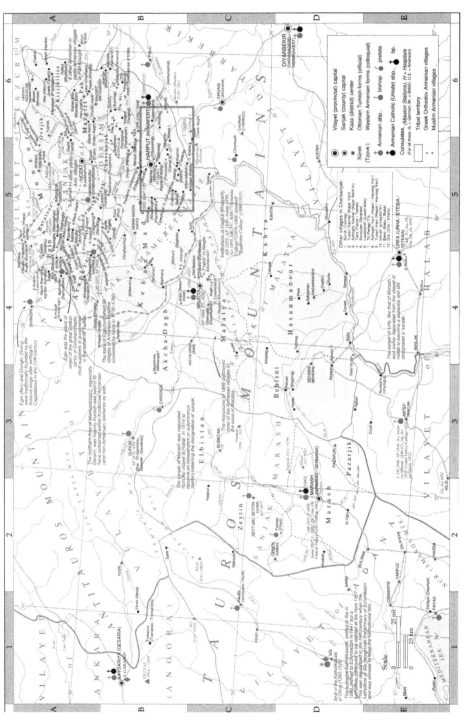

110. The Vilayet of Mamuretülaziz and the Sanjak of Marash. *Courtesy of Robert H. Hewsen,* Armenia: A Historical Atlas. *Original in color.*

to learn from the survivors about their needs. He was appointed as an official agent of the Hnchakian Reformed Party and given the task of visiting the region of Marash, Fundijak and Hadjin. En route, at the town of İslahiye, he was invited to dinner with the *müdür* of the Keferdiz district and his friends, including Boghos effendi Kherlakian, a member of a highly regarded local Armenian family (mentioned again below). The next day, with a Turk and an Arab gendarme as their guides and guards, the party rode on horseback through mountain paths towards Marash, spending the night in the home of the *agha* of the region.

> On the evening of Friday, 27 June, Boghos effendi and I, accompanied by the two gendarmes, arrived at Marash without incident. On the road leading into the town we were welcomed by a number of community members and after greetings, all went together to the home of Khoren Varzhabedian, in the neighborhood of Kyumbet, near the church of St. Sarkis. A rich table was laid out by the Varzhabedian family not only to entertain me but other community members who had come to receive fresh news from Adana. The meeting of a few hours clearly indicated one thing—that those survivors from Marash who had returned to their family homes felt that their lives were not secure.[1]

Boyajian learned that the residents were aware of the impending regime change and held very mixed feelings. They had been happy with British rule and were sorry to see them go. However, they had heard that the Indian soldiers serving the British would be replaced by Armenian legionnaires. This thought made them glad. Even so, living side by side now with people who had been responsible for their deportations and had participated in the earlier massacres in Marash made them deeply uneasy.[2]

> Outwardly everything was normal. Churches were open, pupils at school were attending courses without fear; the teachers—although suspicious and sceptical of the apparent calm in the prevailing situation, succeeded in hiding their uneasiness of mind. A public meeting even took place where

111. Title in Armenian reads: "The Supreme Command of the Army and Military Police." *Photograph courtesy of Ardemis Matteosian. Project SAVE Armenian Photograph Archives.*

112. Shishmanian writes that these women were "rescued by Armenian troops and brought to Cilicia. Refined women, many of them wealthy and from educated classes," they are washing wool for weaving.
John Amar Shishmanian Papers, envelope B, Hoover Institution Archives.

29. XII. 19.

THE RESIDENCY,
CAIRO.

HIGH COMMISSIONER
FOR EGYPT.

Dear Sir,

I thank you for your letter of 25th inst. — with its good wishes for you and your boys, for which I am very grateful. I am sorry, if the gallant conduct of the Armenians was not sufficiently recognized. I know they fought nobly, and I am proud to have had them under my command.

With all good wishes, I am

Yours sincerely,

Allenby. F. M.

113. A letter to Lt. John Shishmanian from General Allenby, expressing his regret that the Armenian legionnaires had not been officially recognized for their contribution. *John Amar Shishmanian Papers, envelope B, Hoover Institution Archives.*

the main speakers were two legionnaires: Stepan Dardouni in uniform and I in mufti. The spacious National Hall was full to the rafters with an inquisitive crowd.

My visit to our compatriots in Marash lasted until August 22. The planned visits to Fundijak and Hadjin were canceled due to extreme insecurity of the roads. Two days before my departure, Dr. Sevian and Dr. Der Ghazarian suggested that I visit the Turkish *mutasarrif* of Marash at his home with them accompanying me. This was ostensibly to present my respects to him but in reality, to ask him to assign two gendarmes and a horse to accompany me to Baghché (Bahçe). The *mutasarrif* received us respectfully and expressed regret that I could not stay longer in order to receive his hospitality in his summer residence garden. Our request was wholly fulfilled. Of the two guards escorting me, one was a Turk and the other a Christian Arab.[3]

Amid increasing signs of danger and violent incidents, Boyajian traveled to the United States at the beginning of October 1919 where he had a special mission to raise awareness and funds for the legionnaires. He was then prevented from returning himself. In his book, the narrative continues through the memoirs of other legionnaires and his own later research.

Two months after Boyajian's visit to Marash, two detachments of the remaining legionnaires were sent there and to Aintab.

114. Woman (unidentified) sharp-shooter of Adana. Some 40 women served along with the legionnaires in Cilicia. "They met with hardships as well as the men, say their officers," writes Shishmanian.
John Amar Shishmanian Papers, envelope B, Hoover Institution Archives.

115. One of the (unnamed) women fighting alongside the legionnaires in Cilicia.
John Amar Shishmanian Papers, envelope B, Hoover Institution Archives.

The Company of legionnaires in which Hovannes Garabedian served traveled from Adana to Marash but then went on to the area's headquarters in Aintab. Garabedian takes up his narrative as his Company leaves Adana.

> Having all our ammunition and provision on our backs, on October 20 we started marching for Marash, which was three days' walking distance. We spent the first night at Kazan-Ali where the legionnaires slaughtered several cows and calves; and all those Turks who came and protested against this act received a good beating and returned to their homes. We spent the second night at El-Oghli. There were no Armenian inhabitants in these two villages. On October 31, we crossed quite a

long bridge on our way to Marash and stopped on the bank of the river for lunch and a short period of relaxation. After bathing and swimming, we continued our expedition and within three hours, we were in Marash. The Armenians of Marash were lined up on both sides of the road, waving French, British and Armenian flags to welcome us. A band in the center was playing the hymns of the Allies and Armenian national songs. Many of them, tears in their eyes, were embracing us; many of them, down on their knees, were kissing the ground and thanking God for this joyful day. Some of them followed us until we reached our military quarters.

On November 5, we left Marash for Aintab. After three days of long marches and crossing through several Turkish villages, we arrived in Aintab on November 8, 1919 and spent the night at the former American College for Armenian students. The next morning, we were ordered to leave for Katma's military camp. Here our battalion was divided into several smaller groups and each group was assigned to a different railroad station. Our group was assigned to stay at the mosquito-infested Koort-Koolak Station, where many of us fell sick because of inclement weather and unhealthy water. On November 14, a train arrived from Aleppo carrying the other battalion of the Armenian legionnaires. One of them got down from the wagon, approached me, introduced himself as Soghomon Gougassian from Perchenk, and wanted to know if there was anyone around here from Perchenk. "I am Perchenktsi, and my name is Hovannes Garabedian," I replied. He said, "There are some Perchenktsis in the wagon. Would you like to come and meet them?"

We walked to the wagon and accidentally, I met my Uncle Dado. We embraced, kissed each other, shed some tears and hardly exchanged a few words before the train started moving. I gave him two Turkish pounds, shook his hand finally for a farewell, hoping to meet again within a few days.

> On December 10, 1919, the black African soldiers, under the French command, replaced us and we returned again to Katma. Here I fell sick and on December 23, the military doctor dispatched me by train to the military hospital of Adana.[4]

Stanley E. Kerr, in *The Lions of Marash*, describes the entry of these legionnaires, setting the scene for what was to come. He relates two different perspectives on the arrival of the French and Armenian detachments, confirming Garabedian's description.

> An Armenian resident of Marash, Nishan Saatjian describes the arrival of the Armenian legionnaires.
>
> Finally, in October, two French detachments arrived at Marash. There were two companies of the Armenian Legion with pointed caps and shining eyes, happy to greet the native Armenians on Cilician soil. Our joy and enthusiasm reached a peak, and the souls of our martyred brothers and sisters were flickering around us. These were happy days, to end too soon![5]

Also included in Kerr's account is a Turkish description of the same event.

> The Armenians went out to meet the French with a display even greater than they had given the British, with a band and a bouquet of flowers. "Damn the Sultan! Damn the Turks! Long live the French and the Armenians," they were yelling. By their actions the Armenians were showing their gratitude to the French, who—they thought—were bringing their independence. The British, after turning Marash over to the French, all departed from Marash.[6]

Kerr goes on to note that leading Turkish citizens of Marash almost immediately sent a complaint to the French commander that incidents were taking place that indicated the Armenians showing "hatred for the Muslims." Putting it into perspective, Kerr adds that the Armenians denied the charges but also writes that it was suggested by outside observers that as the Turkish people were used to having a subservient

Armenian population, they were resentful of the proud (and armed) entry of Armenians who were no longer taking orders from the Turkish government or local chiefs. Indeed, Kerr and Armenian memoirists themselves do give examples of "misbehavior" on the part of a few legionnaires. While not condoning these actions, the commentators note that all members of any army do not always follow the rules, particularly when alcohol is involved. In addition, feelings of revenge were difficult to contain at times.

Revenge was always a latent emotion for the men, with their families and towns decimated. At times however, it was also a more immediate reaction when incendiary incidents occurred to one of them or to Armenians around them. In his moving description of those days, Kerr includes a story told by an Armenian Catholic priest who, walking down a street in Marash, narrowly escaped being killed by a large jagged rock thrown from a balcony. After a gash in his cheek was sewn up and he was speaking about the incident to the French commander, a loud explosion was heard in the town, shaking the building in which they were sitting. A local Armenian had asked the young soldiers to avenge the attack on their priest and one had taken up the challenge. He managed to throw a grenade in the midst of some Turkish town leaders, drinking coffee near the scene of the crime, according to the account.[7]

In November 1919, the British troops were leaving Turkey to

116. Dikranouhi Krikorian. "G. G." on her collar indicates "Giligia Gamavor." When her family was killed, she dressed as a boy and joined the Legion. She hid in caves and behind boulders, and was wounded in battle. Shishmanian, through the Near East Relief, sent her to Fresno to his parents to continue her education. *John Amar Shishmanian Papers, envelope B, Hoover Institution Archives.*

117. Meydan Ekbezir. The Armenian volunteer and the child of a deported, lost Armenian. Shishmanian notes that this is an Armenian Volunteer from South America with an orphan found by Herrian, "Armenian secret agent working for the British."
John Amar Shishmanian Papers, envelope B, Hoover Institution Archives.

move further south, making room for French soldiers to take their place and extend their mandate over the region. Associated with the French Foreign Legion, the Armenian troops assisted in this takeover and at times seem nearly to have been left to their own resources. While the British had not met with significant resistance from Turkish soldiers or citizens in those areas, the French, with far fewer men and employing Armenian soldiers to do their work, did. As Kerr writes, he and other aid workers, American missionaries and doctors were warned by British and Turkish acquaintances not to go to Marash under any circumstances at that time as fighting was expected. An English officer told him bluntly, "Let me advise you—don't go! There will be fighting. We have released our Turkish prisoners and they have been armed. They are preparing to fight the French!"[8]

118. Sarkis Najarian (bottom right) and comrades.
Courtesy of Sona Najarian Touloumjian.

119. Marash embroidery (Marash *kordz*). This remnant was once part of a much larger piece brought to Cyprus with refugees from Marash.
Courtesy of Nouvart Kassouni Panayotides-Djaferis.

The local, national and international scenes continued to shift rapidly. In Turkey, internal politics were reaching a new crisis point with the insurrection, as it was perceived by the central government, of Mustafa Kemal Pasha and the revolution he was seeking to put in place. The British had allowed civil administration to continue under local Turkish leadership but Georges-Picot sent an order that henceforth all would be placed under direct French control. However, Col. Brémond, as governor of the region, realized that this would be difficult or impossible to put in place without more military support. Kerr writes that instead of following what was agreed upon in Paris, he decided to try different approaches in each locale, depending on the attitudes prevalent amongst the leaders of each town or area. There were pro-nationalist Kemalists in Marash and many more in the surrounding villages and mountains. However, supporters of the Istanbul government were dominant in the town. Thus, following a request from Turkish citizens of Marash, Brémond put the town under the direct control of Captain André who was already in charge of the sanjak of Marash.

However, both Kerr and Boyajian note that dissent continued at all levels throughout the town. Both authors mention the Kherlakians, an influential and wealthy Catholic Armenian family, working for the sultan. The Francophile family entertained the incoming Captain André. Kerr describes an evening dinner party at the home of the Kherlakians where Captain André invited one of the daughters to dance with him.

> "I don't like to dance in a city where there are no flags—neither French nor Armenian flags!" she replied.

> On the morning of Friday, 28 November the Turkish lawyer Mehmet Ali, whose window faced the nearby citadel, was astonished to see the French flag flying in place of the Turkish emblem on the citadel's tower. He sat down and wrote an emotional appeal to his fellow Muslims: "It is worthwhile that a little Turkish blood be shed to correct this insult!" He placed copies of this appeal in conspicuous places in the Ulu Jami, or Great Mosque, to which the Muslims were already coming for the Friday prayers. The assembled crowd of more than a thousand agreed that there would be no prayers until the Turkish flag was replaced.[9]

Kerr relates how the men then climbed the path to the citadel and replaced the French flag with the Turkish one, but notes also that French historian Pierre Redan denies that the French flag ever flew there as it would have been "contrary to military custom." However, as will be seen in the memoirs of Sarkis Varadian, in Chapter Eleven, Armenian soldiers also report this scene, as does Abraham Hartunian (in *Neither to Laugh Nor to Weep*). All agree that the incident surrounding the raising of the Turkish flag at the citadel brought about mob scenes and gun fights, including the intimidation of pro-French Turks. Captain André called his headquarters in Aintab to ask for reinforcements and was asked to go to Aintab himself. He and his aide, Monsieur Vahan, went and never returned. Kerr observes that "The importance of the flag incident was that the Turks had defied French authority with impunity."[10]

11

The Battles of Marash or "The Marash Affair"

The scenes in the previous chapter overlap with those described below, showing the destruction of Armenian Marash from perspectives of people caught in the chaos of those moments. A vibrant town with a population determined to rebuild their lives was facing terror again. The Turkish population itself was divided between those who supported Mustafa Kemal, seeking to establish a new Turkish republic, and those who continued to support the sultan. As shown vividly in accounts by Kerr and others, in the skirmishes and battles that wracked the city, some Armenians were helped by their Turkish neighbors, others were targeted and killed by them. But the odds were greatly against the Armenians as the support and already weak communication system of the French army was not activated in time.

Protestant minister of Marash, Rev. Abraham Hartunian writes that the French authorities had assured the Armenians that they would protect them—that any uprising would be over in "two hours." On January 6, he and other leaders of the Marash Armenian community were invited by Turkish religious and community leaders to a meeting to discuss possible ways to avert the crisis all could see coming. They were told, "We request you Armenians to unite with us, your Turkish fellow-countrymen, and to fight with us against the French, force them

120. The exchange of French for British troops at Aintab, November 4, 1919. 18th Indian Lancers withdraw as French and Armenian troops stand at the roadside. *Photograph and caption by Stanley Kerr, Joyce Chorbajian collection. Courtesy of Houshamadyan.*

out of the city, and then to live with us in eternal brotherhood."[1] In hindsight, Hartunian allows that perhaps this should have been considered but at the time, with the French promising to be their protectors, indeed liberators, and the Turkish people so recently their murderers and again threatening them, there did not seem to be a choice at all. After all, there were some 6,000 French troops in Marash.

From mid January, 1920 to the evacuation of the city by the French in February, the city was rocked by ongoing battles between the different forces. In an example of what has been called "total war," the civilian population was targeted; it was not that they were accidentally killed while soldiers fought. In scenes grotesquely reminiscent of 1909 and 1915, thousands of Armenians were killed by gunfire but also by fires set alight by kerosene-doused rags.

Dr. Harutiun Der Ghazarian, a native of Marash, gives an eyewitness account of events, and the dividing up of the Armenian population looking for protection, adding information about the placement of troops.

> A few days before the event the French forces were divided as follows: American orphanage, 80 soldiers; St. Sarkis church, 110 (Armenian volunteers); first Protestant church, 280 soldiers;

121. Armenian orphans pictured on a hillside outside Marash.
Photograph by Stanley Kerr, Joyce Chorbajian collection. Courtesy of Houshamadyan.

Armenian Catholic church, 40 soldiers; Holy Mother of God church, 100 (Armenian volunteers); St. George's church, 50; the Latin monastery, 150 (Algerians); the garrison 1,200 (Armenian volunteers); second Protestant church 150 soldiers; Holy Forty Martyrs church to the south of the town and adjacent areas, 1,500 Senegalese and Armenian volunteer legionnaires.

In the early morning of January 21, on the day of the incident, the Armenian legionnaires had gone towards Bel-Punar to meet the forty carts of munitions and provisions coming for them. Taking advantage of their absence the Turks immediately moved to attack. For safety, the Armenians had gathered near the centers where the volunteers were based. The Turks attacked these centers to annihilate the Armenians. Faced with resistance, they began to set fire to Turkish houses in the vicinity of the Armenians in order to burn the Armenian houses.

The wind and the petrol doused upon the houses caused the propagation of the fire everywhere. The Armenians were forced to demolish the houses near them so that the fire would not reach them.[2]

This firestorm and gun battle is further recorded by legionnaires present. Boyajian writes that "Amongst the descriptions of the battles of Marash, the most moving is the story of the tragic struggle of the twenty-two

122. Baghdasar Odabashian, killed in Cilicia. *Courtesy of the Armenian Museum of America.*

123. Khazaros Atamian, killed in Marash. *Courtesy of the Armenian Museum of America.*

volunteers who had taken refuge in the burnt church of Holy Mother of God [*Soorp Asdvadzadzin*], as recounted by Ajem Ajemian and Manoog Atamian." Note that although Ajemian states that the soldiers told the civilian population not to worry as there were many to protect them, it soon became apparent that really, there were very few and almost no supplies. Ajemian writes:

> It was the third day after Christmas [that is, January 22][3] when at the back of the town, we noticed Turks carrying rifles on horseback descending from the mountains and raiding the town. The bazaar was shut. Armenians from the surrounding houses, upon seeing the armed Turks overrunning the town and with the premonition of a forthcoming danger, began slowly to cram into the church, fearing that soon the expected storm would be unleashed. We reassured them, saying that the great number of French and Armenian soldiers based in town would be able to give them the necessary protection.
>
> Around 9 o'clock gunfire was heard from the neighborhoods near the fort. This gradually became more intense and spread to every part of the town. Within a few minutes, a great multitude of the entire Armenian population of the neighborhood filled the church, the courtyard and the school rooms. The terror was general. There were twenty-two of us volunteers with Sergeant Baghdasar Odabashian at our head. He assigned the position and role of every soldier to be ready for any attack.
>
> The attack had also started near the church where we were. Countless bullets were hitting the walls of the church and school. In order to further strengthen our positions and lay our hands on provisions abandoned by the people in surrounding houses, we covered the walls and passed from house to house, securing the necessary stocks. Provisions would no longer be a worry.
>
> After the attack of the first night, fires started in neighborhoods. The neighborhood of the church of Holy Mother of God could not have been an exception. Fire also started there.

Bullets on one side and fire on the other. How long could we—a handful of volunteers—resist, particularly with a very small supply of cartridges? Each one of us had barely 100–120 cartridges and the enemy had got wind of this fact through the treachery of a woman of ill repute. It is true that the traitor got her punishment by death, but our weakness had also been exposed. We were obliged to use our cartridges sparingly.

The fire burning the houses of our neighborhood was approaching us hour by hour. Some Armenian neighborhoods and churches had already been consumed by the fire. There was no sign of attack from the French side, therefore all hope of anyone coming to our aid was completely extinguished. Our situation was little by little becoming worse. There was a need to somehow send word to the French detachment nearby. Ghevont Bedrosian from Yerznga [Erzincan] became our volunteer messenger. He went and returned disappointed. The French commander had refused all assistance, adding cynically: "I can do nothing. Leave the people to their fate, there is no need for you to die for them. Put down the mules so that they don't fall into the hands of the Turks and you—the soldiers—come here." Although we had deserters, the majority decided to keep our positions and die fighting. That was also the decision of our commander.

However, in order to fight we needed munitions. Our cartridges were diminishing hour by hour, no matter how sparingly we were using them. In order to push back every enemy attack, it was necessary to fire. We put our faith on the success of a second attempt, sending another volunteer to the French *commandant*, at least to receive some cartridges if not military assistance. We were looking for a volunteer, someone who knew how to sneer at death, as we were surrounded and it would have been a miracle to find a safe way of getting out.

After a moment's silence, I [Ajem Ajemian] undertook that dangerous mission. Two Armenian townsfolk who knew the roads well accompanied me. We set out at night with moonlight making our journey more dangerous. It was necessary to be more cautious. If we were able to cross the bridge over the gorge dividing the town, we would feel safe. We had barely walked a few paces over the bridge when a barrage of bullets started from all four sides. The Armenian walking in front of me, seized with terror, threw himself over the bridge. At that very moment, a bullet hit the wall and showered fragments of stone over and around me. My eye was wounded and covered with blood. In turn, I too jumped down from the bridge and sank in water up to my knees. Our other friend was nowhere to be found. He was either wounded or dead.

Finally, we reached the French guardhouse. We presented ourselves to the same *commandant* with whom Ghevont Bedrosian had spoken earlier. We met with the same stone-hearted attitude. He refused to convey any help to the soldiers and nearly one thousand women, elderly people and children besieged in the church of Holy Mother of God. The deterioration of the wounds that I had sustained forced me to check into hospital for treatment, leaving my friends and kinsmen to their fate.

A few days later Manoog Atamian, one of the soldiers at the Holy Mother of God church, having been wounded in the leg while fleeing, arrived limping at the church of the Forty Martyrs (*Karasun Mangants*), where I met him and listened to his tragic story.[4]

Manoog Atamian continues the narrative:

The evening of departure we waited impatiently for your return. It wasn't difficult to guess the failure of your mission when one of the Armenian townsfolk accompanying you entered in a state of breathlessness and voicelessness, terrorized and unable to speak. His tongue was locked. It took two days before he was able to tell us that he had fallen over the bridge at the time of a terrible fusillade. We had lost all hope. We were in a quandary—remain and be destroyed in fire or attempt to rush out with the people and with a sudden unexpected attack confuse the Turks and cut through the line of siege.

Every preparation was made to dart out from the church in the darkness of night. However, it wasn't easy to lead a crowd consisting of women, girls and children in silence. It was impossible to proceed unnoticed. When the group reached the mosque, the Turks started a terrible fusillade. We charged ahead, behind us an unorganized and terrified crowd. A few paces ahead our road was closed with barbed wire. A few Armenian townsfolk and I succeeded in crossing over to the other side of the barbed wire by jumping, however the remaining soldiers and the multitude were forced to retreat towards the church of Holy Mother of God.[5]

During this same period, legionnaires were stationed in the garrison, as mentioned by Dr. Der Ghazarian. Their battle was more conventional in the sense that it was between soldiers, the legionnaires aiming to protect the town as well as the French resources and headquarters. In an article written for *Hairenik*, Sgt. Sarkis Varadian's account of fighting in the Marash region connects with that of Kerr and others and also displays the complex ways in which the distractions of power relationships affected the considerations, priorities and judgments of their French officers. Part of Varadian's account is included here.

When the city of Marash, Turkey, was occupied by the Allies, our company of Armenian legionnaires was waiting for word from headquarters to advance toward Marash and relieve the British occupation troops. According to formulated plans, the British army which occupied Marash without a fight was to withdraw and the second Armenian Legionnaire Battalion along with some French troops would replace the British. When the Armenian legionnaires were within one hour's distance from Marash on the Albistan road, several vantage points were secured by a squad of twenty-five Armenian soldiers, including one additional machine gun section. This same area during the British occupation was protected by 270 cavalry with two machine gun sections.

124. Garabed Kassabian of Philadelphia, killed in Marash. *Courtesy of the Armenian Museum of America.*

125. Legionnaire group including Sarkis Varadian (3rd from right). *Courtesy of Michael Varadian.*

Varadian's squad kept watch outside Marash for six weeks "and then we were relieved by another squad of twenty-five men with two machine gun sections. This small group was not in any position to carry out its mission in view of the fact that since our guard duty period, intelligence had told us about the advancing 6,000 Turkish regulars. The twenty-five men would become a suicide squad." Varadian managed to convince the Captain of the 5th Battalion that help was needed and an additional 50 cavalrymen were sent to assist the legionnaires.

Once in Marash, Varadian and his fellow legionnaires were surprised by an incident (which is also described by Kerr).

> One morning when we were returning from our military drill, while one group of our men was in the Armory and one group outside, we noticed that a French flag was waving above a Turkish fortress. The Turks were drilling in the fortress. One of the Turkish soldiers pulled down the French flag and raised the Turkish flag and soon gunfire was directed toward our Armory. We alerted our troops to prepare to attack the Turks then suddenly the firing stopped. The commander of our Battalion, named Kereti [Queretti], had taken the Turkish Vallee into captivity until peace terms could be accomplished. He didn't expect the Turks to open fire when they were the captured party.
>
> Three days later a Turkish soldier approached our commander with a white flag saying that with the return of the Vallee, the fighting would be completely stopped. The Vallee was then released, and before the Turkish Vallee reached the Turkish military area, the Turks opened fire again, this time on the French-held prisoner. We were in a stagnant period for three days waiting for orders to return fire or to attack. Orders finally came and fighting started on all sides. The Turks attacked us from several directions and each time were driven back by our fire power, suffering huge casualties. Unable to penetrate the Armory, the Turks changed their tactics and started firing upon the schools and homes forcing the civilians to seek refuge in our Armory. We numbered in total approximately one thousand soldiers. The ammunition that was being transported to us by

way of the Dauros Range, was captured by the Turks, forcing us to limit our fighting capabilities according to our existing supplies. A valley separated the two Turkish units attacking us. We had dug in and our trenches and foxholes lined our defensive position. In order to dislodge us, the Turks had to go down into the valley and then advance upon our position. The Turks did just this and as they approached our position, our commander told us to hold our fire and at the last moment, we opened up our attack with machine guns and grenades and decimated the Turkish soldiers. They suffered such heavy casualties that they did not attack again and withdrew to regroup.

Our Commander Kereti, hearing the firing and the battle information, had assumed that we had been overrun and had alternate plans with his officers to evacuate towards Zeitoon where it would be safer. Our troop's French officers were young and inexperienced and they always consulted us on matters. One such officer was sent to us from the commander to verify the extent of our fighting. This commander had great respect for the Turkish soldier and he couldn't stomach the thought that a group of Armenians could defeat the Turks in combat. I informed his messenger to return to headquarters and advise the commander that the Turks had been beaten by the Armenian soldiers and he should now change his opinion of the capabilities of the Turkish soldier. We had in our contingent four hundred French soldiers, veterans of the Western Front who were eligible for discharge and were to be released from Adana. Within the hour the Turks attacked this group and killed many French soldiers who were one day away from receiving their discharges. This same commander was then threatened with a court-martial for not protecting these men. Many families lodged a protest and a trial would be pending when he returned to France.

One day, before the battle of Marash, a Moroccan cavalry with a French officer and an Armenian interpreter (Exnadios Loosavorian) had left from Aintab for Marash. Half-way through their journey they were surrounded by the Kemalist soldiers and ambushed. Fighting continued into the night and in the darkness only three soldiers escaped the ambush. They made their way to our camp and we tended to their needs after interrogation. We had assigned five soldiers for guard duty to protect an American Hospital in our sector. The French commander gave orders to set up the machine gun section in the public square. The Turks observed this from one of their Minarets and directed fire towards the gun emplacement. During the incident, legionnaire Soghomon Pashalian was wounded and the section became pinned down and remained contained until darkness. We then changed the position of the gun to the other end of the compound and further secured its position with sand bags. We soon came under fire from Turkish cannons that had been placed in strategic positions within a half-mile of Marash. These guns were hitting some of our 75 millimeter cannons.

A vantage point was needed badly and quickly. Sgt. Zadie Garabedian (Troy, New York), Corporal Guiregh Atanossian (Cranston, Rhode Island) and Corp. Garbed Kasparian and two additional men along with machine guns mounted a steep hill on the eastern side of Marash and awaited orders. We had no opportunity to give these brave men any kind of relief and they had to remain alert and ready to fire. The weather became very cold and one of the men of the section was badly wounded in a skirmish. Relief was needed and Guiregh Atanossian volunteered to make his way back to headquarters for ammunition and relief. As Atanossian descended the hill, the Turks opened fire on him each time he would make a movement from foxhole to foxhole. We observed through glasses and so did the Turks. They thought they had killed this brave Armenian fighter and I too thought he had been hit. I had lost sight of him after the first volley of rifle fire that was directed toward him. As I looked through my field glasses, I could see Atanossian again racing from position to position and eventually to safety. (I had the pleasure of living next door to this brave comrade of mine in Cranston, R.I. and to raise our two families as one.) Gerry Atanossian returned to his dangerous position after darkness with supplies and successfully evacuated the wounded soldier.

We held our position for twenty-four days and Armenian legionnaires battled the Turkish Army and inflicted tremendous casualties on the Turks each time they tried to advance. The Turks soon tried to envelope us from the eastern side of the city and where the Armenian Armoury was located. We anticipated this and so did Garabedian and Atanossian who reported the attempt and this too ended in disaster for the Turks. During the fighting, three young Armenians had reached us from Zeitoon, asking for supplies for the Zeitoon heroes. We had received our supplies by then and we equipped these brave lads and sent them on their way with haste.

126. Group of Armenian refugees in Marash.
Photograph by Stanley Kerr, Joyce Chorbajian collection. Courtesy of Houshamadyan.

THE BATTLES OF MARASH OR "THE MARASH AFFAIR"

127. Legionnaires on the hillside by Marash.
Photograph by Stanley Kerr, Joyce Chorbajian collection. Courtesy of Houshamadyan.

The Turks seeing the hopelessness of their situation tried another tactic. They sent word to us that their fight is with the French and not the Armenians. This amazed us to no end. "What stupidity," said some of our officers. We then fought alongside our French comrades with more vigor. On the nineteenth day of fighting our communications system was hit and we had no contact from all sides. At approximately eleven a.m. a French plane was hovering above. With white sheets of paper we marked our position and signaled for assistance. The flyer dropped a message saying he received ours and disappeared. At three o'clock another French plane appeared and dropped a message saying that help was on the way. The Turks also got word of this message. The news of help arriving gave us some hope and the pace of the battle increased. During the fighting, the Captain called me to his headquarters and asked me to stay with him and not the troops. I looked at him with disgust and my first thought was that he was going crazy. I asked him how one can give orders from a room and not know what was going on and also informed him that the lives of Armenian soldiers were at stake and a tactical error in his part will cost him his life. He left me and walked away without an answer.

I returned to the troops and quickly checked the progress the Turks had made in trying to envelope us again from the east side. We placed two additional guns on the east side and with Garabedian and Atanossian's sections established a crossfire. We further re-enforced that side by directing some of our 75 millimeter cannons along this crossfire. When the Turks made another assault, they were actually decimated. The Armenian soldiers were fighting with such fury, with revenge in their hearts and the memory of their loved ones the Turks had already killed. On the twentieth day of the siege, another French plane approached and dropped a final message saying that a fully armed division will reach us in two days. The Turks also received this message and immediately offered to discuss peace terms. Our desire was not to discuss peace but to fight on to victory. First they implied surrender and then peace.

We debated what our course of action should be. In a firefight, many civilians could be killed. Within two days after a standstill, an eight thousand force of French troops arrived and relieved us. Upon reaching Marash, they mistakenly opened fire on us and this was soon corrected and they stopped firing. The Turks at this moment were deeply concerned and the new commander had threatened to level Marash to the ground. At five o'clock the next day, without any explanations, word was received by our commander to withdraw from Marash toward Eslaye [İslahiye]. All of the firepower was directed toward the Turkish positions so that our troops were able to move out. We evacuated our positions without casualties and left nothing for the Turks. We rendezvoused below Marash and headed toward Eslaye by way of Davros. This was a three-day march. The weather was very cold and on the second day, it snowed. Many of the civilians marching along with our column froze and some died along the way. It was sad to see our people suffer but some welcomed death knowingly and with such bravery.[6]

Armenian Legionnaires Who Died in Marash

"In the unequal and tragic battle for the self-defence of Marash," Boyajian continues, *"the heroic participation of the Armenian legionnaires claimed its victims, whose remembrance ought to be one of the glorious pages of this memoir. Unfortunately it was not possible to verify the names of all hero-martyrs. We are compelled to reproduce the list of victims of the 7th Company of the Armenian Legion that appeared towards the end of the very interesting article by the legionnaire Krikor Ajemian."*[7]

Sergeant Avedis Akrabian, from Marash

Sergeant Baghdasar Odabashian, from Arapgir

Ghazaros Atamian, from Chmshgadzak

Aleksan Kalusdian, from Baghdad

Garabed Kasabian, from Tokat

P. Karadaghlian, from Hadjin

Melkon Krikorian, from Kilis

Khacher Tanielian, from Gesaria

Markar Zorian, from Kharpert

Dikran Ehramjian, from Yerznga

Misak Tenpelian, from Hadjin

Manuel Tutunjian, from Malatia

Khachik Khozigian, from Divrig

Hagop Garabedian, from Alexandria

Keork Geolebatmazian, from Tokat

Hagop Grboyan, from Suedia

Mihran Muradian, from Van

Kevork Hagopian, from Kilis

Ghevont Bedrosian, from Garin [Erzurum]

Garabed Bodosian, from Bardizag

Stepan Sarian, from Afion Karahisar

Krikor Simonian, from Farghin

Mgrdich Stepanian, birthplace unknown

Khacher Panosian, from Suedia

Corporal Pedbos, French

*Eighteen of the above heroes died in the church of Holy Mother of God (*Soorp Asdvadzadzin*), after fighting to their last cartridge [...], incinerated in the church which had been set on fire. The remaining seven died in various battles in the town.*

The following are also worthy of the roll of honor:

> *Corporal Donabed Shushanian, from Divrig, who after remaining buried under the snow for 12 hours was transferred almost dead to the Adana hospital and breathed his last there.*

In the battles that took place on the road after the retreat from Marash the following were killed:

Lieutenant Bedros Dimlakian, from Suedia

Arshavir Asadurian, from Gesaria

Simon Avakian, from Kharpert

Asadur Boyajian, from Kilis

What happened to those left behind? Rev. Hartunian describes the horror of waking to discover that they had been abandoned. Only a day earlier, the Armenians had believed that the tide had turned; the Turkish rebels had left the town, fearing French reprisals. Now they returned and the massacres started again. Hartunian and his family, with the remnants of his congregation, passed along secret, dark places to join others in the more secure Catholic church. He notes that there were roughly 5,000 there. They removed the French flag from the Catholic and Protestant churches and waited. His own church was burnt down and the crowd of "çete and *bazibocuk*" [bandits, rabble, irregulars][8] were surrounding the Catholic church with torches and guns trained on the building to prevent escape. Kerosene was spread around.

At that moment, he writes, there was a knock and a shout at the door. An American missionary, Mr. Lyman and a Near East Relief official, Dr. Wilson, entered holding a white flag, accompanied by gendarmes. The Americans had spoken with the Turkish leaders of the town and secured the Armenians' safety on the condition that they gave up their arms and promised obedience. Five men, including Hartunian, were chosen to speak with the Turkish leaders.

128. Marash in ruins.
Photograph by Stanley Kerr, Joyce Chorbajian collection. Courtesy of Houshamadyan.

129. A section of Marash near the citadel.
Photograph by Stanley Kerr, Joyce Chorbajian collection. Courtesy of Houshamadyan.

After twenty-three days of war and imprisonment (writes Hartunian), this was my first walk in the streets. But oh! What a horrible scene! Corpses, large and small, corpses of men, women, children, soldiers, littered the snow-covered ground. Even carcasses of animals were scattered all over. The snow was red. Another Armenian section was in flames.[9]

Hartunian writes that upon reaching the meeting, humbling themselves and expressing their respect, "our unforgiveable crime was forgiven.

130. The Armenian Protestant church in ruins, Marash.
Photograph by Stanley Kerr, Joyce Chorbajian collection. Courtesy of Houshamadyan.

131. The Bilezikian family surviving in Marash, 1920. The father, Movses, was working in quarries in Vermont. Wife Yepros has her hand on son Peter's shoulder.
Courtesy of Bethel Bilezikian Charkoudian.

Protection was promised. [...] As long as chivalrous France with her great power was protecting us, we were murdered. When she departed, the Turk had pity and spared the remnant."[10] The 10,000 Armenians remaining in Marash were cared for by the missionaries and Near East Relief for the next two years as they opened schools and cared for the new orphans. Though troubles continued and were constant, including accusations that Hartunian and others had started the Marash wars, the remnant survived. As the Americans too were driven out of the region and the French completely withdrew from Cilicia, most Armenians took the difficult road of migration to places of greater safety and a more secure future. Hartunian writes what many must have been thinking:

Farewell Turkey.

Farewell the places where I was born, grew up, and lived.

Farewell my consecrated and holy temples, foundations of wisdom and knowledge—mounds mixed with the ashes of Armenian martyrs and mixed in their blood ...[11]

12

The Aftermath

> While in the hospital, I received the happy news that the Great Powers [Allied Powers] had officially recognized the Independent Republic of Armenia. Three days after this joyful event, word came that the 25,000 Armenian inhabitants of Marash had, once more, been subjected to massacres and deportations by the Turks. Suddenly, the days of excitement and happiness were replaced by long days and years of sorrow and mourning.
>
> —*The Autobiography of Hovannes Garabedian*

The tragic battles and evacuation of Marash were part of a pattern around the area. Hadjin and other towns and villages had also become scenes of conflict with the returning survivors facing threats from the Kemalists. Boyajian notes that in Hadjin some 8,000 Armenians, out of an original population of 30,000, were trying to rebuild their lives in their birthplace but threats and attacks were making it impossible. He writes that Col. Brémond was petitioned urgently to allow volunteers to go quickly to Hadjin to help. The French authorities were reluctant but eventually allowed 300 to 350 men to go, led by Lt. James Chankalian with Lt. Boghos Der Sarkisian as his adjutant.

The volunteers chafed at the delays blocking their progress as they were stopped halfway in Misis on the pretext of danger from the çete (irregulars or bandits) on the roads. They were ordered to stop again at Sis, their frustration becoming unbearable.

> The enemy had already laid siege to the surrounding villages. However the volunteers who had put their lives at the service of their people's liberation could not remain idle with a calm heart and conscience, while their kinsfolk were waging a life and death battle. Against the will of the French, they attempted to leave Sis, but with their small group and poor armaments, found the line of siege impregnable. Thus the first attempt met with failure and the loss of fifty persons.[1]

Boyajian continues the story with a summary of an eyewitness account written by legionnaire Hovhanness Vekilian. Lt. Vahan Portukalian, who had left for France after demobilization, returned to Cilicia in May 1920 under the insistence of Georges-Picot, charged with a special mission in Misis, as administrator of relief and assistance on behalf of the French. The plan was that some volunteers would be sent for relief of Hadjin. As many young men assigned to him had no military training, Portukalian asked General Dufieux to send him four legionnaires as drill sergeants, suggesting Hovhanness Vekilian, Manoog (Khan) Baghdasarian, Movses Shahbazian and Jack Simonian.

Vekilian writes that in Misis, Captain Thibault, the military head of local French authority, agreed that these four men as well as two newly formed detachments would be under Portukalian's command. These consisted of around 100 soldiers and 50 to 60 mounted troops who, after a short period of training, moved on towards Sis and Hadjin.

> Two legionnaire drill sergeants, Vekilian and Simonian, were appointed leaders of the infantry detachment, while Mgrdich Yepremian, accompanied by legionnaires Garabed Yegavian and Levon Konsyulian and two fighters from the Caucasus, both called Avetis Chavush,[2] were named as brigade heads, assuming command of the mounted detachment.

> Little by little, the cautious, slow progress of the detachment made them aware of the scarcity of their provisions. The detachment commanders decided to purchase sheep from

shepherds they met on the road and, in the event of meeting with resistance, would requisition any number that was necessary. However, before putting this decision into action, intelligence was received that around Paklali, through which both detachments had passed, two shepherds had been slain. As will be seen later, this incident, for which the Armenians bore no responsibility, was the reason why later Vekilian and Simonian, the two brigade heads of the infantry, were tried as murderers by the military tribunal and Portukalian and Yepremian as criminals.

When the infantry detachment approached the fort of Tumlu Kale, sounds of fusillade were heard from the surrounding areas. A group of scouts were sent to assess the situation. Brigade head Boghosian reconnoitred the surrounding areas with three or four legionnaires and battled with the enemy forces. At the same time, the infantry detachment came under attack from the enemy and also, unwittingly, from our mounted detachment who had taken refuge in the fort.

Through the exchange of special signals, the identity of the infantry became known and a group of mounted troops rushed to their help from the fort, putting the enemy to flight. The Armenians sustained one casualty, brigade head Boghosian.[3]

Boyajian writes of the aftermath of this expedition:

A few days after returning to Misis, Vekilian and Simonian were unexpectedly summoned by Captain Thibault and informed that on the order of General Dufieux, they would be sent to Adana, escorted by a sergeant major. Intrigued by the mysterious motivation behind this unexpected order, the two legionnaires grilled the sergeant appointed to guard them and learned that they were under arrest. Had it not been for the good will of Captain Thibault, they would have been sent to Adana in chains.

It was evident that there was a serious accusation against them. After arriving in Adana they were led to the prosecutor and subjected to a harsh and merciless interrogation, being accused of setting fire to peaceful and defenseless villages and killing two shepherds in Paklali. Supposedly, it had been irrefutably proven that the bullets killing the shepherds bore French markings. The accused were imprisoned and remained in prison for 63 days, awaiting their court martial. Lawyer Lt. Haig Azadian took charge of their defense. During the trial, the prosecutor, a French officer, spared no effort to ensure that the accused were condemned on the false testimony of witnesses supplied by the Turks. In his closing speech, the prosecutor demanded the death penalty for the two selfless, devoted soldiers who had fought for the liberation of their fatherland under the French flag.

Fortunately, thanks to the evidence presented by the defense lawyer and rigorous cross-examination of the false witnesses, it was not difficult to establish the groundlessness of the accusations. In his brilliant defense plea, Lt. Azadian also made a brief historical overview of the Armenian people having borne the cross for so long and praised the heroic fight of the Armenian legionnaire. After a short discussion, the court martial proclaimed the acquittal of the accused. Based on the same false intelligence, Portukalian and Yepremian were also arrested and imprisoned after their return to Adana and were to be tried before a military tribunal.[4]

Meanwhile, Cilicia was again being emptied. Boyajian relates that on the night of June 1, the Armenian population of Sis along with resident French authorities were evacuated under the protection of the Armenian legionnaires. The Armenian Legion was the only remaining protection and, as battles continued to rage, the Legion was being dismantled. Boyajian has bitter words for the French: "The attempts to come to the aid of Hadjin had met with failure on account of the French authorities, friend, ally and protector of the Armenians."[5]

132. Students digging trenches around an Armenian school near Adana for protection against Kemalist troops.
John Amar Shishmanian Papers, envelope B, Hoover Institution Archives.

Legionnaire Lt. John Shishmanian, born in Kentucky of Armenian and Scottish–American parentage, became the head of the remaining Armenian Legion troops in Cilicia. In a 1921 interview with *The Christian Science Monitor*,[6] Shishmanian said that his criticisms were not aimed at the dedicated French officers serving locally but at those higher up the ranks in Paris whom he described as "attempting to manage things in the Near East for the selfish purposes of some individual Frenchmen, and without a proper understanding of the real characteristics of the people upon whom great wrongs are being inflicted."

In the interview, Shishmanian observed that the French had a more "inefficient and vacillating policy" than the British and far fewer men, resulting in the French acting out of fear for their own safety. He points out the tensions of that time, noting that he was requested to stay on beyond the order for demobilization as further assistance was needed to protect Adana because the French were concerned that Turkish nationalists would destroy their communication line, the railroad. Shishmanian was asked to organize Armenian volunteers to protect Adana and its surroundings while the colonel took troops to Mersin to drive the Kemalists away from the connecting railroad.

CONTRACT WITH FRENCH GOVERNMENT AT ADANA. NOTE THE SIZE OF FRENCH PAY.

CONTRAT D'ENGAGEMENT

I.- Monsieur CHICHMANIAN est engagé aux Services Administratifs des T.F.O.M. (Cilicie) à compter du 10 Juin 1920.
Il remplira les fonctions d'Inspecteur des Groupements Arméniens d'Adana. Il est placé à cet effet sous les ordres du Gouverneur de la Ville d'Adana.

II.- La durée du contrat sera de trois mois avec faculté de prolongation.

III.- Le rôle et prérogatives de M. CHICHMANIAN sont définis dans la note de service N° 2205/M en date du 13 Juin 1920 du Colonel BREMOND.

IV.- Son traitement fixé à .....1697.90.......... payable au taux officiel des Troupes Françaises du Levant.

V.- Il est entendu avec M. CHICHMANIAN que cet engagement sera caduc après un préavis de 15 jours, si l'autorité supérieure donne l'ordre de l'annuler ou si M. CHICHMANIAN ne donne pas satisfaction dans l'emploi auquel il est affecté.

VI.- Par réciprocité, M. CHICHMANIAN pourra démissionner de ses fonctions et être libre de tout engagement après un préavis de 30 jours; dans ce cas il n'aura droit à aucune indemnité.

VII.- Toutefois, les indemnités des autres officiers étant payables au pair et par suite variant avec le cours du Secteur le total de la solde et des indemnités de M. CHICHMANIAN arrêté à une somme en francs, pourra être revisé en cas de renouvellement de son engagement, si les cours du change appliqués aux autres officiers venaient à être modifiés sensiblement./.

Fait à Adana, le 2 Septembre 1920

Le Colonel Chef du Contrôle Administratif.

Le Postulant

133. Work contract for Lt J. Shishmanian (*"Chichmanian"*), June 10, 1920. Shishmanian was engaged to work as Inspector of the Armenian *"Groupement"* of Adana, under the orders of the Governor of Adana.
John Amar Shishmanian Papers, Hoover Institute

There were 1,000 volunteers and we defended the city for three months. This force was completely armed, equipped, clothed and fed by the Armenians themselves, who made great sacrifices for this purpose. [...] The people cut down their own scanty food to clothe and feed us and we found our arms. [...]

Armenian laborers, including boys and girls who went out to the vineyards and vegetable gardens just outside Adana, began to be kidnapped and killed by the Turks. Soon this was done right in the streets of the city. Many children were killed. The parents came to me. I went to the colonel one day and told him my office was full of weeping women. He said nothing could be done. Later I gave him names of 138 cases, with witnesses and all, and still no action. The result was that on July 10, the whole Christian population got out of hand, to put it mildly. The Armenians, Chaldeans, Assyrians and Greeks simply ran wild, and by midnight nearly all the Turks, except a few hundred around the French governor's residence, had fled to Konya.

After that the French officers decided that the Turks must come back. They told me that the Armenians were ruffians, they massacred the Turks, and the French must control them. The French general told me I must disarm the Armenians. I responded that it would be impossible for me to execute that order. Then he ordered me to give him a list of those with arms and collect the arms into depots. I told him it was impossible to get such a list. [...] After that, French officers would walk into houses and, if they found arms, the men in the house would be arrested and hung. Six or seven Armenians were hanged in that way.

Seeking protection and shelter, many continued to come to Adana as long as the French remained. However, as Shishmanian describes, the French themselves were afraid and were making plans both for an escape route to the sea and for extra provisions for themselves and the Adana population. When the Armenians were invited to harvest the wheat, they responded with energy and enthusiasm. The wheat was

134. Certificate of Good Conduct for Hovsep Ajemian. *Michael Najarian Collection.*

not one large field but a whole plain, populated by small villages. The Armenian National Union in Exile and the Inter-Party Organization set up separate groups for various localities. Boyajian lists these and how they were divided between political parties:

The Dashnak group led by Minas Veradzin occupied the Armenian village of Abdoghlu which had been set on fire by the çete a few weeks previously and whose inhabitants had fled to Adana. The Reformed Hnchakians set up two groups. The first under the command of the legionnaire Chakeji occupied the village of Tashjek, on the bank of the Seyhan and the second under the command of the legionnaires Haytugents and Hayguni established itself in Solaklu, on the road to Karatash. The Ramgavar group under the command of an Armenian from the Caucasus occupied the Mirmanda village and the environs. The Hnchakian group, under Yeretsian's command, established itself in Akharja farmstead.[7]

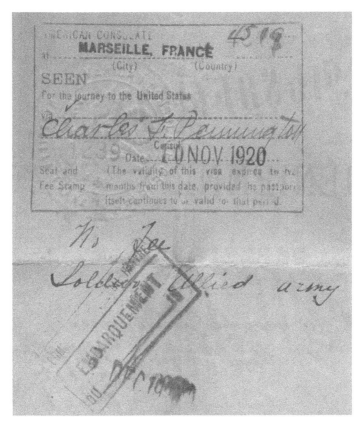

135. Stamp of the American Consulate of Marseilles on the reverse of the Armenian passport of Nishan Najarian. *Michael Najarian Collection.*

136. Nishan Najarian. *Michael Najarian Collection.*

Located between the Seyhan and Ceyhan rivers, the region was called Yureyli. With the arrival of the organized Armenian returnees and their protectors, the local Turks abandoned their homes and animals and fled to the mountains. "Thus," Boyajian writes, "spontaneously a separate Armenian district was created, occupied solely by Armenian forces who, taking advantage of the flight of the Turks, gathered the entire harvest of the plain and transferred it to Adana."[8]

However, as Shishmanian related in his interview, the situation was more complex than this suggests, in terms of safety. It was also very much more complex politically, both internally and on an international scale. Boyajian writes that the leader of the Dashnak group, Minas Veradzin, proclaimed an independent republic in the name of the entire population of Cilicia on August 2. He sent a proclamation

137. Elected and appointed leaders of the Armenian National Union in Exile of Adana. Seated from left: Garabed Ashikian (treasurer), Dr. D. Mnatsaganian (chairman), Lt. John Shishmanian (Commander of the Armenian Forces of Cilicia), Firooz Khanzadian. Standing from left: Aram Mndigian, Dr. Salibian, Setrag Guebenlian (vice-chairman). *Courtesy of Ardemis Matteosian.*

138. Mersin, Cilicia, May 1921 (from left) Hovhanness Vekilian (Cyprus), following discharge from the Armenian Legion, Lt. Boghos Der Sarkisian, wearing the uniform of the Turkish gendarmerie in which he also served, Lt. James Chankalian. *Photo courtesy of Vahram Goekjian, Project SAVE Armenian Photograph Archives.*

and report to the Dashnak party and to Mihran Damadian, telling him to immediately inform the French authorities. However, Damadian, in discussion with the Armenian National Union and the Inter-Party Organization, thought this too provocative and decided to keep the proclamation quiet. He sent representatives, headed by Lt. Chankalian, to convince Veradzin of "the seriousness of that action and its probable grave consequences." Veradzin agreed not to make any more moves until he had orders from community leaders.[9]

According to a more detailed account by Garapet Moumdjian, this is not how the situation ended. Soon afterwards, the French sent soldiers to the headquarters of Veradzin and demanded that the ANU expel him. The ANU complied and Veradzin was exiled by the French.[10] Soon afterwards, on August 5, Damadian himself issued a proclamation of independence, writing in his memoirs that he had been quietly encouraged to do so by Col. Brémond who promised to pass it on to his superiors in Beirut. Again, a visit by French soldiers ended the short moment of independence on the plain of Adana.

The declaration also marked another end. Boyajian writes that barely a month after these proclamations of independence, Col. Brémond, who had always been recognized as a friend of the Armenians, was made to resign from his post and recalled to France. In a declaration dated September 4,[11] Brémond writes that he has received a letter dated the same day from the commander of the 1st Division informing him that as he (Brémond) has spent 19 months in the East, the High Commissioner has decided that he should return to France to give essential intelligence on the implementation of the peace treaty with Turkey in Cilicia.

Three days later, Col. Brémond invited representatives of the communities to a reception where he delivered a speech, including this excerpt:

> You who have witnessed the actions I have undertaken amongst you know that I have always strived to be just and equitable towards everyone, without discriminating between race and nationality. You know how laughable are the lies bandied about me, making me appear as someone favoring this side or the other.[12]

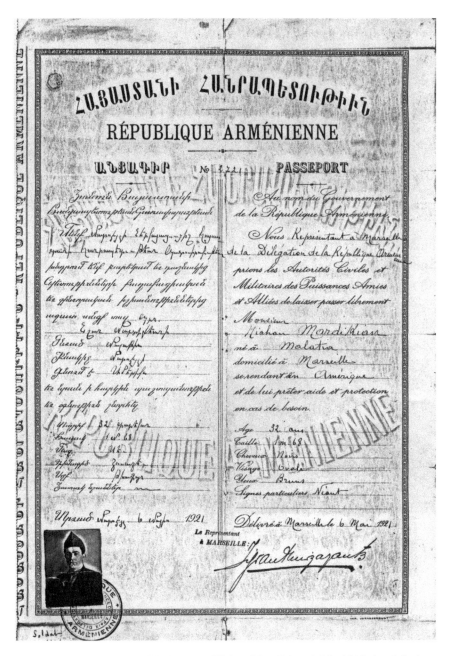

139. Armenian passport of legionnaire Nishan Mardikian. *Michael Najarian Collection.*

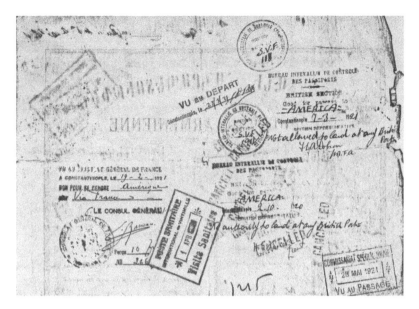

140. Stamps on the passport of Nishan Mardikian, showing passage from Constantinople, through France to the United States. Two handwritten notes on these stamps indicate that he had no "authority to land at any British port." *Michael Najarian Collection.*

141. The passport of Angèle Adjemian, whom Nishan Mardikian married in Constantinople in February, 1921. The stamps show that she began her journey to the United States via Greece and Italy. *Michael Najarian Collection.*

Commenting on Brémond's speech, Boyajian notes that the colonel was pronouncing these words when Adana was already besieged, when the Armenian Legion was undergoing its final disbanding and when the French had already "sold Cilicia to the Turks."[13] Following a letter of appreciation sent to Col. Brémond from General Dufieux, Boyajian continues:

> Thus, day by day the protection given to the Armenians by the French was weakening. Col. Brémond's *hayasirutyun* (affection for Armenians) was unquestionable. If the verdict on the independence of Cilicia depended on him, there is no doubt that his decision would have been in favor of the Armenians. His words of farewell were not insincere. [...]

> It was hard to hear more beautiful and expressive words of farewell on those days when France had taken the decision to sacrifice the Armenian [sic] for its pro-Turkish policy, the result of which was not only the final disbanding of the Armenian Legion, but also the dissolution of civil defense forces organized locally for the protection of the region.[14]

The Armenian Legion Ends

The signing of the Treaty of Sèvres on August 10, 1920, paved the way for the final demobilization and official discharge of what was left of the Armenian Legion. Without any protection at all, neither the Armenians nor other Christian minorities in the area were able to withstand the new battles as the nationalists under Mustafa Kemal eventually won their war of independence.

Boyajian had foreseen this moment and alluded to it in preceding chapters. At this point in his narrative, he turns to the valedictory words of the French as the last of the legionnaires prepared to depart. When reading these words, it is important to remember that at that point, some of the most prominent legionnaires—Portukalian, Shishmanian and others—were either still in French military prison or had just been released. With more than a touch of irony, Boyajian writes the following.

To make one swallow a pill with sweet words would have been the most pleasing way. And in the mouth of a French official that sweet tongue appeared very natural, no matter how much the words had lost their meaning and had put on a fake robe which nevertheless was radiant, dazzling, transparent, and beautifully entwisted. Here is the declaration issued by the General Commander of the Occupying Army of the East [General Henri Gouraud] on the complete disbanding of the Armenian Legion, under which all the principal officers have put their signatures:

"Ceyhan, August 19, 1920. Officers, non-commissioned officers, corporals and soldiers! The disbanding of the Armenian Legion frees you from the undertaking in favor of France which you generously signed in 1916 and 1917. You left your family homes to stand next to the Allies. Now that on your way back you are called to pass through the world, you will be justified in sharing the pride and reputation of those in the ranks of the nation who for three years exerted every effort to re-establish the freedom endangered by our common enemy.

142. Military parade in Adana on the eve of the final demobilization.
Courtesy of Ardemis Matteosian.

"In September 1918, Arara offered you the opportunity to participate in the victory of the Allied armies. Afterwards, France will obligingly confess that during darker times she was able to rely on the same selfless devotion and the same bravery of her legionnaires. This union that manifested itself during glorious days and dire times seals for eternity a profound fellowship, soldering together the hearts of Armenian and French combatants. They fell together in Marash, for the common ideal of justice and peace. The image of our brave men lying side by side in a shroud of snow symbolizes our warm cordiality. I bow deeply to their supreme sacrifice.

"How many brave legionnaires fell unrecognized under inglorious circumstances? Their simple death is such a laurel that would surpass all glories. France knows what bravery is and glorifies the humble, modest man who fought and fell without ostentation, without a witness, without a story. The plain of Ceyhan witnessed your latest heroic exploits—such as the displacement of the cannon at Yaparlak, the attack on Ibrahim Bey's farmstead, the capture of Manguet—which speak sublimely of your merits. The lands stretching from Aintab to Mersin, from the Euphrates to the Taurus were glorified with your many great military deeds.

"Officers, non-commissioned officers, corporals and legionnaires! On the eve of taking leave from you, I hasten to express my deep gratitude for your awe-inspiring service. I shall retain the imperishable memory of your bravery and ardor. France the magnanimous will remember with pride that she has had the honor of entrusting bayonets to the children of Armenia which they put to use with fervor. Would that the blood that has been shed and this particular heroism were not in vain.

"Brave legionnaires, inspired by the lessons of history, you should keep in mind the lessons imparted to you by the French, that is the benefits of discipline, which will guide you towards the realization of your desires. I wish you happiness in your family homes and prosperity for your homeland which is so precious for you. Farewell officers, non-commissioned officers, corporals and legionnaires.

"Commander-in-Chief of the Occupying Army of the East, General Gouraud; Commander of the First Division, General Dufieux; Commander of the Regiment of the Armenian Legion, Colonel Flye Sainte Marie, Battalion Commander Bojar."[15]

Boyajian follows this passage with his own sardonic summary of the speech:

You enlisted voluntarily, fought bravely, gave many casualties whose blood sanctified not only an anonymous, unknown hill in Palestine—Arara—but also the plains and the ravines, the mountains and the hills, the lakes and the rivers of Cilicia, and now you are leaving. Godspeed. [...]

This is the gist of General Gouraud's and his colleagues' beautiful but hollow words. No one asks why the Armenian young man "magnanimously" signed a contract to fight under the French flag and participate in the victory of the Allied armies. What gains did that victory procure for him or his deported and persecuted kinsfolk? Why should one immortalize Arara, this wretched hill rising in a foreign country, who had not been worthy of any mention throughout history? What price the Armenian victory in the battle waged against the Turk? What was the consequence of the supreme sacrifice of the 21 [sic] heroes buried on the flank of Arara?[16]

Recalling the funeral oration given by Lt. Col. Romieu at the burial of those fallen at Arara, Boyajian reminds the reader that he said:

I vow before your tomb, this tomb which we will turn into a monument to glory and we will call it the Graveyard of Arara, uniting in that name the memory of our dead, their sacrifice, and the horizon which that victory shall open for the national aspirations of their compatriots.[17]

143. Sunrise over Alexandretta (possibly taken by Lt. Shishmanian). Shishmanian was held prisoner on board a ship in this harbor after his arrest for insubordination in Cilicia. His father, supervisor of the Port Said railway, was able to join with British officers in securing his release.
John Amar Shishmanian Papers, envelope B, Hoover Institution Archives.

Boyajian notes that the pledge lasted a very short time, forgotten only a few months after Armenian soldiers had reached the land of Cilicia and again, justice and human rights for the indigenous Armenians were forgotten. Remembering a visit to Adana by High Commissioner Georges-Picot on March 13, 1919, he also questions the ceremony held to honor some of the legionnaires, conferring military crosses upon them. He argues that while it is good that at least these few men received recognition, it is completely inadequate and incomprehensible that more men were not decorated. As some 80 legionnaires were wounded at Arara and a further 600 had fought heroically and played a part in the victory, according to General Allenby, he continues, why have the services of the legionnaires in Cilicia not been similarly recognized? "Would it not have been a worthy deed to suitably appreciate them before demobilization, not for the defense of the Cilician soil but for relieving the French from a difficult predicament on many occasions? There were many instances."

From December 17, 1918 until May 28, 1919 the only army occupying Cilicia was the Armenian Legion. Apart from civil servants, there was not a single French soldier until that date. It was the legionnaires that totally occupied the Plain of Cilicia. And when the English withdrew from Marash, Kilis and other towns of Mountainous Cilicia, only then did Algerian and some French soldiers join the Armenian legionnaires. According to the existing agreement between the National Delegation and the French government, in the case of disbanding the Armenian Legion, the discharged legionnaires, should they want it, would have been sent to countries from where they had set out to be recruited under the French flag.[18]

Instead, the men were left to return home, alone or in groups as they were able, towards the end of 1920 and early 1921. Some men did receive assistance to reach "home" but others received nothing.

> And thus the legionnaires were going away crestfallen, bitter and in despair. They were leaving the soil that their comrades in arms and before them hundreds of thousands had irrigated

144. Lt. John Shishmanian (center) leaving Cilicia after his release from arrest and confinement in Alexandretta. Initially not allowed to take his personal belongings, here he is pictured with his suitcase, an "old revolutionary" (sic) on the left, and his orderly on the right. *John Amar Shishmanian Papers, envelope B, Hoover Institution Archives.*

with their blood. They were leaving with their dreams shattered, their expectations in tatters, their trust cruelly exploited. They were going away unable to avenge their slain, starved, kidnapped, violated mothers, sisters, newly wed brides, tender children, grandfathers with one foot in the grave, brothers with towering height and endowed with the beauty of Adonis, and their embittered fathers.[19]

As mentioned earlier, following demobilization, Vahan Portukalian had been sent back from France to continue with the French military in Adana, directing French assistance during the evacuation of the region. This heartbreaking work prolonged the anguish for Portukalian, as shown in letters he wrote to a friend, M. Kourken Tahmazian, in Paris. Edited by Raymond Kevorkian, these letters express the sorrow and anger of witnessing the destruction of a people and a dream. A few extracts follow:

14 November, 1921.

My dear friend,

With the execution of the [Ankara] Accord of October 20 the evacuation of Cilicia has effectively begun. As soon as the news spread, the exodus of Christians began in proportions that no one could have imagined. Up to today, in Adana alone, they have given out 18,000 "laissez-passer". If one counts an average of three people per laissez-passer (there are often five or six), this makes around 45,000 people who are going.

It's useless to tell you about the crowding at the station—I don't know what is happening at Mersin—the Armenian quarters, so populated, even overpopulated, even two weeks ago, look like deserts. [...]

This evening, more than two thousand people jostled with each other in front of the passport office. [...] Does anyone in France have an idea of the suffering of these past fifteen years? Plundered, burnt down, massacred in 1909, Christians dress their wounds as they are able. With admirable patience, they rebuild their homes and reorganize their life a little. Five years roll by. Again, a new, even more terrible catastrophe. Mobilization with arbitrary requisitions, emptying shops and farms, taking linen and kitchen utensils from homes, and above all, attacking the purse under a thousand pretexts; then the mobilization of men waiting for mass deportation and the annihilation of the race. These sad wrecks make their way back, attempting to take shape in the shadow of the French flag.

May 27, 1922. [Portukalian now writing from Greece, on his way home.]

The exodus of the Armenians of Cilicia has passed almost unnoticed in France. Public opinion, so eager with generous impulses, has no suspicion of this poignant drama. [...] A few agency dispatches have brought up the "guarantees" related to minority rights promised by the Turkish nationalists and speak of an unjustifiable panic among the Armenians. They explain this panic as being instigated by outside intrigues against French influence. [...] There was no panic in Cilicia, but rather the unanimous will of the Christians to escape at all costs from the Turkish administration, as soon as they heard the news of the evacuation of the French troops. How can one again question the disposition of the Turks in regard to the Armenians? How can one forget a series of bloody events that have taken place, ranging over a long historical period? And those that took place under the French occupation itself? [...] at Marash, there were 12,000 Armenians that the Turks exterminated as soon as the French evacuated the town. At Hadjin, after an admirable resistance of eight months, organized and maintained for the honor of the French flag, only 400 soldiers breaking out on the road to Adana, as well as the entire population, some 8,000 souls, massacred with a brutality beyond the borders of horror. Idem, the 5,000 Armenians and Greeks from the surrounding villages. At Zeitoon, the legendary citadel, already 3,000 Armenians have paid with martyrdom for the faith they put in the promise of the Allies. [...] What is the point of continuing to list these? [...]

Believe me, I do not feed myself with illusions or paradoxes. I feel myself drained of what I would call my capacity for indignation. One could say, aside from that, that indignation is not a political position. I do not preach discouragement at all but rather that patience joined with effort should continue. The reign of the absurd—which flourishes today in the question of the Middle East—will not last forever. Stability, the logic of things, will again take the upper hand.[20]

Despite these deep doubts, anger and disappointments, the legionnaires maintained their ideals and desire to somehow rebuild Armenian communities, albeit in new environments and among strangers. Not allowing the bitterness to consume them, legionnaires went on to lead productive lives. Around the diaspora, returning legionnaires become community leaders, helping to rebuild old and create new spaces and institutions for Armenians to come together and create, in William Saroyan's words, "a new Armenia."

Epilogue

The abrupt exit of first the British and then the French led to mass migration of the surviving Armenians in the region. Today we know that there were many in the region who did stay, either willingly or by force, embedded in Kurdish, Turkish or Arab life to save themselves and their children. The homelands appeared utterly emptied of Armenians and Armenian life with the exception of a handful of families in the larger towns, such as Mersin, and two clusters of Armenian villages mentioned earlier, just south of Cilicia: those of Musa Dagh and those of Kessab.

Many legionnaires originally from the areas of Musa Dagh and Kessab returned to join the surviving villagers in their heroic efforts to rebuild their lives. Prior to the Genocide, these villages and others in the area had been thriving with predominantly or wholly Armenian populations.

From 1918 as World War I ended, the refugees began returning from Port Said to the six villages[1] on the slopes of Musa Dagh (in Armenian, *Musa Ler*) and the nearby village of Suedia. After two decades of renewed life in the villages, during which a dispute over the boundaries of modern Turkey was ongoing, the French ended their mandate and transferred the Hatay region to the Republic of Turkey. The decision took effect on June 29, 1939, leaving the villagers of Musa Dagh with the choice of becoming Turkish citizens or being moved by the French to a rocky area in the Bekaa Valley of Lebanon. Given recent memories, nearly all villagers opted to leave and settled in the new town of Anjar, Lebanon, whose six districts are named after the villages of Musa Dagh.

145. Legionnaires from Kessab, including Zerone Hagopian (back row, middle), return to their birthplace to help returning survivors rebuild.
Courtesy of Arpi Hagopian Haboian.

In the twenty-first century, there are still some 140 Armenians in the village of Vakif and the annual celebration of the Feast of the Assumption draws Armenians (many descendants of the Musa Daghtsis) from around Turkey and the world to join them.

Though the border between Turkey and Syria briefly changed to include the villages of Kessab, the current border returned the villages to Syria but considerable farm and grazing land, a monastery and the sacred place on Jebel Aqra (or Mount Cassius) remained in Turkey. However, since 1918 and the return of surviving Kessabtsis to their villages, there has remained a constant majority presence of Armenians, with the exception of a few months in 2014 with the invasion and destruction of property by Al Qaeda and other irregulars during the Syrian war.

Hagop Cholakian writes that legionnaires began arriving soon after the surviving Kessabtsis. The first to arrive were Ovsia Saghdejian ("Kara Oghlan" or "Dayi") and Misak Giragossian ("Missako" or "Sakkali") walking day and night from Mersin, in uniform and with guns, through many Turkish villages, pretending to be customs officers. Later, other legionnaires began to arrive and helped secure the safety of the villages.

From 1918, mostly under the leadership of the returning former legionnaires, independent rule was established in Kessab, lasting until 1922 (see the Appendix, biography of Ovsia Saghdejian). The villagers elected officials, established administrative and judicial bodies and their own army to protect the population. Legionnaire Movses Shahbazian, writing in his own memoirs, states firmly that the work that the returning legionnaires did in Kessab's self-defense in those years was equally important to anything they had done while in the Legion itself.[2] Other minorities including Greeks and Alevis sought refuge in Kessab. When the French firmly established their colonial rule over Syria and Lebanon, self-rule ended though the mountainous position of Kessab made it more isolated and difficult for outsiders to control completely. Several of the legionnaires who devoted themselves to re-establishing community life in Kessab were remembered as legendary figures for many decades afterwards.

George Azad Apelian, a child in the mid 1950s in Keurkune, another of Kessab's villages, remembered *Gamavors* arriving for a September reunion and celebration.

> Their arrival created much excitement among the villagers, particularly among the youngsters: seeing the men in their military fatigues and carrying ammunition and rifles was a thrill for all. The *Gamavors* celebrated their victory at the Battle of Arara seated next to the village spring, feasting on food over white sheets spread on the meadow. They sang about the *Gamavors*.

George had memorized the old song that ended with:

From Arara to Cilicia
Are reminders of the Volunteers
On the tomb of the Volunteer
There is no wreath, however.[3]

Elsewhere in the new diaspora, the returning legionnaires also turned their energies and talents towards their communities and families. With

146. A picnic in Providence, Rhode Island, August 21, 1929. Legionnaires join with comrades, family and community. *Courtesy of the Armenian Museum of America.*

147. A picnic in Whitinsville, Massachusetts, 1932. Members of the Armenian Legion pose with community members and other soldiers who served as volunteers on other fronts in World War I and in the US armed forces. General Sebouh Nersesian, who led forces on the Caucasian Front at Sardarabad, is seen in the second row, center; behind the flag. *Courtesy of the Armenian Museum of America.*

the tremendous losses within families during the Genocide, community became extended family. Adjusting to life in the new countries and cities, former legionnaires and their families along with other Armenian men and women helped each other create churches, local centers of political parties, schools, and compatriotic unions as well as other cultural and civic organizations. These formed an institutional and international framework for the diaspora in addition to the continuing importance of informal family ties and friendships.

The legionnaires continued to visit each other regularly, whether in other cities or countries, keeping their ties, memories and ideals alive. As noted above in Kessab, picnics brought large crowds together and quickly became a regular part of the legionnaires' new lives where they could share camaraderie. Photographs of these events show *Gamavors* or volunteers from the different fronts of the war, standing together, comrades in victory at Arara, Sardarabad, Musa Dagh, supporting each other in the defeat of their hopes for Cilicia, encouraging each other in the challenges of integration and rebuilding.

148. Legionnaires gather in Lawrence, Massachusetts, 1922.
Courtesy of the Armenian Museum of America.

A Legionnaires' Association was formed with its first publication emerging in 1919, commemorating the first anniversary of Arara. By 1923, Nishan Najarian, whose life inspired this book, had become the first chairman of the Armenian Legionnaire Association, based in Boston. On the fifth anniversary of Arara he and other former legionnaires published another edition of the journal *Arara*, with further descriptions of their battle experiences but mainly paying tribute to those who died and the dedication of all who served. Some reflected on lessons learned and what they hoped to pass on.

Manoog Khan Baghdasarian alluded to the innocent and misplaced hopes that he and others had placed on outside powers.

> Since the time of its genesis until today the Armenian race has understood in essence that it hasn't had an external friend and wasn't going to have one in future. We have to apply balm with our own hands to our pulsating wound. We have to be our own best friends. Let our children aspire to have a model human society and system of government a century later.[4]

Looking at the divisions predating the Genocide and those continuing afterwards, Sharam Stepanian, an officer in the Association, hoped that the new communities would somehow work together. "Let's reflect amongst ourselves. Let's forget senseless party political, clique and individual quarrels; they proved to be highly disastrous for the Armenian people."[5]

On a practical level, the writer calling himself *Viravor Ashough* [the Wounded Troubadour], invites the readers to consider not only those who have left this earth but those who continue suffering from the wounds received in battle.

> Come, dear reader, let's leave these fresh graves with funereal sorrow and go back a few miles to hospitals behind the battle lines where our living martyrs are suffering. Approach with mindful steps, crouch at the tiny opening of the tent and come in. Lying on this first bed is a young man from Suedia, one arm is broken and his mother and sisters as well as young bride and children are impatiently waiting for his return in the refugee tents of Port Said.

149. The officers of the Armenian Legionnaire Association, 1923. Center: Nishan Najarian, chairman; clockwise from top right: Mihran Guzelian, treasurer; Kh. Krikorian, assistant secretary; K. Assadourian, vice-chairman; Sharam Stepanian, secretary. *Michael Najarian Collection.*

150. Legionnaires raised funds to assist those comrades who had suffered injuries. Here the New York branch of the Armenian Legionnaire Association publishes a poster to raise money in aid of disabled Armenian legionnaires (price 25 cents). *Courtesy of Arsen Haroian. Project SAVE Armenian Photo Archive.*

This other is a young man from Sepasdia with a broken leg and who, alas, has no one in this world; the great storm of the Catastrophe (*Yeghern*) has taken away all of them. The third is a young man from Gesaria whose legs are both amputated.[6]

The children and grandchildren of the legionnaires report that there was great respect for these men and an appreciation of the sacrifices they were known to have made but that little was known of what they actually did. This is not unusual and it is fair to assume that these same relatives are correct in saying that the legionnaires did not seem very eager to talk with them about it. Dickran Boyajian wrote and published his own memoirs, with those of others, some 40 years later. Many of his comrades did not begin to write until roughly the same amount of time had passed. As new studies are showing, their examples of active participation, both physical and intellectual, social and emotional bonds of family and friendship, a future-orientation or a focus on building new

151. Stepan Piligian was sent by his father to the United States from a village in Sepastia just before the Genocide. He joined the Legion and towards the end, while stationed in Adana, met his future wife, Turfanda Yergatian. They married and made their way to the US via Marseilles, settling in Indian Orchard, Massachusetts.
Courtesy of the Armenian Museum of America.

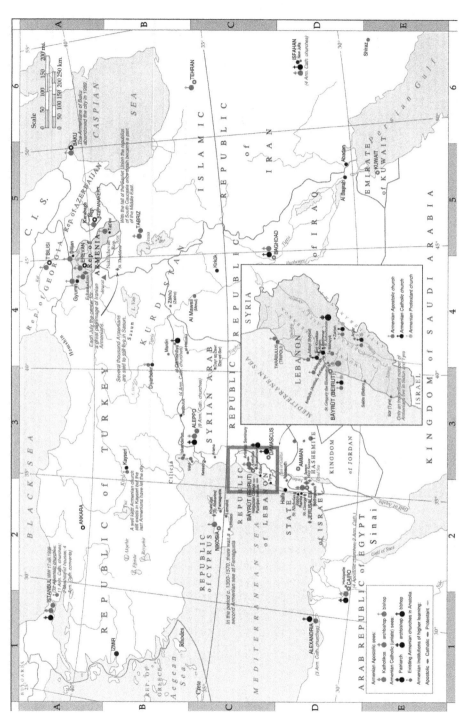

152. The Armenian Diaspora in the Middle East since 1918. *Courtesy of Robert H. Hewsen, Armenia: A Historical Atlas.* Original in color.

153. *Gamavor* friends and comrades at a picnic in Massachusetts in later years. *Michael Najarian Collection.*

institutions and organizations, all help the healing process or at least keep the painful memories at a more healthy distance.

The Armenian legionnaires' stories are still relevant today. Dedication to a cause always requires focus and devotion but is never guaranteed to end as one hopes. What do we learn from those who come before us? How do we pick up the pieces and start again, if our initial goal is not reached? The legionnaires, of all ages and from around the Armenian world of the time, were a very mixed group, bringing different talents and perspectives, trained to work together but also sharing a fundamental tie with each other, a sense of great loss but also of intense attachment to their people and their land. When it was apparent that Cilicia would not become an autonomous Armenian region, the legionnaires turned their attention to what could be done to ensure that future generations would grow to know and appreciate their heritage as well as becoming citizens contributing to their new countries, to become Armenians in new ways, in new places. The legacy of the Armenian legionnaires is their example of selflessness, courage and dedication.

Appendices

A. SHORT BIOGRAPHIES

Men came to the Legion in very different ways and their paths afterwards diverged considerably. However, each shared a continuing dedication to human rights and dignity. Here we present a few sample short biographies.

DICKRAN BOYAJIAN
by Marc Mamigonian

154. Dickran Boyajian, author's portrait in *Haygagan Lekeone*.
Courtesy of Baikar Press.

Dickran Boyajian (1895–1975) was born in the village of Armujan near Palu in the Diyarbakır region of the Ottoman Empire. When he was 15 years old he left his home and after nearly a year of travels in Europe, stowed away on a steamer from Liverpool headed for Boston and then Providence, Rhode Island where he joined an uncle in 1911 (see Chapter Seven).

After working various odd jobs, he found employment as a typesetter for the Armenian newspaper *Bahag (Pahak)*, published at that time in Providence, while also attending school. In 1916 he entered Brown University but transferred to Boston University in 1917 when *Bahag* merged with *Azk (Azg)* and relocated to Boston.

In July 1917, Boyajian was among the Armenians in the United States who volunteered for the Légion d'Orient (later the Armenian

Legion), functioning as part of the French military forces in the Near East. He saw action in Palestine and became private secretary to the head of the Legion's medical group, Dr. Roland. He was discharged in 1919, but remained in Cilicia to observe conditions among the surviving Armenians. He returned to the United States in 1920 to assist in raising funds for the Cilician Armenians but then found he was not allowed to return. In 1921 he translated *La Cilicie en 1919–1920* by Col. Édouard Brémond, chief French administrator in Cilicia, published as *Giligia 1919–1920* (Boston: *Tbaran Bahag*, 1921).

Boyajian began law school at Northeastern University in 1920 and graduated in 1924. He received his Master's in law from Boston University in 1925, passed the Rhode Island and Massachusetts bar examinations, and practiced law from 1930 until going into semi-retirement late in life.

An active participant in Armenian–American religious and civic institutions, Boyajian served many times as a Diocesan delegate from St. James Armenian Church in Watertown, Massachusetts, chairing diocesan assemblies on two occasions (1955 and 1962) and participating in National Ecclesiastical Assemblies in Etchmiadzin. He was recognized as the Diocese Man of the Year in 1972, and received the St. Gregory the Illuminator Medal from His Holiness Vazken I, Catholicos of All Armenians. He served for many years with the Armenian General Benevolent Union (AGBU), including as a member of the Central Board, was a Grand Commander of Knights of Vartan, a member of the Armenian Democratic-Liberal Party (Ramgavar) District Committee, and was a Founding Member of the National Association for Armenian Studies and Research (NAASR), which he also served as a member of the Board of Directors and as co-chairman of its national advisory board.

In addition to the book quoted at length in this volume, he wrote and translated many articles and books including *Armenia: The Case for a Forgotten Genocide* (1972), a pioneering work on the Armenian Genocide at the time of its publication.

While still in Adana, Boyajian met and married Ardemis Janjigian (see Chapter Eight) who shared his life of service to the Armenian community of New England and worldwide.[1]

VAHAN PORTUKALIAN
by Gagik Stepan-Sarkissian

Vahan Portukalian was born in Marseilles on July 29, 1887. His father, Megerdich Portukalian, was a political activist and one of the founders of the Armenagan party. In exile from Van in the Ottoman Empire, M. Portukalian settled in Marseilles where he published the influential magazine *Armenia*.

After studying medicine and law, Vahan Portukalian enlisted in the French army during World War I. As an officer he took part in battles in the Champagne region and was awarded the Croix de Guerre before he was sent to the Middle East. He served in the Légion d'Orient (later Armenian Legion) with the rank of second lieutenant. After the disbanding of the Legion, Portukalian was put in charge of the French Assistance Services in Cilicia entrusted with the difficult task of ensuring an orderly handover of his duties during the French evacuation.

Following the French departure from Cilicia in early 1922, Portukalian was appointed a magistrate at the Appeal Court in Aleppo. Following Syrian independence, Portukalian returned to France in 1947 and settled in Aix-en-Provence, where he pursued his legal career, eventually retiring as the President of the Appeal Court of the city. He died on July 7, 1974.

Portukalian never published his memoirs on the Armenian Legion but contributed a series of articles to the Paris-based Armenian newspaper *Haratch* on the events in Palestine and Cilicia during and after World War I.

HAGOP AREVIAN

From *The Mirror Spectator*, September 3, 2009.
"ALMA Armenian Legionnaire Traveling Exhibition Begins Nationwide Tour."

155. Home page of the Hagop Arevian website.
Courtesy of www.hagoparevian.com. Credit: Haniel Rivière

[Hagop Arevian] was born in 1894 in a small village near Sebastia (Turkey) [...] His family miraculously survived the massacres ordered by Sultan Abdul Hamid in 1894–1896, and moved to the capital of Constantinople (Istanbul), where Hagop's father, Nazareth, obtained work as a port supervisor. [...]

Hagop received his education in Mekhitarist schools in the capital, and in 1914 went to Alexandria, Egypt, to join his older brother. With the outbreak of World War I, he resolved to fight for the Allies and went to Marseilles, France, to volunteer for the French Foreign Legion. After training in Algeria, he joined the French Army in France. On leave in Paris, he met Boghos Nubar Pasha and learned of the plans to form the Armenian Legion [...]

Arevian, now a corporal first class, returned to the battlefield in France and was seriously wounded at Vitry-le-François. Receiving the valued Croix de Guerre, he was detached from the Foreign Legion in 1917 and assigned to the Armenian Legion, which was then training in Cyprus. After helping to train the Armenian volunteers in Cyprus, Arevian joined the Legion as it marched to Palestine [...] As a member of the Fifth Battalion, Arevian participated in the Legion's victory at the Battle of Arara [...]

Marching north with General Allenby's forces, Arevian joined other legionnaires in rescuing Armenian women and children who had survived the death marches of the Genocide. The Armenian Legion was assigned to occupy Cilicia [... and] Arevian was subsequently stationed in Adana, the center of the French occupation in Cilicia, where he served for the following two years.

[When] France turned Cilicia over to the Turkish nationalists [and] quietly disbanded the Armenian Legion, [...] Arevian (now a citizen of France) returned to Egypt, where he married and established a family and a successful business.

In 1939, Arevian became an early supporter of the French resistance against Nazi Germany and became one of the first members of General de Gaulle's Free French Forces. From 1940 to 1945 he organized a hospice for soldiers of the resistance, a museum of the war, and created a circle of benefactors and volunteers to assist the French military. In recognition of these services, he was awarded the French Medal of Resistance in 1946, and over the next decade concentrated on his business in Egypt.

In 1956, however, his life was disrupted once again as he and his wife were expelled from Egypt, given only 48 hours to pack and leave the country. He moved to Paris, where he became an Officer of the Légion d'honneur and was given the privilege of rekindling the flame at the Monument of the Unknown Soldier at the Arc de Triomphe in 1959. He died in Paris in 1965.[2]

OVSIA SAGHDEJIAN
by Vahe H. Apelian

156. Ovsia Saghdejian, more widely known as Daye or within the family, Daye Baboog, in older age in Kessab. *Courtesy of Sevag B. Panossian.*

Extracts from *Daye—A Kessabtsi Legend Remembered*[3]

Ovsia Saghdejian was born in 1887 in [...] Kaladouran, the coastal village of Kessab, where the Saghdejian family had their own hamlet known as Saghdejlek. [...] He left for America before the 1915 Armenian Genocide and [later] volunteered from America to enlist in the Armenian Legion under French command, taking part in the famed Arara battle on the Palestinian front.

He continued to serve in the Armenian Legion under French command. However upon witnessing the French government renege [on] the promises it had made to the Armenians for a secure homeland in Cilicia, he left the Legion and with his compatriot Missak Guiragossian, returned to Kessab and took refuge in his ancestral village, Kaladouran, organizing a defensive force consisting largely of the former legionnaires who had the training and the material for self-defense. The group undertook the security of Kessab and made a point of ceaselessly appearing in different locations at different periods of the day, but mostly under the cover of the night, leaving the impression that armed Armenian forces were stationed throughout Kessab safeguarding the security of the inhabitants who had survived the Armenian Genocide and were returning to their ancestral homes to start their lives anew. [...]

During [the period of self-rule], Ovsia Saghdejian was not elected to any office and yet for the Kessabtsis he personified the spirit and the will that safeguarded and made this self-governing entity a functioning reality in Kessab. It is thus that the legend of the *Daye* was born. His name, Ovsia Saghdejian, henceforth started to fade into oblivion while the stature of *Daye* started to emerge larger than life. The late Bishop Terenig Poladian wrote in his eulogy of *Daye* that the Kessabtsis noted with confidence that as long as *Dayen* (The Daye) was alive and well, no Turk would dare attack Kessab.

His compassion for the welfare of the Genocide survivors was not only manifested in his fiercely independent will to resort to arms for self-defense. He also established an orphanage and took care of over thirty young orphaned boys and girls. He resorted to every means to fund the orphanage, [...] setting his arms aside and roaming from village to village, asking for sustenance whenever the funds became insufficient [...]. It is also said that he acted as a matchmaker and found suitable mates for many of his orphans and he married the last orphan.

In late 1922, the French government took over the command of the region and dissolved the local self-proclaimed governing entity of Kessab. The French authorities also issued an arrest warrant for *Dayen* on the allegation that he was spearheading desertion activities from the French army. During this period *Dayen* was compelled to live a semi-nomadic life in Kessab always entrusting his fellow Kessabtsis with his whereabouts.

157. Hagop Panossian (left), also known as Onbashi, poses with his cousin Dzeron/ Joseph. Their original family name was Boyunumushakian. They had changed it to Panossian upon immigration to the USA, most likely in 1911. After demobilization, the cousins went to Kessab, and assisted in protecting and rebuilding their native village with the returning survivors of the Genocide.
Courtesy of Razmik Panossian.

B. LETTERS AND DECLARATIONS

Many letters, declarations and excerpts from treaties are included throughout Boyajian's *Haygagan Lekeone*. Examples of these are given below.

Led by Mihran Damadian, representatives of the Christian minorities, Armenian, Greek, Syriac, Syrian, Chaldean, met in Adana and decided to proclaim the independence of Cilicia under French protection. The declaration—in French—was issued on August 4, 1920 and Dickran Boyajian gives the Armenian translation of this document on pages 346–51. An abridged version in Armenian, also provided by Boyajian, is translated here.

OFFICIAL DECLARATION TO THE ARMENIAN PEOPLE[4]

Today, August 4, 1920, at noon, the Representative of the United Armenian Delegation, the Armenian National Union, the religious heads of the three Armenian denominations, the religious and civil delegates of Greek, Syriac, Chaldean and Syrian communities collectively called upon Col. Brémond, Head of Administrative Control in Cilicia and solemnly presented him with an official document signed by the above-mentioned in the name of all Christians of Cilicia, declaring the independence of Cilicia from the Turkish state and endowing it with an autonomous administration under French protection.

The Head of French Control showed a greatly sympathetic attitude and whilst promising to relay to his government this important document which was destined to open a new era in the contemporary annals of Cilicia, gave strict orders to us to exhort our people to remain calm and orderly.

The official national bodies consider it their duty to exhort all people to show complete orderliness, refraining from all kinds of demonstrations and gatherings, as are already forbidden by the state of siege regulations.

Through their decent behavior and by absolutely refraining from any unlawful acts towards the Turkish and Muslim population of the town, from insobriety and generally from any action likely to disrupt the public peace, the Armenians must effectively show that they are a politically mature people and worthy of liberty that they demand and proclaim unanimously with their fellow Christian countrymen.

For popular celebration of this declaration of independence, it is only allowed to bedeck Christian buildings and establishments with flags, preferably with the French flag.

INTER-CHRISTIAN SPECIAL COUNCIL

Adana, 4 August 1920

LETTERS OF COMMENDATION

Dickran Boyajian collected excerpts from letters of commendation written by officers working with the Armenian Legion. He begins by stating:

In Cilicia the Armenian legionnaire was involved in battles a hundred times more bloody than Arara: Marash, Aintab, Sis, İslahiye, Dort-Yol, Osmaniye, Misis, Baghché (Bahçe), Haruniye, Bozanti, the entire length of the Amanos and Taurus mountain chains and the large and small towns, hamlets and villages of Cilicia Pedias [the Plain of Cilicia] are witnesses to their heroism. Let the French testify:

I have the honor to inform you that the Armenian Legion under the command of Lt. Col. Flye Sainte Marie gave the proof of an excellent conduct during the operations to capture Aintab and Marash, in which it played a major role.

Col. Brémond (December 30, 1919).

The Command of the French army is proud of the legionnaires' excellent military deportment. They stirred feelings of perfect satisfaction with their meticulous and faultless accomplishment of the highly difficult task entrusted to them.

Col. Flye Sainte Marie (December 30, 1919).

This (Armenian) nation has lost none of its moral vigour. The Armenians and Greeks around Osmaniye can feel proud of the bravery they demonstrated. The Armenians leaping out of their trenches on 5 June to attack the enemy merited the commendation of the colonel. By this action, the Armenians demonstrated that they could fight bravely, while at the same time providing the proof of their faith in the authentic values and spirit of their race. In the near future, the Armenians and Greeks will savor the fruits of their bravery.

Lt. Col. [C. J. E.] Andrea, military commander of Jebel Bereket, June 9, 1920.

Boyajian concludes: "That 'near future' never came near and the Armenian legionnaire and the Armenian fighter were deprived of the pleasure of savoring the 'fruit of their bravery'."[5]

C. "THE FRENCH RECORD IN CILICIA"
from *The Christian Science Monitor*, 1921
An interview with
legionnaire Lieutenant John Shishmanian[6]

Evidence accumulates that when a true history of the Near East during the last five years comes to the printed page, there will be revealed to the world a record of inefficiency, expedience, cupidity and promise-breaking by those from whom the Christian peoples of that part of the world had every right to expect fair dealing and salvation from the Turk, which will astound the world's sense of justice and righteousness.

The historian who seeks proof of the injustice inflicted upon those Christians may find some of it in the experience of Lieutenant John Shishmanian, native of Kentucky, U.S.A., of Scotch and Armenian ancestry; American ambulance driver in France preceding entrance of the United States into the war; wounded at Verdun; second lieutenant in the French Army; instructor of Armenian troops on the island of Cyprus; commanding officer of Cilician Armenian Volunteers, organized to defend the Christians in the City of Adana, Cilicia; while still wearing the uniform of a French officer, and without specific excuse, except the political expediency of the Treaty of Sèvres, "railroaded" out of Cilicia by his own superior French officers, and only set free when an inquiry by the Secretary of the State of the United States had apparently convinced the French of the urgent advisability of denying that he had ever been so much as arrested.

Lieutenant Shishmanian told the story in detail to a representative of *The Christian Science Monitor*. He made it clear that he did not mean to criticize adversely the French officers in Cilicia as being responsible for the policy under which the Turks and Kurds have been favored and the Armenians, Chaldeans, Assyrians and Greeks oppressed. Responsiblility for this, he held, rests with higher officials in Paris, whom he described as attempting to manage things in the Near East for the selfish purposes of some individual Frenchmen, and without a proper understanding of the people upon whom great wrongs are being inflicted.

"I was born in Kentucky," said Lieutenant Shishmanian, "and years ago had experience with the Kentucky militia in feud troubles. Before we entered the war I went to France as a member of the American ambulance field service. Some time after that, in order to see active service, I enlisted in the French Army and rose to the rank of second lieutenant. After serving at Verdun, I was ordered, with about a score of other French officers, in January 1918, to go to Cyprus and drill Armenian troops into an Armenian legion.

"This drilling was done in Cyprus to conceal the organization of the Armenian legion from the Turks. There were about 5,000 men, 1,600 from America, and they saw service in Palestine and Syria, and later occupied Cilicia for the French.

"The legion was organized because France was short of troops and had to have Armenians to help keep the Turks engaged on the Palestine front; and also because France was afraid that without sufficient troops there she would lose her prestige in the Near East; and because of her desire, after the Sykes–Picot treaty, to have good reason to say a strong word in her own behalf, after the war, in connection with the Near East.

"Remember that more than 200,000 Armenians were brought back from exile, under the British and French regime, and were encouraged to rebuild their homes in Cilicia. That was just after the armistice, and that was how Sis, Hadjin, Urfa, Marash, Adana and other places were repopulated. During the year and a half when the Cyprus Legion [sic], almost alone, occupied Cilicia, these people were perfectly happy and safe.

"Now, as soon as the British had evacuated Cilicia, the trouble began. The French have shown a stupid, inefficient and vacillating policy in everything they have done in Cilicia. But they had so few men in comparison with the number the British had that they were terrified. Because of this they kept concentrating the people in the towns, and this prompted the Turks, when they saw that we would not attack, to guerrilla warfare.

"Take the case of Marash. The 6,000 French troops evacuated that city after the Turks had flown the white flag. Let me emphasize that: the French evacuated after, not before, the Turks had signaled for truce.

"The situation today is the result of the same policy. All the Armenians have been disarmed, in the sense that none is allowed to go on the streets armed, and he is not supposed to have arms even to defend himself from attack.

"Now the Cyprus Legion [sic] was due to be demobilized last June. The demobilization order came. My service expired June 5. I asked permission to go home. The French colonel in Adana told me that 20,000 Kemalists were coming against the city. The only communication with Europe lay through Mersina, and the Turks, he said, might destroy that railroad any day.

"In Adana at that time there were almost 100,000 people. The inhabitants of Sis, Aintab, Urfa, and other places, back to which they had been brought by the British and French, had now been forced to seek refuge in Adana: the place was much overcrowded and the people were on the verge of starvation. There were attacks by the Kemalists almost daily.

"The colonel said that he was organizing a big column to go to Mersina and drive the Kemalists off the railroad along the way. He asked me to organize Armenian volunteers to defend the city during the column's absence and made me their commanding officer.

"There were 1,000 volunteers and we defended the city for three months. This force was completely armed, equipped, clothed and fed by the Armenians themselves, who made great sacrifices for this purpose. When the colonel asked me to raise the volunteers, he provided me with no arms or equipment. I was told to go out and hustle for them. I did, any way I could. The people cut down their own scanty food to clothe and feed us and we found our arms. Our 1,600 defended the city against the daily and nightly attacks of some 15,000 or 20,000 Kemalists for three months.

"On the night before the French left Adana, during the first week in July, the colonel asked the Armenians to furnish 2,000 more volunteers before dawn. The request was made at 9 o'clock. The volunteers had to be found, assembled, armed, equipped, officered. The Armenian notables said this was impossible, the time was too short. The colonel said it must be done.

"That night the Armenians hustled around and did their very best,

158. This photo from a French-Armenian newspaper (unidentified, undated) shows Makrouhi Helvajian Apovian (left) posing with a friend. Born into a prominent family in Marash, Makrouhi witnessed the beheading of members of her family but escaped with her baby sister. The girls were taken to an orphanage by the Red Cross but Makrouhi joined the legionnaires in their struggle. She later told her daughter of the dangerous missions they ran, transporting guns and ammunition through underground tunnels and fighting alongside the men. Through this photo, a family friend in the United States discovered that she was still alive. He sent her money to come to the United States with her young sister and, after a short period, asked her to marry him. They settled in New Jersey and raised two children.
Photo courtesy of Dr. Caroline Apovian.

but by dawn, only 85 new volunteers had been found. Now I understand that General Gouraud has recently reported that although Armenians keep declaring that they can furnish men for an army in Cilicia, when he called for 2,000 for the relief of Tarsus, they furnished only 18! But he should also tell of the preposterously unreasonable shortness of time imposed upon them, and that when given more time later, they did the job and did it efficiently.

"And here is what the job was, what the colonel wanted those extra men for. He wanted them to go down into the wheat plain south of Adana, clear it of Turks so that the wheat could flow into the city and, something quite important to him, to open up and keep open the automobile road to the seaport of Karatash, for an avenue of escape for his staff and anyone else who wanted to come along, in case the big column toward Mersina was defeated.

"It should be stated that this area could have been occupied and cleared of the brigands or Kemalists long before this time and a continuous supply of wheat assured the city. But for reasons best known to the French, this was not done until after they had prevailed upon the Near East Relief to supply flour six months longer.

"After the column came back, Armenian laborers, including boys and girls who went out to the vineyards and vegetable gardens just outside Adana, began to be kidnapped and killed by the Turks. Soon this was done right in the streets of the city. Many children were killed. The parents came to me. I went to the colonel one day and told him my office was full of weeping women. He said nothing could be done. Later I gave him names of 138 cases, with witnesses and all, and still no action. The result was that on July 10, the whole Christian population got out of hand, to put it mildly. The Armenians, Chaldeans, Assyrians and Greeks simply ran wild, and by midnight nearly all the Turks, except a few hundred around the French governor's residence, had fled to Konya.

"After that the French officers decided that the Turks must come back. They told me that the Armenians were ruffians, they massacred the Turks, and the French must control them. The French general told me I must disarm the Armenians. I responded that it would be impossible for me to execute that order. Then he ordered me to give him a list of those with arms and collect the arms into depots. I told him it was impossible to get such a list. Apparently the French did not want to try to do this work themselves. After that, French officers would walk into houses and, if they found arms, the men in the house would be arrested and hung. Six or seven Armenians were hanged in that way. And it was such a hanging that eventually led to my release.

"There were no French white troops in Adana to speak of. They will not go out to Asia Minor. The French forces are mostly Senegalese Negroes and Algerians. The former fight well and are loyal, but the latter are Muhammedans and desert in great numbers to the Turks, always managing to take arms and ammunition with them, even machine guns, which is rather remarkable."

Notes

NB: 'DHB' refers to Dickran H. Boyajian, *Haygagan Lekeone* [*The Armenian Legion*], Watertown, MA: Baikar Press, 1965. DHB followed by page number(s) will be used throughout to indicate where more information can be obtained in the book and/or the source of a particular quote.

Note on the Contents of
The Armenian Legionnaires

1 To contact the Museum (now called the Armenian Museum of America) for information about this exhibition, visit the website www.armenianmuseum.org or write to info@armenianmuseum.org.

Chapter 2 The Armenian Legion at the Crossroads of Colonial Politics

1 The Armenian National Delegation was established in 1912 in order to defend Armenian interests at a time when the Allied/Entente Powers were advocating reforms in favor of the Christian population of the Ottoman Empire's Eastern provinces, decades after the first diplomatic initiative undertaken at the Berlin Congress in 1878. Boghos Nubar was appointed head of the delegation by the Catholicos Kevork V, and by the end of 1912, had settled in Paris. Thereafter he deployed intense diplomatic activity, especially with Allied governments during the war.

2 Boghos Nubar, *Papers and The Armenian Question, 1915–1918*. Trans. Vatche Ghazarian. Waltham, MA: Mayreni Publishing, 1996: 59.
3 Boghos Nubar, *Papers*, 212.
4 A selection of books and articles for further reading is included in the bibliography.

Chaper 3 Recruitment and the Voyage

1 DHB 23.
2 *The Autobiography of Hovannes Garabedian* (unpublished), Michael Najarian Collection.
3 Interview conducted by the Zoryan Institute, 1984, later donated by the family to the Armenian Museum of America as part of the Legionnaires' Archive.
4 As remembered by Sarkis Najarian's daughter, Sona Najarian Touloumdjian, Nicosia, Cyprus, 2016.
5 Interview conducted by the Zoryan Institute, 1984, later donated by the family to the Armenian Museum of America as part of the Legionnaires' Archive.
6 Guévork Gotikian. "La Légion d'Orient et le mandat français en Cilicie (1916–1921)." *Revue d'Histoire Arménienne Contemporaine* 3 (1999): 251-324. www.imprescriptible.fr/rhac/tome3.
7 DHB 41.
8 DHB 48.
9 DHB 49–54.
10 Sarkis Najarian, personal papers.
11 DHB 56–7.
12 DHB 58.

Chapter 4 Training in Cyprus

1 Gotikian, 1999.
2 DHB 60.
3 DHB 62.
4 Interview conducted by the Zoryan Institute, 1984, later donated

by the family to the Armenian Museum of America as part of the Legionnaires' Archive.
5   DHB 66.
6   DHB 66–8.
7   DHB 71.
8   Adrian Barracks or *Baraques Adrian*, named after the engineer Louis Adrian who designed them, were easily put together from prefabricated modules, constructed of wood and tin. Flexible and sturdy, serving multiple purposes, the lower walls flared out, providing more floor space.
9   DHB 76.
10 DHB 77–8.
11 DHB 78–9.
12 DHB 79–80.
13 Andreko Varnava describes several incidents in "Famagusta during the Great War: from backwater to bustling." In Michael J. K. Walsh (ed.) *City of Empires: Ottoman and British Famagusta*. Cambridge: Cambridge Scholars Publishing, 2015, 103–5. Another serious incident is described in Nina Hierodeacon Kyriakou, Ροδινη Αυγη – Μνήμες Τρικώμου της Νίνας Ιεροδιακόνου Κυριάκου [*Pink Dawn: Memories of Trikomo*]. Another Greek Cypriot source giving both general information about the legionnaires' history, camp, and location also includes mention of discord among the legionnaires themselves, bringing about the re-situating of one of the camp sites, can be found at https://ammohostos.wordpress.com/category/αρμένιοι.
14 DHB 82.
15 DHB 90.
16 DHB 92.

Chapter 5 Palestine and Preparation for Battle

1   DHB 95.
2   DHB 96–8.
3   DHB 101.

4 DHB from *Haratch*, August 15, 1964.
5 *The Autobiography of Hovannes Garabedian* (unpublished).
6 DHB 109.

Chapter 6 The Battle of Arara

1 *Arara: dedicated to the fifth anniversary.* Boston, Massachusetts, 1923: 6.
2 *The Autobiography of Hovannes Garabedian* (unpublished)
3 From Mihran Guzelian. "Heroes of the Battle of Arara." Unpublished memoir, translated by Varad Varadian. Michael Najarian Collection.
4 *Arara: dedicated to the fifth anniversary.* Boston, Massachusetts, 1923: 9.
5 Mihran Guzelian. *The Armenian Mirror-Spectator* September 27, 2010. https://mirrorspectator.com/2010/09/27/remembering-the-battle-of-arara-september-19-1918.
6 DHB 125.
7 DHB 125.
8 Gotikian, 1999.
9 DHB 130.
10 DHB 137.
11 From Guzelian, "Heroes of the Battle of Arara."
12 DHB 155.
13 DHB 138–9.
14 DHB 139–52.

Chapter 7 The Next Stages: Beirut

1 DHB 157–8.
2 DHB 160–4. From an article originally published in *Baykar* in 1958.
3 DHB 166.
4 DHB 170.
5 DHB 173.
6 DHB 174–7.

Chapter 8 To Cilicia, the "Promised Land"

1 DHB 187.

2 *The Autobiography of Hovannes Garabedian* (unpublished)
3 DHB 181.
4 DHB 191.
5 Karnig Tourian. "My Memoirs" [in English and Armenian]. Nicosia, 1999: 2–4.
6 DHB 191–2.
7 DHB 194.
8 *Coutelas* was one of 13 Claymore-class destroyers launched in 1907.
9 DHB 195–7.
10 DHB 178–9.
11 DHB 201–4.
12 As remembered by Sarkis Najarian's daughter, Sona Najarian Touloumdjian, Nicosia, Cyprus, 2016.
13 *Ibid*.
14 Levon Saryan. "A Brief History of the Armenian Legion of World War I." Presentations made in Racine, WI, Chicago and Evanston, IL, 2010.
15 DHB 203–4.
16 DHB 206.

Chapter 9 Repatriation and Increasing Uncertainties

1 This letter, also mentioned in Vahram Shemmassian, "The repatriation of Armenian refugees from the Arab Middle East, 1918–1920." In Richard G. Hovannisian and Simon Payaslian (eds), *Armenian Cilicia*. Costa Mesa, CA: Mazda Publishers, 2008, is found in full in DHB 207–8.
2 See Shemmassian, "The repatriation" for a detailed discussion of the French, British and Armenian perspectives and proposals on repatriation.
3 *Ibid*. 425.
4 *Ibid*. 427–8.
5 *Ibid*. 447.
6 DHB 209.
7 DHB 210.

8   DHB 210–11.
9   DHB 212.
10 Boyajian does not give any indication of who is suspected of killing Dr. Roland.
11 DHB 213.
12 DHB 214.
13 DHB 215.
14 DHB 217.
15 Though he does not indicate, we assume that Boyajian found this letter during his own research for his book.
16 DHB 217–19.
17 DHB 221.
18 DHB 225.
19 DHB 231–3.
20 DHB 237.
21 DHB 241.
22 DHB 241–2.
23 DHB 242–6.
24 DHB 247.

Chapter 10 The Transfer of Power in Marash

1   DHB 252.
2   DHB 254–7 include letters written (a) by community leaders of Marash to the head of British Secret Intelligence Service in Marash asking for punishment for those responsible for massacres in the region, and (b) by the Armenian National Union of Marash to General Allenby to extend protection to the Armenians of the region. Both letters are reproduced in full.
3   DHB 258–9.
4   *The Autobiography of Hovannes Garabedian* (unpublished).
5   Stanley E. Kerr. *The Lions of Marash: Personal Experiences with American Near East Relief*. Albany, NY: State University of New York Press, 1973: 62.
6   *Ibid.*

7 *Ibid.* 64.
8 *Ibid.* 57.
9 *Ibid.* 71.
10 *Ibid.*

Chapter 11 The Battles of Marash or "The Marash Affair"

1 Abraham Hartunian. *Neither to Laugh Nor to Weep: An Odyssey of Faith, A Memoir of the Armenian Genocide*. Trans. Vartan Hartunian. Belmont, MA: Armenian Heritage Press, National Association for Armenian Studies and Research, 1999: 113.
2 DHB 288–9.
3 Armenian Christmas in Marash, was then celebrated on January 19. Today, except in Jerusalem, Armenian Christmas is celebrated on January 6.
4 DHB 280–4.
5 *Ibid*.
6 Sgt. Sarkis Varadian. *Hairenik Daily* on 09/17/61 in Armenian. Translated by Varad Varadian.
7 DHB 295–7.
8 Hartunian is always clear that there were Turks who did not participate in the mob scenes and these terms are left untranslated in his book, perhaps because it is so difficult to express.
9 Hartunian, *Neither to Laugh*: 149.
10 *Ibid.* 149.
11 *Ibid.* 180.

Chapter 12 The Aftermath

1 DHB 301.
2 Although Boyajian does not mention this, "Chavush" could be a nickname denoting rank, rather than these men's actual family name.
3 DHB 301–3.
4 DHB 304–5.
5 DHB 320.
6 Printed in full in the Appendices. From "The French Record in

Cilicia" (originally in *The Christian Science Monitor*, 1921). *The New Armenia* (Boston, MA) 13, no. 2 (March–April 1921): 22–4. Also, Armenian translation printed in *Hayrenik* (Boston, MA) on March 21, 1921 and printed in DHB 340–2.
7   DHB 343–4.
8   DHB 344.
9   *Ibid.*
10 Garabet K. Moumdjian. "Cilicia under French administration: Armenian aspirations, Turkish resistance and French stratagems." In Richard G. Hovannisian and Simon Payaslian (eds), *Armenian Cilicia*. Costa Mesa, CA: Mazda Press, 2008: 483.
11 See Appendices for text of Col. Brémond's September 4, 1920 declaration (DHB 365–6).
12 *Ibid.*
13 DHB 368.
14 DHB 369.
15 DHB 372–3.
16 DHB 376.
17 DHB 377.
18 DHB 381–2.
19 DHB 384–5.
20 Raymond Kevorkian. "L'évacuation française de la Cilicie en 1921 vue par officier Vahan Portoukalian." 1999. *Revue d'Histoire Arménienne Contemporaine* 3 (1999): 345 ff. www.imprescriptible.fr/rhac/tome3/p2b#correspondance. Translated by Gagik Stepan-Sarkissian.

Epilogue

1   Kabusia (Kaboussieh), Yoghunoluk, Bitias, Vakif, Kheter Bey, and Haji Habibi.
2   Movses Shahbazian. *The Armenian Volunteer Movement 1917–1920*. Kessab, Syria, 1965: 25.
3   http://kessabheritage.blogspot.co.uk/2013.
4   *Arara*, 1923:16.

5 *Ibid*. 18.
6 *Ibid*. 27.

Appendices

1 A selection of books and articles for further reading is included in the bibliography.
2 For full article see www.mirrorspectator.com/2009/09/03/alma-armenian-legionnaire-traveling-exhibit-begins-nationwide-tour; see also www.hagoparevian.com.
3 http://kessabheritage.blogspot.co.uk/2013/07/daye-kessabtsi-legend-remembered.html.
4 DHB 351–2.
5 DHB 376–7.
6 DHB 340–2.

Bibliography

Arslanian, Artin H. "British wartime pledges, 1917–1918: the Armenian case." *Journal of Contemporary History* 13, no. 3 (July, 1978): 517–30.

Barr, James. *A Line in the Sand: The Anglo-French Struggle for the Middle-East 1914–1918*. New York: W. W. Norton & Co., 2012.

Beylerian, Arthur. *Les Grandes Puissances, L'Empire Ottoman et les Arméniens dans les archives françaises (1914–1918)*. Paris: Publications de la Sorbonne, 1983.

Bloxham, Donald. *The Great Game of Genocide: Imperialism, Nationalism, and the Destruction of the Ottoman Armenians*. Oxford: Oxford University Press, 2007.

Boghosyan, Samvel A. "Մեգիդոյի Ճակատամարտը եւ Հայկական Լէգէոնը." ["Megidoyi chakatamarte yev haykakan legeone"]. *VEM Pan-Armenian Journal* 6 (12), no. 3 (47) (September, 2014): 135–57.

Boyajian, Dickran. *Հայկական Լէգէոնը: Պատմական Յուշագրութիւն* [*Haygagan Lekeone: Badmagan Hushakrutiun*]. Watertown, MA: Baykar Press, 1965.

Brémond, Édouard. *La Cilicie en 1919–1920*. Paris: Imprimerie Nationale, 1921.

Cholakian, Hagop. *Քեսապ* [*Kessab*]. Vol. I. Aleppo: Hamazkaine Syrian Regional Committee Publication, 1995.

Gotikian, Guévork. "La Légion d'Orient et le mandat français en Cilicie (1916–1921)." *Revue d'Histoire Arménienne Contemporaine* 3 (1999): 251–324. www.imprescriptible.fr/rhac/tome3.

Hartunian, Abraham. *Neither to Laugh Nor to Weep: An Odyssey of Faith, a Memoir of the Armenian Genocide*. Trans. Vartan Hartunian. Belmont,

MA: Armenian Heritage Press, National Association for Armenian Studies and Research, 1999.

Hewson, Robert H. *Armenia: A Historical Atlas.* Chicago: University of Chicago Press, 2000.

Hovannisian, Richard G. "The Allies and Armenia, 1915–1918." *Journal of Contemporary History* 3, no. 1 (January, 1968): 145–68.

———. "The postwar contest for Cilicia and the 'Marash Affair'." In Richard G. Hovannisian and Simon Payaslian (eds), *Armenian Cilicia.* Costa Mesa, CA: Mazda Publishers, 2008: 495–534.

Hovannisian, Richard G. and Simon Payaslian (eds). *Armenian Cilicia.* Costa Mesa, CA: Mazda Publishers, 2008.

Jackson, Simon. "Auxiliary troops, global recruitment: the Légion d'Orient and the origins of the French mandate in Syria." In Alison Carrol and Ludivine Broch (eds), *France in an Era of Global War, 1914–1945: Occupation, Politics, Empire and Entanglements.* Basingstoke, England: Palgrave Macmillan, 2014: 133–52.

Karamanougian, Aram. "Հայկական Լէգէոնը պատմական, իրաւական ու քաղաքական հարցերու լոյսին տակ եւ վաւերագրեր." [HaygaganLekeone badmagan, iravagan u kaghakagan hartseru luysin dag yev vaverakrer"]. Haigazian Armenological Review 5 (1971): 39–89.

Kerr, Stanley E. *The Lions of Marash: Personal Experiences with American Near East Relief.* Albany, NY: State University of New York Press, 1973.

Kevorkian, Raymond. "L'évacuation française de la Cilicie en 1921 vue par l'officier Vahan Portoukalian." *Revue d'Histoire Arménienne Contemporaine* 3 (1999): 345 ff. www.imprescriptible.fr/rhac/tome3/p2b#correspondance.

Kredian, Armin. "The Armenian community of Egypt: World War I and Genocide 1914–1919." *Haigazian Armenological Review* 35 (2015): 201–48.

Krikorian, Robert O. "In defense of the homeland: New England Armenians and the Légion d'Orient." In Marc Mamigonian (ed.), *Armenians of New England: Celebrating a Culture and Preserving a Heritage.* Belmont, MA: Armenian Heritage Press, 2004: 25–33.

Mesrobian, Arpena S. "Like One Family": The Armenians of Syracuse. Ann Arbor, Michigan: Gomidas Institute Books, 2000.

Moumdjian, Garabet K. "Cilicia under French administration: Armenian aspirations, Turkish resistance and French stratagems."

In Richard G. Hovannisian and Simon Payaslian (eds), *Armenian Cilicia*. Costa Mesa, CA: Mazda Press, 2008: 457–94.

Nassibian, Akaby. *Britain and the Armenian Question: 1915–1923*. London: St. Martin's Press, 1984.

Nubar, Boghos. *Boghos Nubar's Papers and the Armenian Question 1915–1918: Documents*. Ed. Vatche Ghazarian. Waltham, MA: Mayreni Publishing, 1996.

Shahbazian, Movses. Հայ Կամաւորական Շարժումը Առաջին Աշխարհամարտին, 1917–1920 [*Hay Gamavoragan Sharzhume Arrachin Ashkharhamardin, 1917–1920*]. Kessab, Syria [printed in Lebanon], 1965.

Shemmassian, Vahram. "The repatriation of Armenian refugees from the Arab Middle East, 1918–1920." In Richard G. Hovannisian and Simon Payaslian (eds), *Armenian Cilicia*. Costa Mesa, CA: Mazda Publishers, 2008: 419–56.

Suny, Ronald Grigor. *They Can Live in the Desert but Nowhere Else:"A History of the Armenian Genocide*. Princeton, NJ: Princeton University Press, 2015.

Tachjian, Vahé. *La France en Cilicie et en Haute-Mésopotamie. Aux confins de la Turquie, de la Syrie et de l'Irak (1919–1933)*. Paris: Editions Karthala, 2004.

——. "The Cilician Armenians and French policy, 1919–1921." In Richard G. Hovannisian and Simon Payaslian (eds), *Armenian Cilicia*. Costa Mesa, CA: Mazda Publishers, 2008: 539–56.

Tatarian, M., Կամաւորի մը Յուշերը. [*Gamavori me hushere*] Antelias, Lebanon: Catholicate of Great House of Cilicia Press, 1960.

Tauber, Eliezer. "La Légion d'Orient et la Légion Arabe." *Revue Française d'Histoire D'Outre-Mer* 81, no. 303 (1994): 171–80.

Torossian, Sarkis. *From Dardanelles to Palestine: A Story of Five Battle Fronts in Turkey, and Her Allies, and a Harem Romance*. Boston, MA: Meador Publishing Co., 1947.

Torosyan, Shmavon T. Կիլիկիայի Հայերի Ազգային-Ազատագրական Շարժումները 1919–1920 թ.թ. [*Kilikiayi Hayeri Azgayin-Azatagrakan Sharzhumnere 1919–1920 t.t.*]. Yerevan: Yerevan State University Press, 1987.

Varnava, Andrekos. "Imperialism first, the war second: the British, an Armenian Legion, and deliberations on where to attack the

Ottoman Empire, November 1914–April 1915." *Historical Research* 87, no. 237 (August, 2014): 533–55.

———. "French and British post-war imperial agendas and forging an Armenian homeland after the Genocide: the formation of the Légion d'Orient in October 1916." *The Historical Journal* 57, no. 4 (November, 2014): 997–1025.

———. "The politics and imperialism of colonial and foreign volunteer legions during the Great War: comparing for Cypriot, Armenian, and Jewish Legions." *War in History* 22, no. 3 (2015): 344–63.

———."Famagusta during the Great War: from backwater to bustling." In Michael J. K. Walsh (ed.) *City of Empires: Ottoman and British Famagusta*. Cambridge: Cambridge Scholars Publishing, 2015: 91–111.

Dickran H. Boyajian: Sources and References
compiled by Marc Mamigonian
(in order of publication date)

Yeghisheh [*The History of Vartanank*]. Trans. Hovhannes Zovickian and Dickran H. Boyajian. New York: The Delphic Press, 1952.

Boyajian, Dickran H. *A Light Through the Iron Curtain*. New York: Vantage Press, 1957.

[An account of Boyajian's 1955 trip to Armenia as a delegate to the National Ecclesiastical Assembly at which Vazken I was elected as Catholicos.]

"D. H. Boyajian to be honored." *Armenian Mirror-Spectator*, September 23, 1961: 1, 4.

"New honors for Dickran Boyajian on Oct. 29." *Armenian Mirror-Spectator*, October 28, 1961: 1.

Boyajian, Dickran H. *Armenia: The Case for a Forgotten Genocide*. Westwood, NJ: Educational Book Crafters, 1972.

"Dickran H. Boyajian—Author, Speaker, Community Leader—Dies." *Armenian Mirror-Spectator*, May 10, 1975: 1–2.

File "Dickran H. Boyajian." National Association for Armenian Studies and Research (NAASR).

Glossary

Agha In the Ottoman Empire, title used for a wealthy property owner with a degree of local authority.

Armenian Apostolic Church An independent branch of Eastern Christianity, founded in the early years of the fourth century, the Armenian Apostolic Church is considered the national church of Armenians around the world and the earliest kingdom to adopt Christianity as its religion.

Armenian Catholic Church An Eastern Rite Catholic church, autonomous since 1740, the Armenian Catholic Church is in full communion with Catholics worldwide and recognizes the supreme authority of the Pope. Its liturgy is given in classical Armenian.

Armenian Democratic Liberal Party (Ramgavar) A political party beginning as the *Armenagan* Party in 1885, its name changed in 1921 to *Ramgavar Azadagan Goosagtsootiune* when it merged with two other political parties. The *Armenagan* Party was founded by Mgrditch Portukalian, father of Vahan Portukalian, mentioned many times in *The Armenian Legionnaires*.

Armenian Evangelical Church Following attempts at reformation within the Apostolic Church, the Armenian Evangelical Church was established in Constantinople in 1846. The church had strong support from missionaries from the United States and had a great impact on education for Armenians across the Empire. (Sometimes called the Armenian Protestant Church.)

Armenian General Benevolent Union (AGBU) Founded in 1906 in Cairo, Egypt, by Boghos Nubar and Yervant Aghaton, the AGBU began as a humanitarian and cultural organization, quickly spreading around the world. By 1909, the AGBU was receiving major donations from Armenian individuals and assisting survivors of the massacres taking place across Cilicia. During and following the Genocide, the AGBU again came to the aid of survivors, organizing orphanages and medical assistance, working independently and alongside the Allied Forces and others to provide relief.

Armenian Revolutionary Federation (*Dashnaktsoutiune*) An Armenian socialist and nationalist political party, also called the *Dashnaktsoutiune*, was founded in 1890 in Tiflis, Georgia. In the Ottoman Empire, the ARF's long-term goal was autonomy for the Armenian homelands and while there were attempts at cooperation with members of the opposition in Ottoman politics, such as the Young Turks, before 1912, the ARF supported resistance bands and defense units where raids and massacres were taking place.

Catholicos The highest ecclesiastical office of the Armenian Apostolic Church. During the early twentieth century there were two Catholicoi, one based in Etchmiadzin, now in the Republic of Armenia (Catholicos of All Armenians), one in Sis, Cilicia. After the Genocide, the loss of Sis resulted in the seat of the Catholicos of the Great House of Cilicia moving to Antelias near Beirut in 1930.

Cilicia In Armenian, *Giligia*. The medieval Armenian kingdom (1080–1375), south of the historic homelands, northwest of the Gulf of Alexandretta. Armenian migration towards the area of Cilicia had begun during the Byzantine Empire in the sixth century CE. Under pressure from further invasions by successive powers, Armenians continued to move, seeking refuge. The invasions of the Crusaders, however, brought a useful alliance for the Armenians of Cilicia, including intermarriages. The tombstone of the last king, Levon, is in St Denis, north of Paris.

Effendi (Turkish) Title of respect usually given to non-Muslims, also used by Armenians with each other.

Fellahin From Arabic, meaning peasants, workers of the soil and sometimes, colloquially, simply the dispossessed.

Gamavor (Armenian) Volunteer, in this case, the men who volunteered to join as legionnaires.

Hamidian Massacres Between 1894 and 1896, atrocities and pogroms were carried out against Armenians in the Ottoman Empire by Turkish armed forces and Kurdish irregulars. Oppressive new legislation and taxes found resistance among Armenians, supported by the Armenian Revolutionary Federation and Hnchakian Party. While few Armenians were part of this resistance movement, the government of Sultan Abdulhamid feared its spread and reacted with massacres and repression. Waves of killings of thousands of Armenians followed protests, such as the Ottoman Bank seizure in 1896.

Hnchakian or Social Democrat Hnchakian Party A political party founded in 1887 by Armenian students in Geneva, Switzerland. The name "Hnchak" means clarion or bell, signaling enlightenment and the desire to awaken the Armenians to their mistreatment in the failing Ottoman Empire. Its founders, like those of the Armenian Revolutionary Federation, wished to foster an autonomous if not independent state.

Kemalist At the time of *The Armenian Legionnaires*, Kemalist forces were inspired by the leadership of Mustafa Kemal who sought to replace the Ottoman monarchy with a republican state, based on secular, nationalist principles. Kemal and his followers also fought to remove all outside forces, such as the French and British, from what would become the Republic of Turkey and with them, any minorities, such as the Armenians, who resisted or had been allies of the Europeans.

Müdür (Turkish from Arabic) Administrator of a small group of villages, the level below the *kaymakan* who governs the *kaza* – a city and its surrounding villages.

Mutasarrif An appointed post, administrator of a Sanjak.

Sanjak The provinces or vilayets of the Ottoman Empire were divided into administrative districts called sanjaks.

Suediatsi Suedia (or Suediya) was a village south of the six villages of Musa Dagh (in Armenian, Musa Ler). The Armenian suffix "tsi" indicates belonging to that village. Throughout D. M. Boyajian's book, the men of Musa Dagh are often referred to as Suediatsis. In other places "Musa Daghtsi" is used. The reason for this is unclear, but it was common vernacular usage at the time, continuing on years after the Genocide.

Vartanants A day set aside to commemorate Vartan Mamigonian and the Battle of Avarayr. St. Vartan led Armenian forces to prevent the Persians from forcing a conversion of the population to Zoroastrianism. Vartan and his troops lost but it was a pyrrhic victory for the Persians as they lost so many troops that they could no longer continue the forced conversion, thus delivering a victory in the longer term to the Armenians, who remained Christian.

Vilayet A province of the Ottoman Empire, composed of sanjaks.

List of Illustrations

1.	Upon discharge from the Legion, Nishan Najarian returned to Massachusetts, bringing with him a mother and daughter, survivors of the Genocide. He later married Arshalous and they raised four children together.	viii
2.	Title page of Dickran H. Boyajian's *Haygagan Lekeone* [*The Armenian Legion*]. *Courtesy of Baikar Press.*	x
3.	George Kolligian and comrades. *Courtesy of the Armenian Museum of America.*	x
4.	Légion Armenienne. Poste d'Erzine (also known as Yeşilkent), a town in the Hatay district on the Turkish coast. *Michael Najarian Collection.*	xi
5.	Dickran Boyajian, author of *Haygagan Lekeone: Badmagan Hushakrutiun* [*The Armenian Legion: A Historical Memoir*]. *Courtesy of the Armenian Museum of America.*	xiv
6.	Banner publicizing the 2001 exhibition at the Armenian Museum of America. *Courtesy of the Armenian Museum of America.*	xiv
7, 8.	Postcard to Khan B. from "G." *Courtesy of Ardemis Matteosian (daughter of Khan B.).*	xv
9.	Original diary cover of Khazaros Gopoian, overprinted in English by his son and translator, Stephen Gopoian. *Courtesy of Ardemis Matteosian.*	xviii
10.	Diary frontispiece. In Armenian – "Notes of a Gamavor" by Kh. Gopoian. *Courtesy of Ardemis Matteosian.*	xviii
11.	Khazaros Gopoian with legionnaire comrades. *Courtesy of the Armenian Museum of America.*	xix
12.	Hagop Minasian, Beirut. *Michael Najarian Collection.*	xx
13.	Entry of the French Cavalry into Adana. *AGBU Nubar Library, Paris.*	xxi
14.	Plaque of portraits of Armenian legionnaires. *Courtesy of the Armenian Museum of America.*	2
15.	A portrait from the plaque, enlarged by his family, of legionnaire Hagop Shakarian. *Courtesy of Mayda Shakarian Tartarian.*	2
16.	Page one of a booklet published in Boston in 1916, advising Armenians in the United States on how to organize paramilitary training in preparation for fighting for the homelands when the opportunity arose. Company G, Boston. *Courtesy of Ardemis Matteosian.*	5

17.	Rescue at Musa Dagh. Survivors of the 53-day siege are taken to the French ship *Guichen* and on to Port Said, Egypt. *Courtesy of Sona Najarian Touloumjian.*	5
18.	Some 40 women fought alongside the legionnaires in Cilicia; unnamed "sharpshooter." *John Amar Shishmanian Papers, envelope B, Hoover Institution Archives.*	6
19.	Kegham Aghjayan. *Courtesy of the Armenian Museum of America.*	7
20.	Boghos Nubar, Chairman of the Armenian National Delegation.	9
21.	Volunteers gather in New York before sailing to France and onward to Port Said. *Michael Najarian Collection.*	18
22.	Survivors of the Musa Dagh resistance at Port Said refugee camp. *AGBU Nubar Library, Paris.*	19
23.	Légion d'Orient. Armenian volunteers, 1918. *Photograph courtesy of the Armenian Revolutionary Federation Archive. Project SAVE Armenian Photograph Archives.*	20
24.	Officers of the French Foreign Legion. Lt. Col. Romieu is third from right, first row. *Courtesy of Ardemis Matteosian.*	21
25.	Flag for the 3rd Company, Légion d'Orient, made by Armenian women at Port Said. *John Amar Shishmanian papers, envelope B, Hoover Institution Archives.*	22
26.	Armenian Legion on maneuvers near Adana. Photo by H. M. Berberian, Adana; legionnaire Aram Hovsepian is fourth from left. *Photo courtesy of Barkev Hovsepian. Project SAVE Armenian Photograph Archives.*	23
27.	"The Proposed Partition of Turkey According to Various Secret Allied Agreements, 1916–1918." *Courtesy of Robert H. Hewsen,* Armenia: A Historical Atlas. Original in color.	25
28.	Legionnaires from Musa Dagh. *Courtesy of Karen Kludjian.*	27
29.	Mihran Guzelian. *Courtesy of the Armenian Museum of America.*	29
30.	Sarkis Najarian. *Courtesy of Sona Najarian Touloumjian.*	29
31.	Vagharshag Vartabed Arshagouni. *Courtesy of the Armenian Museum of America.*	30
32.	American–Armenian men hoping to join the Légion d'Orient wait in Patterson, New Jersey, ready to sail to France and onwards to Port Said. *Courtesy of Ardemis Matteosian.*	31
33.	Dzerone Hagopian, originally from Kessab, Syria, joined the Legion from the United States. *Courtesy of Arpi Hagopian Haboian.*	32
34.	Kaspar Menag, legionnaire. *Courtesy of the Armenian Museum of America.*	32
35.	The *Espagne* transported some of the legionnaires from New York to France.	33
36.	Painting of the *Amiral Orly* sinking in the Mediterranean Sea. *Courtesy of Sona Najarian Touloumjian.*	35
37.	Diran Patapanian. *Courtesy of the Armenian Museum of America.*	36
38.	The journeys of legionnaires traveling from the United States. *By Anieka Sayadian.*	37
39.	"*Certificat d'Engagement*" showing that Nishan Mardikian has been accepted into the Légion d'Orient. *Michael Najarian Collection.*	40
40.	The first departure of legionnaires from Port Said, en route to Cyprus. *AGBU Nubar Library, Paris.*	41

LIST OF ILLUSTRATIONS

41. Armenian Legion tents pitched at Monarga, Cyprus. 1917. *Michael Najarian Collection.*   44
42. Lt. Col. Louis Romieu. *Courtesy Ardemis Matteosian.*   44
43. Adrian Barracks, Monarga, Cyprus. The back of the photo is signed by Romieu, noting the building is the "Foyer du soldats." *AGBU Nubar Library, Paris.*   45
44. Legionnaire musicians in Monarga. Mgrditch Garinian with mandolin. *Courtesy of Mrs. V. S. Gulezian. Michael Najarian Collection.*   48
45. Kantara Castle, north of Monarga in the mountains. The legionnaires visited "Levon's Castle." *Courtesy of Susan Paul Pattie.*   50
46. Inscribed on back of photo: "Future Armenian soldier." *Michael Najarian Collection.*   52
47. Armenian legionnaires holding the French flag with Armenian inscription: "May God Protect the Armenians." Parade commemorating *Vartanants*, Cyprus, March 1918. *John Amar Shishmanian papers, envelope AB, Hoover Institution Archives.*   52
48. Men marching on parade, honoring the Armenian national holiday, *Vartanants*. *John Amar Shishmanian papers, envelope A, Hoover Institution Archives.*   54
49. Legionnaires. *Michael Najarian Collection.*   54
50. Lt. John Shishmanian with fellow legionnaire at Salamis, Roman ruins north of Famagusta, Cyprus. *John Amar Shishmanian papers, envelope B, Hoover Institution Archives*   55
51. Karnig Berberian and fellow legionnaires. *Courtesy of the Armenian Museum of America.*   56
52. Lt. John Shishmanian "with my boys." *John Amar Shishmanian papers, envelope B, Hoover Institution Archives.*   57
53. Ardashes Arakelian and comrades. *Courtesy of the Armenian Museum of America.*   59
54. Lt. Vahan Portukalian, Lt. John Shishmanian and Lt. Papazian. *John Amar Shishmanian Papers, envelope B, Hoover Institution Archives.*   62
55. A. Ajemian, Cairo, June, 1918. *Michael Najarian Collection.*   64
56. Lt. Hagop Arevian. *Courtesy of the Armenian Museum of America.*   64
57. H. Derderian, B. Zakarian, N. Karnakian. It was common for photographs to be taken of men posing, as if in battle. *Photo Khazaros Gopoian Collection, Courtesy of the Armenian Museum of America.*   66
58. Hovannes Garabedian and comrade. *Courtesy of the Armenian Museum of America.*   68
59. Legionnaires Haig Panossian and Ardasher (family name unknown). *Courtesy of the Armenian Museum of America.*   69
60. Camouflaged tent of Lt. Shishmanian on the ridge of Arara where he spent 15 nights. *John Amar Shishmanian Papers, envelope B, Hoover Institution Archives.*   70
61. "Armenian–American legionnaires refused to give up this American flag and carried it through Palestine, Syria, and into Cilicia. Lt. Arevian is tall man on left; Manasse, standing under the flag, was killed in the Battle of Arara." *John Amar Shishmanian Papers, envelope B, Hoover Institution Archives.*   71
62. To the firing line. *John Amar Shishmanian Papers, envelope B, Hoover Institution Archives.*   72

63. *The Gamavor*, published in Cairo in 1928, 10th anniversary of Arara. 74
64. Khazaros Gopoian, author of "Notes of a Gamavor." *Courtesy of Ardemis Matteosian.* 76
65. Two pages from the diary of Khazaros Gopoian, showing the battlefront of Arara. *Courtesy of Ardemis Matteosian.* 76
66. Mihran Guzelian. *Courtesy of the Armenian Museum of America.* 78
67. Mardiros Jingirian, killed in the Battle of Arara, with Stepan Piligian. *Courtesy of the Armenian Museum of America.* 81
68. Hovannes Kouyoumdjian, killed in the Battle of Arara. *Courtesy of the Armenian Museum of America.* 81
69. Kourken Zildjian, killed in the Battle of Arara. *Courtesy of the Armenian Museum of America.* 82
70. Sgt. Arditti and Dr. Grunberg. *John Amar Shishmanian Papers, envelope A, Hoover Institution Archives.* 82
71. Message to the legionnaires and officers from General Allenby, telling of his thanks and appreciation for their great deeds, gallantry and dedication. *Courtesy of Ardemis Matteosian.* 84
72. Legionnaires gather to bury their comrades. *John Amar Shishmanian Papers, envelope B, Hoover Institution Archives.* 84
73. Burial site at Rafat–Arara. *John Amar Shishmanian Papers, envelope B, Hoover Institution Archives.* 85
74. Six Armenian officers decorated for bravery in battle. Portukalian, Sahatjian, Papazian; Bablanian, Shishmanian, Arevian. *John Amar Shishmanian Papers, envelope B, Hoover Institution Archives.* 88
75. Cover of *Arara*, 1923, showing a possible design for the future reburial site of those who fell at Arara. *Courtesy of National Association for Armenian Studies and Research (NAASR).* 89
76. Dr. Roland, the Chief Medical Officer of the Armenian Legion, is described in *Arara* 1919. 92
77. Starting north along the Mediterranean Sea. *John Amar Shishmanian Papers, envelope B, Hoover Institution Archives.* 93
78. Hagop Arevian and members of his battalion. *Courtesy of Ardemis Matteosian.* 94
79. Refugees in Palestine, trying to go home. *John Amar Shishmanian Papers, envelope B, Hoover Institution Archives.* 95
80. Freight carriers for the Legion. *John Amar Shishmanian Papers, envelope B, Hoover Institution Archives.* 96
81. Villagers speaking with legionnaires along the road. *John Amar Shishmanian Papers, envelope B, Hoover Institution Archives.* 96
82. Lt. Portukalian and Lt. Papazian. *John Amar Shishmanian Papers, envelope B, Hoover Institution Archives.* 97
83. Lt. John Shishmanian at Beirut Hospital. *John Amar Shishmanian Papers, envelope B, Hoover Institution Archives.* 99
84. Nurses at Beirut Hospital. *John Amar Shishmanian Papers, envelope B, Hoover Institution Archives.* 100
85. Armenian legionnaires with Sikh soldiers from the British Army. *Courtesy of Ardemis Matteosian.* 101
86. The city of Adana. Fire symbols show destruction in 1909. *Courtesy of Robert H. Hewsen*, Armenia: A Historical Atlas. Original in color. 105

LIST OF ILLUSTRATIONS

87. Aram Hovsepian. *Photo courtesy of the Armenian Museum of America.*   106
88. Legionnaires salute the flag at the new station, Adana. *Michael Najarian Collection.*   107
89. Legionnaires gather at the Adana restaurant of the Tourian family. *Courtesy of Anahid Tourian Eskidjian.*   109
90. Shishmanian labels this a sketch of an old Armenian castle in Cilicia. *John Amar Shishmanian Papers, envelope B, Hoover Institution Archives.*   114
91. Brothers and sister, Nishan, Yeghsabet and Sarkis Najarian, Beirut. *Courtesy of Sona Najarian Touloumjian.*   117
92. Armenian legionnaires in Adana. Photo by H. Fermanian. *Courtesy of Sona Najarian Touloumjian.*   118
93. Back of Sarkis Najarian's group photo with note to his aunt. *Courtesy of Sona Najarian Touloumjian.*   118
94. Armenian girls, tattooed by Arab Bedouin, found (Shishmanian states "bought") by legionnaires and brought to doctors in Cilicia. *John Amar Shishmanian papers, envelope B, Hoover Institution Archives.*   120
95. Sarkis Saryan, Simon Sarkisian, wife Shamiram and baby George Sarkisian. New York, 1931. *Courtesy of Judith Saryan.*   122
96. Sgt. Doud. *John Amar Shishmanian papers, envelope B, Hoover Institution Archives.*   125
97. Military Police of the Armenian Legion, Adana, Turkey, 1919. Photo by H. Berberian. Manoog "Khan" Baghdasarian was a volunteer in the military police of the French Armenian Legion. *Courtesy of Ardemis Bagdasarian Matteosian. Project SAVE Armenian Photography Archives.*   126
98. In Aleppo, the first group of survivors prepare to return to their homes. *AGBU Nubar Library, Paris.*   129
99. The vilayet of Adana. *Courtesy of Robert H. Hewson,* Armenia: A Historical Atlas. Original in color.   131
100. Early morning in Adana. American flag flying over Near East Relief building and below, workers going to the vineyards. *John Amar Shishmanian papers, envelope B, Hoover Institution Archives.*   132
101. Nurse Marie Dertadian worked at the French Hospital in Adana. *Courtesy of Ardemis Matteosian.*   133
102. Captain James M. Chankalian, decorated with the *Médaille Militaire. Courtesy of the Armenian Museum of America.*   134
103. Legionnaires. *Courtesy of Michael Najarian Collection.*   136
104. Hovsep Ajemian. *Courtesy of Michael Najarian Collection.*   137
105. Military Police pass belonging to Hovsep Ajemian. *Courtesy of Michael Najarian Collection.*   138
106. Neshan Mardikian, Certificate of Good Conduct, April, 1919, Adana. *Courtesy of Michael Najarian Collection.*   140
107. Old Roman bridge across the Djihan (Ceyhan) river. Lt. Shishmanian's headquarters were at the left end of the bridge. *John Amar Shishmanian Papers, envelope B, Hoover Institution Archives.*   142
108. Legionnaires and children near Adana. *Courtesy of Michael Najarian Collection.*   144
109. Marash, 1919. Photograph by Stanley E. Kerr. Under the protection of the British and French troops, Armenian deportees return   146

to Marash from exile in the Syrian desert. *Photo courtesy of Rev. Vartan Hartunian. Project SAVE Armenian Photograph Archives.*

110. The Vilayet of Mamuretülaziz and the Sanjak of Marash. *Courtesy of Robert H. Hewsen, Armenia: A Historical Atlas. Original in color.* — 147

111. Title in Armenian reads: "The Supreme Command of the Army and Military Police." *Photograph courtesy of Ardemis Matteosian. Project SAVE Armenian Photograph Archive.* — 149

112. Women "rescued by Armenian troops and brought to Cilicia. Refined women, many of them wealthy and from educated classes," washing wool for weaving. *John Amar Shishmanian papers, envelope B, Hoover Institution Archives.* — 149

113. A letter to Lt. John Shishmanian from General Allenby, expressing his regret that the Armenian legionnaires had not been officially recognized for their contribution. *John Amar Shishmanian papers, envelope B, Hoover Institution Archives.* — 150

114. Woman (unidentified) sharp-shooter of Adana. *John Amar Shishmanian papers, envelope B, Hoover Institution Archives.* — 151

115. One of the (unnamed) women fighting alongside the legionnaires in Cilicia. *John Amar Shishmanian papers, envelope B, Hoover Institution Archives.* — 152

116. Dikranouhi Krikorian. "G. G." on her collar indicates "Giligia Gamavor." *John Amar Shishmanian papers, envelope B, Hoover Institution Archives.* — 155

117. Meydan Ekbezir. An Armenian volunteer and the child of a deported, lost Armenian. *John Amar Shishmanian Papers, envelope B, Hoover Institution Archives.* — 156

118. Sarkis Najarian and comrades. *Courtesy of Sona Najarian Touloumjian.* — 157

119. Marash embroidery (Marash *kordz*), remnant of a much larger piece brought to Cyprus with refugees from Marash. *Courtesy of Nouvart Kassouni Panayotides-Djaferis.* — 158

120. The exchange of French for British troops at Aintab, November 4, 1919. 18th Indian Lancers withdraw as French and Armenian troops stand at the roadside. *Photograph and caption by Stanley Kerr, Joyce Chorbajian collection. Courtesy of Houshamadyan.* — 161

121. Armenian orphans pictured on a hillside outside Marash. *Photograph by Stanley Kerr, Joyce Chorbajian collection. Courtesy of Houshamadyan.* — 162

122. Baghdasar Odabashian, killed in Cilicia. *Courtesy of the Armenian Museum of America.* — 163

123. Khazaros Atamian, killed in Marash. *Courtesy of the Armenian Museum of America.* — 163

124. Garabed Kassabian of Philadelphia, killed in Marash. *Courtesy of the Armenian Museum of America.* — 168

125. Legionnaire group including Sarkis Varadian. *Courtesy of Michael Varadian.* — 168

126. Group of Armenian refugees in Marash. *Photograph by Stanley Kerr, Joyce Chorbajian collection. Courtesy of Houshamadyan.* — 172

127. Legionnaires on the hillside by Marash. *Photograph by Stanley Kerr, Joyce Chorbajian collection. Courtesy of Houshamadyan.* — 173

128. Marash in ruins. *Photograph by Stanley Kerr, Joyce Chorbajian collection. Courtesy of Houshamadyan.* — 177

LIST OF ILLUSTRATIONS

129. A section of Marash near the citadel. *Photograph by Stanley Kerr, Joyce Chorbajian collection. Courtesy of Houshamadyan.* — 178
130. The Armenian Protestant church in ruins, Marash. *Photograph by Stanley Kerr, Joyce Chorbajian collection. Courtesy of Houshamadyan.* — 179
131. The Bilezikian family surviving in Marash, 1920. The father, Movses, was working in quarries in Vermont. Wife Yepros has her hand on son Peter's shoulder. *Courtesy of Bethel Bilezikian Charkoudian.* — 179
132. Students digging trenches around an Armenian school near Adana for protection against Kemalist troops. *John Amar Shishmanian papers, envelope B, Hoover Institution Archives.* — 185
133. Work contract for Lt J. Shishmanian (*"Chichmanian"*), June 10, 1920. Shishmanian was engaged to work as Inspector of the Armenian *"Groupement"* of Adana, under the orders of the Governor of Adana. *John Amar Shishmanian papers, Hoover Institute* — 186
134. Certificate of Good Conduct for Hovsep Ajemian. *Michael Najarian Collection.* — 188
135. Stamp of the American Consulate of Marseilles on the reverse of the Armenian passport of Nishan Najarian. *Michael Najarian Collection.* — 189
136. Nishan Najarian. *Michael Najarian Collection.* — 190
137. Elected and appointed leaders of the Armenian National Union in Exile of Adana: Garabed Ashikian (treasurer), Dr. D. Mnatsaganian (chairman), Lt. John Shishmanian (Commander of the Armenian Forces of Cilicia), Firooz Khanzadian, Aram Mndigian, Dr. Salibian, Setrag Guebenlian (vice-chairman). *Courtesy of Ardemis Matteosian.* — 191
138. Mersin, Cilicia, May 1921: Hovhanness Vekilian (Cyprus), following discharge from the Armenian Legion, Lt. Boghos Der Sarkisian, wearing the uniform of the Turkish gendarmerie in which he also served, Lt. James Chankalian. *Photo courtesy of Vahram Goekjian, Project SAVE Armenian Photograph Archives.* — 192
139. Armenian passport of legionnaire Nishan Mardikian. *Michael Najarian Collection.* — 194
140. Stamps on passport of Nishan Mardikian, showing passage from Constantinople, through France to the United States. Two handwritten notes on these stamps indicate that he had no "authority to land at any British port." *Michael Najarian Collection.* — 195
141. The passport of Angêle Adjemian, whom Nishan Mardikian married in Constantinople in February, 1921. The stamps show that she began her journey to the United States via Greece and Italy. *Michael Najarian Collection.* — 195
142. Military parade in Adana on the eve of the final demobilization. *Courtesy of Ardemis Matteosian.* — 197
143. Sunrise over Alexandretta (possibly taken by Lt. Shishmanian). *John Amar Shishmanian Papers, envelope B, Hoover Institution Archives.* — 200
144. Lt. John Shishmanian leaving Cilicia after his release from arrest and confinement in Alexandretta. *John Amar Shishmanian Papers, envelope B, Hoover Institution Archives.* — 201
145. Legionnaires from Kessab, including Zerone Hagopian, return to their birthplace to help returning survivors rebuild. *Courtesy of Arpi Hagopian Haboian.* — 206

146. A picnic in Providence, Rhode Island, August 21, 1929. Legionnaires join with comrades, family and community. *Courtesy of the Armenian Museum of America.* — 208
147. A picnic in Whitinsville, Massachusetts, 1932. Members of the Armenian Legion pose with community members and other soldiers who served as volunteers on other fronts in World War I and in the US armed forces. General Sebouh Nersesian, who led forces on the Caucasian Front at Sardarabad, is seen in the second row. *Courtesy of the Armenian Museum of America.* — 208
148. Legionnaires gather in Lawrence, Massachusetts, 1922. *Courtesy of the Armenian Museum of America.* — 209
149. The officers of the Armenian Legionnaire Association, 1923. Center: Nishan Najarian, chairman; clockwise from top right: Mihran Guzelian, treasurer; Kh. Krikorian, assistant secretary; K. Assadourian, vice-chairman; Sharam Stepanian, secretary. *Michael Najarian Collection.* — 211
150. Legionnaires raised funds to assist those comrades who had suffered injuries. Here the New York branch of the Armenian Legion Organization publishes a poster to raise money in aid of disabled Armenian legionnaires (price 25 cents). *Courtesy of Arsen Haroian. Project SAVE Armenian Photo Archive.* — 212
151. Stepan Piligian was sent by his father to the United States from a village in Sepastia just before the Genocide. He joined the Legion and towards the end, while stationed in Adana, met his future wife, Turfanda Yergatian. They married and made their way to the US via Marseilles, settling in Indian Orchard, Massachusetts. *Courtesy of the Armenian Museum of America.* — 213
152. The Armenian Diaspora in the Middle East since 1918. *Courtesy of Robert H. Hewsen, Armenia: A Historical Atlas. Original in color.* — 214
153. *Gamavor* friends and comrades at a picnic in Massachusetts in later years. *Michael Najarian Collection.* — 215
154. Dickran Boyajian, author's portrait in *Haygagan Lekeone. Courtesy of Baikar Press.* — 218
155. Home page of the Hagop Arevian website. *Courtesy of www.hagoparevian.com. Credit: Haniel Rivière.* — 221
156. Ovsia Saghdejian, more widely known as Daye, or within the family, Daye Baboog, in older age in Kessab. *Courtesy of Sevag B. Panossian.* — 223
157. Hagop Panossian, also known as Onbashi, poses with his cousin Dzeron/Joseph. *Courtesy of Razmik Panossian.* — 225
158. Photograph from a French-Armenian newspaper (unidentified, undated) showing Makrouhi Helvajian Apovian posing with a friend. *Photo courtesy of Dr. Caroline Apovian.* — 232

Index

Page numbers in *italics* refer to figures or their captions; "n" after a page number indicates the endnote number.

Abdoghlu, 189
Abdulhamid II, Sultan, 4, 221
Adana, 3, 104, *131*, *132*, 222; Armenian Legion on maneuvers near Adana, *23*; Armenian legionnaires in, *118*, 185, 187, 231–3; arriving in, 107; Christian population of, 187, 233; City of Adana, *105*; entry of the French Cavalry into, *xxi*; French evacuation of, 202, 231; French friendly disposition towards the Turks, 187, 233; Janjigian's restaurant, 107–8; Kemalists and, 185, *185*, 231; leaders of the Armenian National Union in Exile of Adana, *191*; legionnaires salute the flag at the new station, *107*; military parade on the eve of the final demobilization, *197*; Military Police, 126–7, *126*; refugees settlement in, 130–5; Shishmanian, John, Lieutenant, 185, *186*, 187, 229, 231; students digging trenches for protection against Kemalist troops, *185*; Turkish attacks on, 187, 196, 231, 233; *see also* Cilicia
Adana massacre (1909), 4
Adjemian, Angèle, *195*
Adrian Barracks (*Baraques Adrian*), *45*, 49, 237n8
Aghayigian, Haygaz, 34
Aghjayan, Kegham, 7
Aintab (Gaziantep), 3, 85, 109, 159, 170, 198, 227, 231; Armenian legionnaires at, 151–2, 153; exchange of French for British troops at, *161*
Ajemian, Ajem, *64*, 164–6
Ajemian, Hovsep, *137*, *138*, *188*
Ajemian, Krikor, 175
Akharja, 189
Akrabian, Avedis, 175
Albistan road, 167
Aleppo, 3, 115, 121; Armenian refugees leaving Aleppo and returning home, 129–30, *129*; mandatory migration from Aleppo, 130

Alevis, 207
Alexandretta, 104, 109; French occupation, 110; proposals for landing at, 9–10, 11, 14–15; sunrise over, *200*
Alexandretta Incident, 110–14, 138; 4th Battalion, disbanding of, 110, 113, 138, 139; Armenian insubordination, 111–12; imprisonment, 111, 113; internment camp, 113; military tribunal and punishment, 113
Algerian soldiers, 201, 234; Algerian riflemen/ *tirailleurs*, 110, 113; disputes between Armenian legionnaires and, 109–13; killing by, 113; replacing Armenian legionnaires with Algerian Muslim soldiers, 123; *see also* Alexandretta Incident
Ali, Mehmet, 159
Allenby, Edmund, General, 1, 23, 141, 142, 200, 222; Battle of Arara, 21, 23, 80, 83, *84*, 200; letter to Lt. John Shishmanian from, *150*; message to legionnaires and officers from, *84*
Allies/Allied Powers (Entente Powers), 8, 181, 203; Armenian Legion and, 8, 9, 10, 11–12, 14, 143; proposed partition of Turkey according to Allied Agreements, *25*; relations between, 1, 8, 123, 135, 145; *see also* France; Great Britain; Russia
Amerigian, Arsham, 85
Amirian, Ardavast, 28
Anatolia, 10
André, Captain, 159
Andrea, C. J. E., Lt. Col., 228
Anjar, Lebanon, 205
Ankara Accord, 202
Antakya, 3
Antaramian, Simon, 85
Antranig, General, xvi, *126*, 138
Apelian, Vahe H., 223–4
Apkarian School, 133
Arakelian, Ardashes, *59*

259

Arara (journal), 79, *89*, *106*, 210
Arditti, Joseph, Lieutenant, 80, *82*
Arevian, Hagop, Brigade Master, *64*, *71*, 94, *94*, 221–2; decorated for bravery in battle, *88*
Armenia: Armenians after British and French withdrawal, 205; autonomous Armenia, 10, 15; independence of, 3, 7, 8, 28; Independent Republic of Armenia, 181; Ottoman Empire, 3–7; Six Provinces, 10, 205
Armenian Apostolic Church, 27, *30*, 130
Armenian diaspora, 204, 207, 209; Armenian Diaspora in the Middle East since 1918: *214*; community as extended family, 209
Armenian Evangelical Church, 27
Armenian General Benevolent Union (AGBU), 27, 219
Armenian Genocide (1915), 6, 75, 148, 209, 210; Armenian resistance, 6–7, 9, 12; British and French positions on, 11; Cilician Armenians, 6, 9, 10, 11, 12, 14, 24; justification of, 64–5; Ottoman Empire, 6, 11; revenge for, 13, 17, 28, *30*, 32, 75, 77, 78, 110, 155, 174; survival during, 119, 121; survivors of, vii, 6, 128–9, 224, *225*; survivors returning home, 128–9, 224; *see also* deportation; refugee
Armenian Kingdom of Cilicia (1199–1375), 3, *22*
Armenian Legion, 3; "baptism of fire", 20–3; betrayed by the French and the British, 3, 8, 26, 103; dissolution of, 24, 137–8, 140–1, 142–3, 184, 196–204; infantry regiment, 19; *Légion Arménienne*, 24, 102; military leadership of, 17; organization of, 16–20, 139; plaque of portraits, *2*; reorganization of the Eastern Legion, 101–102; transformation into the Armenian National Army, 137, 139; World War I, 1, 8; *see also* Armenian Legion, establishment of; Armenian legionnaires; *Légion d'Orient*
Armenian Legion, establishment of: 1916 establishment, 8, 15; 1916 Sykes–Picot Agreement, 13–14, 15, 16; Allies, 8, 9, 10, 11–12, 14, 143; Armenian, British and French clashes over, 8, 11, 15, 18, 19–20; Armenian National Delegation and, 11, 13, 15, 17; background, 3–7; the British, 10–11, 12–13, 16; first battalion, 17; first months of World War I and earliest proposals, 9–11; the French, 10, 11, 12–13, 15, 16, 230; great power diplomacy and 11–16; *Légion d'Orient*, 8, 15, 17, 24; Musa Dagh resistance at Port Said camp, 9, 12–13, 14, 16; obstacle against the establishment of, 14; purpose of, 8; *see also Légion d'Orient*
Armenian Legionnaire Association, 74, 210; New York branch of, *212*; officers of, *211*
Armenian legionnaires, xi, *54*, *136*, *144*, 215–16, 217; age range of, 46; ambiguous judicial status of Armenian soldiers, 17; Armenian legionnaires with Sikh soldiers from the British Army, *101*; Armenian volunteers, 20; camaraderie, 46, 209; disappointment and frustration, 24, 45–7, 57–8, 61, 64, 104, 136, 139, 144, 201–202, 204; final months of work, 145; French officers hostile attitude towards, 63–4, 110, 111, 136; from army-in-waiting towards the actual battlefield, 67–72; insubordination, 63–5, 111–12, 139, *200*; jokes, 46, 93; lack/scarcity of food, 60, 63, 93, 97, 100, 136, 139, 231; legacy of, 24, 216; letters of commendation, 227–8; music, singing and dancing, 34, 47–8, *48*, 49, 93, 94, 110, 153, 159, 207; punishment of, 63, *106*, 110, 111, 113; recognition of, *88*, 125, *134*, 200, 227–8; wheat, harvest of, 187–9, 191; *see also the entries below for* Armenian legionnaires; demobilization of legionnaires; prison
Armenian legionnaires after demobilization, 205–16, *215*; 1922 gathering in Lawrence, Massachusetts, *209*; 1929 picnic in Providence, Rhode Island, *208*; 1932 picnic in Whitinsville, Massachusetts, *208*; as community leaders, 204, 207, 224, *225*; healing process, 215; returning home, 201–2, 204, *206*, 206–7, 223–4; *see also* Armenian Legionnaire Association; demobilization of legionnaires
Armenian legionnaires, recruitment, 3, 13, 26, 138; Armenian refugees, 13, 16, 17; Armenians from Egypt, 14, 18; Armenians from France, 14, 26, 27, 31–2, 220; Armenians from United States, 14, 18, *18*, 27, 28–30, *31*, 33–9, *213*, 218, 223; *Certificat d'Engagement*, *40*; enlistment limit proposed by French officials, 16, 18; French refusal of new enlistings, 138, 139; Frenchmen, 19; journeys of legionnaires traveling from the United States, 33–9, *38*; motivations for enlisting, 26, 27, 28, *32*, 75; Musa Dagh refugees from Port Said camp, 16, 17, 27, *27*; prisoners of war 13, 16–17; process of enlistment, 17–18, 26, 27, 31, 33; selection process, 18, 31, 33
Armenian Museum of America (Armenian Library and Museum of America), ix, xi; exhibitions, ix, xi, xiii; "Forgotten Heroes", traveling exhibition, xiii, *xiv*; Legionnaires' Archive, ix
Armenian National Committee (ANC), 26, 27, 28, 31, 33
Armenian National Delegation (AND), 11, 13, 15, 17, 235n1; deployment of the Armenian Legion in Palestine, 19–20; disbanding the Armenian Legion, 137–8, 140
Armenian National Security Council of Egypt, 13
Armenian National Union, 137, 141, 188, 193, 226; leaders of the Armenian National Union in Exile of Adana, *191*

260

INDEX

Arshagouni, Vagharshag Vartabed, Armenian priest, *30*, 80
Arslanian, Arshag, 85
Asadurian, Arshavir, 176
Ashikian, Garabed, *191*
Ashtaraketsi, Yenovk, 100, 115–16, 123–4
Assadourian, K., *211*
Assyrians, 187, 229, 233
Atamian, Khazaros, *163*, 175
Atamian, Manoog, 164, 166–7
Atanossian, Guiregh (Gerry), Corporal, 171–2, 174
Atatürk, Mustafa Kemal, General, 158, 160, 196
Avakian, Simon, 176
Ayram, 104
Azad Apelian, George, 207
Azadian, Haig, Lieutenant, 184
Azan, Captain, 58, 63–5, 83

Babayan, Mardiros, 85
Bablanian, officer decorated for bravery in battle, *88*
Baghdasarian, Manoog "Khan", *xv*, 126, *126*, *133*, 182, 210
Baikar Press (*Baykar Press*), ix, xiii
Bailloud, General (inspector-general of the French troops in Egypt), 19
Bartevian, Sooren, 65–6, 67
Battle of Arara (Battle of Megiddo, Palestine, 1918), 1, 21–3, 24, 28, 73–90, 108, 198, 199, 222, 223; aircraft at, 79; Allenby, Edmund, General, 21, 23, 80, 83, *84*, 200; American–Armenian legionnaires, 73, 86; Armenian officers decorated for bravery in battle, *88*; anniversary of, 73, *74*, 210; Azan, Captain, 83; battlefront of Arara, *76*; Boyajian, Dickran, 73–5, 79, 80, 83, 85–6, 87–8, 199; burial of Armenian legionnaires, 77, 79–80, 83, *84*, *85*, 199; defeat of German–Ottoman forces, 22, 77, 78–9, 80; firing line, *72*; Garabedian, Hovaness, 28, 75, 77; German forces, 21, 22, 78, 80; Guzelian, Mihran, 78–80, 86–7; the injured, 23, 80; losses at, 23, 71, 75, 77, 80, *81–2*, 85–7, 199; medical station, 72, 79, 80; Megiddo Campaign, 1, 9, 21; night before the assault, 73; prisoners of war, 75; reburial of the fallen, 87–8, *89*, 90; Romieu, Louis, Lt. Col., 22, 23, 80, 83, 199; *The War Dead and their Origins*, 85–6; *see also* Palestine; Rafat
Bedié (site near Arara), 88
Bedigian, Hagop, 85, 86–7
Bedouins, 114, 119; tattooing women, 119, *120*
Bedrosian, Ghevont, 165, 166, 176
Beirut, 59, 91–102, 109; freight carriers for the Legion, *96*; incident at, 100–1; Spanish flu, 95, 97–8, 100; starting north along the Mediterranean Sea, *93*; trip to, 92–7; villagers speaking with legionnaires along the road, *96*
Beirut Hospital, *99*; nurses at, *100*
Bekaa Valley, Lebanon, 205
Bel-Punar, 162

Berberian, Karnig, *56*
Bertie, Francis, Sir, 10
Beylan, 109, 110
Bilezikian family surviving in Marash, *179*
Bitlis, 3, 10
Bodosian, Garabed, 176
Boghosian, Brigade head, 183
Bouloudian, Boghos, 85
Boyajian, Asadur, 176
Boyajian, Dickran, *xiv*, 24, 65, 91–2, 126, 135–7, 142–3, 218–19, *218*, 227–8; Adana, 107–8, 109; Alexandretta Incident, 110–13; *Armenia: The Case for a Forgotten Genocide*, 219; *The Armenian Legion/Haygagan Lekeone*, ix, x, xiii, xiv, 26, 102, 212, 226; Armenian Legion, dissolution of, 141, 142–3; Battle of Arara, 73–5, 79, 80, 83, 85–6, 87–8, 199; Cyprus, training in, 45–7, 48, 51, 53, 56, 57–8; demobilization of, 146; disbanding of the Armenian Legion, 196–9; insubordination, 63–5; Janjigian, Ardemis, 108, 219; Janjigian family, 108; journey on the *L'Espagne*, 33–4; Marash, 146, 148, 151, 159, 163, 175–6; medical station, 72, 219; Mersin, 107; mother's death, 56; Port Said, 41–2; reburial of the fallen in Arara, 88, 90; United States, trip to, 151, 219
Bozanti, 115, 123, 227
Brémond, Édouard, Colonel, 103, 158–9, 181, 196, 226, 227; *La Cilicie en 1919–1920*, 219; Farewell speech to the legionnaires, 193, 196; "Governor of Armenia and Cilicia", 103, 114; "Governor General of Occupied Enemy Northern Zone Territories", 114; return to France, 193
Brusa, 50
Bursa, 115
Bzarian, Dikran, 86

Cambon, Paul (French Ambassador to London), 15
Catholicos Kevork V (of Etchmiadzin), 15, 235n1
Catholicos Sahag II Khabayan (Sahak Khapayan, of Cilicia), 130
Caucasian Front, 10, 14, *208*
Chakeji (legionnaire), 189
Chaldeans, 187, 226, 229, 233
Chankalian, James, Lieutenant, 130, 133, 134–5, *134*, 181, *192*, 193
Chavush, Avetis, 182
children, 22, *48*, *52*, 94, 95, 97, 107, *144*, 187, 233; Armenian girls, tattooed by Arab Bedouins, *120*; orphan, 115, 130, 133, 135, *156*, *162*, 180, 224; orphanage, 114, 116, 130, 161, 224, *232*; search for Armenian women and, 114–23, 222
Chiljian, Kevork, 86
Chnkoosh, 85, 86, 94
Chobanian, Arshag, 11
Cholakian, Hagop, 206
Christian population, 187, 202, 203, 226–7, 229, 233

261

The Christian Science Monitor, 185, 229–34
church, 165; church of Holy Etchmiadzin, at St. James church, 88; Holy Forty Martyrs church, 162, 166; Protestant church, Marash, 161, 162, *179*; St. Sarkis church, 148, 161; *see also* Holy Mother of God Church
Cilicia, 1, 10, 12, 14–15, 59, 135; 1918–20 French Occupation, 23–4, 230; 1919 as successful year for returning Armenians, 146; Armenian Genocide, 6, 9, 10, 11, 12, 14, 24; Armenian legionnaires occupy the region, 101, 103–27, 200–1, 222, 230; Christian population of, 187, 202, 203, 226–7, 229, 233; France and, 14, 19, 142, 180, 229, 230; French–Armenian relations in, 130, 135; French evacuation, 202–203, 220; French peace treaty with Turkey, 193, 196, 222; as the goal for Armenian legionnaires, 103; independence of, 103, 109, 124, 196, 215; independence, declaration of, 191, 193, 226–7; occupation by British soldiers, 110; old Armenian castle in Cilicia, sketch of, *114*; search for Armenian women and children, 114–23; Turks in, 135–6, 230; withdrawal of British troops, 135, 142, 146, 230; women, *6*; *see also* Adana
Clausen, John, Sir and British High Commissioner, 43
Clayton, Gilbert, Brigadier General and Intelligence Officer, 13, 15
Clemenceau, Georges (French Prime Minister), 18, 19
Constantinople (Istanbul), 3, 6, 11, 86, 115, 139, 221; capitulation of, 10
court martial, *see* military tribunal
Crete, 36, 38
Cypriot Muleteers, 54
Cyprus, training in, 1, 26, 43, 45, 221–2, 230; Armenian disappointed and dissatisfaction, 45–7, 57–8; boredom, 50, 57; Boyajian, Dickran, 45–7, 48, 51, 53, 56, 57–8; brawls and incidents, 51, 52–5; the British, 43, 57; discrimination against the Armenians, 47, 49; drinking, 51, 53, 55; the French, 43, 57; friendship, 56–7; leaving Monarga, 59; legionnaires/French officers relationship, 56–7; military camps in Cyprus, 17, 45; Monarga/Boğaztepe, 43, *44*, 45, *45*, *48*, *50*, 51, 53, 59, 61; Musa Dagh, legionnaires from 45, 46–7, 57; music and singing, 47–8, *48*, 49; Romieu, Ferdinand, Lt. Col., 43, 48–9, 55; routine in the camp, 46; Shishmanian, John, Lieutenant, 230; training activities, 47; wrestling, 47, 50–1; *see also* Adrian Barracks; training

Damadian, Mihran, 28, 141, 193, 226; letter to the remaining legionnaires, 143
Dardanelles, 10, 11
Dardouni, Stepan, 30–1, 46, 151

Dashnak–Dashnaktsoutiune (Armenian political party), 27, 71, 189, 191, 193; Armenian Revolutionary Federation, 27, *30*
Dauros Range, 170
David-Beauregard, Captain, 113
Davros, 174
Dayr Balut, 72
Declassé, Théophile, 11
demobilization of legionnaires, 24, 125, 135–44, 146, 185, *225*, 231; beginning of, 123–4; disarmament, 123; forced to leave, 139; military parade on the eve of the final demobilization, *197*; suspension of, 138; Treaty of Sèvres, 196; *see also* Armenian legionnaires after demobilization
deportation, 6, 24, 30, 121, 136, 148, *156*; Cilician Armenians, 9, 11, 12, 14; repatriation of deported Armenians, 129; return to Marash from exile in the Syrian desert, *146*; *see also* Armenian Genocide
Der Ghazarian, Harutiun, Dr., 151, 161–3, 167
Der Hagopian, Manoug, 85
Der Kaprielian, Mardiros, 85
Der Sarkisian, Boghos, Lieutenant, 181, *192*
Derderian, H., *66*
Derderian, Nigoghos, 85
Dertadian, Marie, *133*
desertion, 39, 61, 121, 165, 224
Dilikjian Delligian, Sarkis, 85
Dimlakian, Bedros, Lieutenant, 176
Diyarbakır/Dikranagerd, 3, 10, 33, 114, 121, 218
Dort-yol (the town of Oranges), 194, 227
Doud, Sergeant, 124–5, *125*
Dufieux, General, Commander of the First Division, 182, 183, 196, 199

Eastwood, Lt. Col., 112
Egypt, 12; Armenians from Egypt, enlistment of, 14, 18; Cairo, 41–2, 91; *see also* National Union of Egypt; Port Said
Ehramjian, Dikran, 175
Ekbezir, Meydan, *156*
El-Oghli (village), 152
Entente, Entente Powers, Triple Entente, *see* Allies/Allied Powers
Ersin, 104
Erzurum, 3, 10, 48, 176
Eslaye (Islahiye), 174
Europe, 4, 7, 11; World War I, 88, 90

Famagusta (Ammosoxtos/Mağusa), 43, 59; Roman ruins north of Famagusta, *55*; street fight in, 51, 53
fedayee (resistance bands), xvi
fellahin, 111
Flye Sainte-Marie, Jean, Colonel and Commander of the Regiment of the Armenian Legion, 146, 199, 227–8
France, 1, 6, 145, 185; Armenian Legion and, 10, 11, 12–13, 15, 16, 230; Armenian Legion, betrayed by, 3, 8, 26, 103, 123, 184, 185, 196, 222, 223; Armenian Legion as colonizing tool 8, 24; Armenians from

INDEX

France, enlistment of, 14, 26, 27, 31–2, 220; French flag in Marash, 159, 169, 177; friendly disposition towards the Turks, 24, 109, 123, 136, 187, 233; mandatory migration from Aleppo, 130; Middle East, division between the British and the French, 103, 123, 145; Musa Dagh, rescue at, 5, 7, 9, 12; pro-Turkish policy, 196; withdrawal of French troops, 180, 205; *see also* Cilicia; Marash

French Foreign Legion, xvi, 17, 26, 28, 30, 108, 130, 157, 221; Officers of, *21*

French Foreign Ministry, 12, 26

French Mandate, 28, 157, 205

Fundijak, 148, 151

Gallipoli campaign, 10, 12, 13

The Gamavor, Cairo, *74*

Gamavors (Volunteers), viii, xvi, 1, 31, 41, 121, 207, 209, *215*

Garabedian, Dado, 153

Garabedian, Hagop, 175

Garabedian, Hovaness, 28, 67–9, *68*, 104, 107, 152–4; *The Autobiography of Hovannes Garabedian*, 181; Battle of Arara, 28, 75, 77

Garabedian, Zadie, Sergeant, 171, 172, 174

Garinian, Mgrditch, *48*

Gazianteb, *see* Aintab

Geolebatmazian, Keork, 175

Georges-Picot, François, Consul General of France in Beirut, 101, 158, 182, 200

Germany, 14; Battle of Arara, 21, 22, 78, 80; German submarine, 34–5

Ghugasian, Ghughas, 85

Giragossian, Misak, 206–207

Gopoian, Khazaros, *xviii, xix, 76*

Gopoian, Stephen, *xviii*

Gotikian, Guévork, 31, 43, 80, 83

Gougassian, Soghomon, 153

Gouraud, Henri, General and Commander in Chief of the Occupying Army of the East, 197–9, 232

Grboyan, Hagop, 175

Great Britain, 1, 6, 10, 145, 185; Armenian Legion and, 10–11, 12–13, 16; Armenian Legion, betrayed by, 3, 8, 26, 103; Armenian Legion as colonizing tool 8; British occupation of Ottoman lands, 128; mandatory migration from Aleppo, 130; Middle East, division between the British and the French, 103, 123, 145; Port Said and, 9, 12–13, 130; withdrawal of British troops, 135, 142, 146, 155, 167, 201, 205, 230

Greeks, 51, 53, 111, 187, 203, 207, 226, 228, 229, 233

Grunberg, Dr., *82*

Guebenlian, Setrag, *191*

Guzelian, Mihran, 28, *29, 78, 211*; Battle of Arara, 78–80, 86–7

Hadjin, 126, 148, 151, 175, 181, 230; Boyajian, Dickran, 182–4; massacre at, 203; military forces sent for relief, 182–3; Paklali incident, 183–4; threats and attacks on returning survivors, 181–2

Hagopian, Dzerone, *32, 206*

Hagopian, Kevork, 175

Haifa, 93, 98

Hairenik Daily, 167

Hamelin, General, 138

Hamidian Massacres (1895–6), 4

Haratch, 61, 97, 220

Hartunian, Abraham, Rev., 160, 161, 176–8, 180; *Neither to Laugh Nor to Weep*, 159

Hatay, 145, 205; Poste d'Erzine/Yeşilkent, *xi*

Havounjian, Misak, 85

Hayguni (legionnaire), 189

Haytugents (legionnaire), 189

Helvajian Apovian, Makrouhi, *232*

Herrian, Roupen, 53

Hnchakian/Reformed Hnchakian (Armenian political party), 27, 71, 148, 189

Holy Mother of God Church (*Soorp Asdvadzadzin*), 162, 164; attack on, 164–7, 176; French refusal of assistance, 165, 166; *see also* Marash, battles of

Hovsepian, Aram, *23, 106*

Hyusenig, 85

Inter-Party Organization, 188, 193

Ismailia, 59, 61, 66, 67

Janjigian's restaurant (Adana), 107–108

Jingirian, Mardiros, *81*, 85

Jinks, Rebecca, *120*

Kalusdian, Aleksan, 175

Kantara Castle, 49–50, *50*

Karadaghlian, P., 175

Karnakian., N., *66*

Kasparian, Garbed, Corporal, 171

Kassabian, Garabed, *168*, 175

Kassabian, Sarkis, 86

Kastellorizo, 59; life on, 60

Katma military camp, 153, 154

Kazan-Ali (village), 152

Kehiaian, Hagop, 86

Kemal Pasha, Mustafa, *see* Atatürk, Mustafa Kemal

Kemalists, 181, 196, 233; Adana and, 185, *185*, 231; Marash and, 158, 160, 171

Kereti, Commander, 169, 170

Kerr, Stanley E., Dr., 155, 157, 158, 159, 160, 167, 169; *Lions of Marash* 145, 154

Kessab, 3, 130, 205, 206–7, 209, 223–4, *225*; independent rule at, 207, 224; legionnaires from, *32*, 33, 86, *206, 223*

Ketsemanian, Varak, xiv, 8–25

Kevorkian, Raymond, 202

Khanzadian, Firooz, *191*

Kharpert, 28, 50, 85, 175, 176

Kherlakian, Boghos effendi, 148

Kherlakian family, 159

Khozigian, Khachik, 175

Kinosian, Stepan, 79

Kiskinian, Sahag, 86

263

Kolligian, George, *x*
Konsyulian, Levon, 182
Konya, 115, 187, 233
Koort-Koolak Station, 153
Kouyoumdjian, Hovannes, *81*, 86
Krikorian, Dr., 112
Krikorian, Dikranouhi, *155*
Krikorian, Kh., *211*
Krikorian, Melkon, 175
Kurdish, 3, 6
Kurds, 6, 114, 229
Kyrenia Mountains, 45, 49

Lebanon, 145, 207
Légion d'Orient (Eastern Legion), xvi, 1, 8, 15, 17, 22, *40*, 43, 80, 83, 218, 220; Armenian volunteers, 20, *31*; renamed as *Légion Arménienne*, 24, 102; *see also* Armenian Legion; Armenian Legion, establishment of the Levant, 12, 13, 14, 15, 19, 24
Levantine campaigns, 8
Lloyd George, David (Prime Minister of the United Kingdom), 19
Loosavorian, Exnadios (Armenian interpreter), 170–1
Lyud (Lod), 87

Mamigonian, Marc, 218–19
Mamuretülaziz, 3, 10, *147*
Manasse, *71*
Marash, 30, 109, *146*; Armenian legionnaires at, 151–3, 154–5, 157, 167, 169, *173*, 227; Armenian refugees in Marash, *172*; Armenians in, 145, 153, 180; Boyajian, Dickran, 146, 148, 151, 159, 163, 175–6; British withdrawal from, 167, 201; French flag, 159, 169, 177; French withdrawal from, 180; Kemalists in, 158, 160, 171; Marash embroidery, *158*; regime change and mixed feelings, 148, 158–9; Sanjak of Marash, *147*, 159; Turkish complaints involving Armenian legionnaires, 154–5; Turkish flag, 159, 169; Turkish/French/ legionnaires fight, 157, 159; *see also* Marash, battles of
Marash, battles of, 160–80, 198; aircraft at, 173, 174; Armenian legionnaires fight the Turks, 167, 169–74; Armenian legionnaires who died in Marash, 175–6; Armenian orphans outside Marash, *162*; civilian population as target, 161, 162–5, 166, 167, 169, 174, 176–7; destruction of Armenian Marash, 160, 180; evacuation of the city by the French, 161, 174, 176, 181, 203, 230; French refusal of assistance, 165, 166; Holy Mother of God Church, attack on, 164–7, 176; the left behind, 176–80; losses at, *163*, *168*, 174, 175–6, 178; Marash in ruins, *177*, *178*; massacre and deportation, 180, 181, 203; Protestant church, 161, 162, *179*; section of Marash near the citadel, *178*; Turks' attacks, 162–3, 164–74, 176–7, 203; *see also* Marash

Mardikian, Nishan: Armenian passport of, *194*, *195*; *Certificat d'Engagement*, *40*; Certificate of Good Conduct, *140*
Mardin, 121
Maxwell, John, General and Commander of the British troops in Egypt, 13, 15
Megiddo, *see* Battle of Arara
Mejdel, Palestine, 20, 65, 69
Mejdel-Yaba (village), 87
Mejidel, 67, 69
Menag, Kaspar, *32*
Mersin, 3, 104, 116, 117, 185, 198, 202, 205, 206; Boyajian, Dickran, 107
Mesha (site near Arara), 88
Mesopotamia, 10, 12, 140, 145
Messirlian, Dzeron, 86
Middle East, 1, 26, 204; Armenian diaspora in the Middle East since 1918: *214*; divided between the British and the French, 103, 123, 145
military parade, 47, *52*, *54*, 56, 68, *197*
military tribunal, 46, 63, 124, 170; Alexandretta Incident, 113; Paklali incident, 183–4
Minasian, Hagop, *xx*
The Mirror Spectator, 221–2
Misis, 181, 182, 183, 227
missionary, 3–4, 6, 157, 177, 180
Mnatsaganian, D., Dr., *191*
Mndigian, Aram, *191*
Monarga (Boğaztepe, Cyprus), 43, *44*, 45, *45*, *48*, *50*, 51, 53, 59, 61; *see also* Cyprus, training in
Moumdjian, Garapet, 193
Mudros Armistice, 23, 103
Muradian, Krikor, 114–15
Muradian, Mihran, 175
Musa Dagh (Musa Ler), 3, 13, 41, 45, 46–7, 205, 209; end of French mandate and Bekaa Valley, Lebanon, 205; rescue at, *5*, 7, 9; resistance against the Armenian Genocide, 7, 9, 12; siege, *5*; Werfel, Franz: *Forty Days of Musa Dagh*, 7, 9; *see also* Port Said
Musa Dagh, legionnaires from, 16, 17, 27, *27*, 41, 45, 61, 63, 65, 205, 206; desertion, 61, 63; Suediatsis, 27, 45, 46, 47, 57

Najarian, Arshalous, vii, *viii*
Najarian, Carolann, ix, xiii
Najarian, K. George, vii–viii, ix, xiii
Najarian, Michael, Sr., ix
Najarian, Nishan, vii, *viii*, ix, 117, *117*, 119, *190*; Armenian passport of, *189*; chairman of the Armenian Legion Association, 210, *211*
Najarian, Sarkis, 28, *29*, 116–17, *117*, *118*, 119, *157*; joining the Armenian Legion, 30; journey from America, 34–9, 41; migration to United States, 30
Najarian, Siranoush, 117, 119
Najarian, Sona, 116, 117
Najarian, Yeghsabet, *117*, 119
Nargizian, Khosrov, 70–1
National Union of Egypt, 61, 87; legionnaires/ National Union rapprochement, 65–7

INDEX

Nazerian, Hampartsume, 87
Near East Relief, *132*, *155*, 177, 180, 233
Nersesian, Sebouh, General, *208*
Nevrooz, Dr. (head of Armenian National Union), 66
Nubar Pasha, Boghos, Chairman of the Armenian National Delegation, 8, *9*, 10, 11, 15–16, 19, 24, 83, 141, 221, 235n1; letter from Armenians refugees to, 128–9; letter to General Allenby, 141–2; *see also* Armenian Legion, establishment of

Odabashian, Baghdassar, Sergeant, *163*, 164, 175
Ottoman Empire, 4; Armenian Genocide, 6, 11; Armenians in, 3–6; British occupation of Ottoman lands, 128; capitulation of Ottoman forces, 23; Six Provinces/vilayets, 3, 6, 10; *see also* Turks

Palestine, 88, 90, 145, 219, 230; deployment of Armenian Legion in, 19–20, 61; refugees in, *95*; *see also* Battle of Arara
Panosian, Khacher, 176
Panossian, Dzeron/Joseph, *225*
Panossian, Hagop, *225*
Panossian, Haig, *69*
Papazian, Lieutenant, *62*, *88*, *97*
Paris Peace Treaty (1919), 16, 158
Pashalian, Soghomon, 171
Patapanian, Diran, 34, *36*
Pedbos, French Corporal, 176
Pianelli, First Lieutenant, 58
picnic, *30*, *208*, 209, *215*
Piédpapé, de, Colonel and Commander of the French Forces in Cilicia, 146
Piligian, Stepan, *81*, *213*
Piran (village), 121
Port Said, Egypt, 31, 33, 39; Armenian women at, *22*; dissolution of the Armenian Workers' Camp, 137; first departure of legionnaires from, en route to Cyprus, *41*; *Gamavors* at, 41–2; Great Britain and, 9, 12–13, 130; Musa Daghtsi legionnaires, incidents related to, 61, 63–5; refugees returning home from, 205; survivors of Musa Dagh resistance at Port Said refugee camp, 9, 12–13, *19*, 41, 205; training at, 45
Portukalian, Megerdich, 220
Portukalian, Vahan, Lieutenant, 48–50, 61, *62*, 63, *97*, 100–1, 139, 220; 1920 return to Cilicia, Adana, 182, 202, 220; biography, 220; decorated for bravery in battle, *88*; demobilization, 182, 202, 220; legionnaires/National Union rapprochement, 65–7; letters from, 202–4; military tribunal and prison, 183, 184, 196; reorganization of the Eastern Legion, 101–2; Spanish flu, 97–8
prison (Armenians sentenced to), 63, *106*; Alexandretta Incident, 111, 113; arrest warrant for *Dayen*, 224; Paklali incident,
184; Portukalian, Vahan, Lieutenant, 184, 196; Shishmanian, John, 196, *200*, 229

Rafat, 21, 71, 75, 79, 80, 87–8; burial site at, *85*; *see also* Battle of Arara
Ramgavar (Armenian Political Party), 27, 189, 219
Red Cross, 98, *232*
Redan, Pierre, 159
refugee: Armenian refugees in Marash, *172*; Cilicia, 136; enlistment as legionnaires, 13, 16, 17; mandatory migration from Aleppo, 130; orphanage, 114, 116, 130, 161, 224, *232*; Palestine, *95*; repatriation, 136; returning home, 224, *225*; returning home from Aleppo, 129–30, *129*; returning home from Port Said, 205; Roland, Louis, Dr. and, 130, 133, 135; settlement in Adana, 130–5
Renié, Colonel, 63
Roland, Louis, Dr., 72, 79, 80, 92, *92*, 103, 108, 135, 219; Armenian refugees and 130, 133, 135; death, 135; wedding of, 91
Roman bridge across the Djihan (Ceyhan) river, *142*
Romieu, Louis, Lt. Col., 16, 18, *21*, *44*; Battle of Arara, 22, 23, 80, 83, 199; Cyprus training, command of, 43, 48–9, 55; early retirement, 145–6; legionnaires/National Union rapprochement, 65, 66; Musa Daghtsi desertion and, 61
Roques, Pierre, General and French Minister of War, 16
Russia, 1, 19
Russian Army, 7, 10, 14, 15

Saatjian, Nishan, 154
Sabahgulian, Stepan, 28
Saghdejian, Ovsia (*Daye*), 206–207, 223–4, *223*
Sahatjian, officer decorated for bravery in battle, *88*
Salibian, Dr., *191*
Sardarabad, *208*, 209
Sarkisian, George, *122*
Sarkisian, Shamiram, *122*
Sarkisian, Simon, 121, *122*, 123
Saroyan, William, 204
Saryan, Levon, 121
Saryan, Sarkis, *122*
Schlinker, Louis, Lieutenant, 56
Senegalese legionnaires, 162, 234
Sevian, Dr., 151
Shahbazian, Movses, 182, 207
Shakarian, Hagop, *2*
Shemmassian, Vahram, 129
ship: *Amiral Orly*, 34–39, *35*; *Coutelas*, French warship, 112; *Guichen*, French ship, *5*; *L'Espagne*, French ship carrying volunteers, 33–4, *33*; Musa Dagh, rescue at, *5*, 7, 9, 12; *Saint Brieuc*, French ship, 59
Shishmanian, John, Lieutenant, *55*, *57*, *62*, 65, 70, *88*, 124, *191*, 196; 1921 interview with *The Christian Science Monitor*, 185,

265

191, 229–34; Adana, 185, 187, 229, 231; Adana work contract, *186*; arrest for insubordination, *200*, 229; at Beirut Hospital, *99*; comments on pictures or figures, *71*, *85*, *114*, *149*, *151*, *155*, *156*; Cyprus, training in, 230; decorated for bravery in battle, *88*; as head of Armenian Legion troops in Cilicia, 185; headquarters of, *142*; leaving Cilicia after his release from arrest, *201*; letter from General Allenby, *150*
Shushanian, Donabed, Corporal, 176
Sikh soldiers from the British Army, *101*
Simonian, Jack, 182, 183–4
Simonian, Krikor, 176
Sinanian, Onnik, 60
Sis, 182, 227, 230, 231; evacuation under protection of Armenian legionnaires, 184
Sivas, 3, 10, 123
Spanish flu, 95, 97–8, 100
Stepan-Sarkissian, Gagik, ix, xiii, 220
Stepanian, Mgrdich, 176
Stepanian, Sharam, 73, 210, *211*
Suedia, 85, 86, 175, 176, 205, 210
Suez Canal, 61, 67
The Supreme Command of the Army and Military Police, *149*
Sykes, Mark, Sir, 129
Sykes–Picot Agreement (1916), 13–14, 15, 16, 101, 230
Syria, 14, 145, 206, 207; Christian minority, 226; Syrian volunteers, 69–70, 75, 83, 111
Syriacs, 226

Tahmazian, M. Kourken, 202
Takakjian, 87
Tanielian, Khacher, 175
Tarsus, 123, 232
Tashjek, 189
Taslakian, Misak, 86
Tavitian, Kevork, 112
Tenpelian, Misak, 175
Thibault, Captain, 182, 183
Toprak Kaley, 104
Torosian, Garabed, 92–7
Tourian family/restaurant, 108–9, *109*
Tourian, Karnig, 108–9
training, 13, 140; by French officers, 16; paramilitary training, *5;* Port Said, 45; *see also* Cyprus, training in
Treaty of Sèvres, 196, 229
Trekjian, Boghos, 86
Tumlu Kale, 183
Turkey, 158; boundary issues, 205, 206; proposed partition of Turkey according to Allied Agreements, *25;* Republic of Turkey, 3, 123, 205, 206; Turkish flag, 159, 169
Turkish National Movement, 24
Turkism/pan-Turkism, 4, 6
Turks, 229; Adana, Turkish attacks on, 187, 196, 231, 233; Alexandretta Incident, 111; Cilicia, Turks in, 135–6, 230; creating problems between Armenian legionnaires and Algerian soldiers, 109–10; crimes perpetrated against the Armenians, 135–6; French friendly disposition towards, 24, 109, 123, 136, 187, 196, 233; Paklali incident, 183, 184; reluctancy to return Armenian homes, farms and businesses, 129; *see also* Armenian Genocide; Kemalists; Marash, battles of; Ottoman Empire
Tutunjian, Manuel 175

United States: American flag, *71*, *132*; Armenian migration to, 4, 7, 30, 121, *213*, *225*; Armenians from United States, enlistment of, 14, 18, *18*, 27, 28–30, *31*, 33–9, *213*, 218, 223; journeys of legionnaires traveling from the United States, 33–4, *38*; legionnaires returning to, vii, 121, 123, 151, *195*, *213*; paramilitary training, *5*
Urfa, 230, 231

Vakif (village), 206
Van, 3, 7, 10, 175, 220
Varadian, Sarkis, 159, 167, *168*, 169–74
Varnava, Andreko, 53–4, 55
Varzhabedian, Khoren, 148
Vekilian, Hovhannes, 182, 183–4, *192*
Veradzin, Minas, 189, 191, 193
Viravor Ashough (the Wounded Troubadour), 210, 212
The Volunteer, Cairo, 73

Wadi Balut, 71
weaponry, 72, 75
Werfel, Franz: *Forty Days of Musa Dagh*, 7, 9
wheat, 187–9, 233
women, 6, *22*, 94, 95, 107; abduction and adoption of, 115; Armenian refugees in Marash, *172*; Egyptian Armenian ladies, 42; fighting alongside the legionnaires, *152*, *155*, *232*; rape of, 6, 111; rescue of Armenian women, 134–5, *149*; search for Armenian women and children, 114–23, 222; sharp-shooter, *6*, *151*; tattooing women, 119, *120*
World War I, *33*, 53, 205, *208*, 221; Armenian Legion, 1, 8, 9–11; Europe, 88, 90

Yegavian, Garabed, 80, 182
Yenice, 115, 123
Yepremian, Mgrdich, 182, 183, 184
Yeretsian (legionnaire), 189
Yergatian, Turfanda, *213*
Young Turk movement, 4
Yureyli, 191

Zakarian, B., *66*
Zanoyan, Melkiseteg, 86
Zeitoon, 170, 172, 203
Zildjian, Kourken, *82*, 86
Zorian, Markar, 175
Zoryan Institute, ix